POVERTY IN INDIA

POVERTY IN INDIA

S. N. Verma

DPS
PUBLISHING HOUSE
New Delhi (India)

POVERTY IN INDIA

First Published 2011
ISBN 978-93-80388-91-5

Published by

D.P.S. PUBLISHING HOUSE

Room No. 213, 7/28, Mahavir Street,
Ansari Road, Darya Ganj,
New Delhi- 110002
email: prashant_pbd@yahoo.co.in
dpspublicationhouse@gmail.com
Mobile: 011-23251264, 91-9811734184

Printed in India

Published by DPS Publishing House, New Delhi and Printed at Vishal Kaushik Printers, Delhi.

PREFACE

Poverty in India is widespread with the nation estimated to have a third of the world's poor. According to a 2005 World Bank estimate, 42% of India falls below the international poverty line of $1.25 a day (PPP, in nominal terms Rs. 21.6 a day in urban areas and Rs 14.3 in rural areas); having reduced from 90% in 1980. According to the criterion used by the Planning Commission of India 27.5% of the population was living below the poverty line in 2004–2005, down from 51.3% in 1977–1978, and 36% in 1993-1994.

Since the 1950s, the Indian government and non-governmental organizations have initiated several programs to alleviate poverty, including subsidizing food and other necessities, increased access to loans, improving agricultural techniques and price supports, and promoting education and family planning. These measures have helped eliminate famines, cut absolute poverty levels by more than half, and reduced illiteracy and malnutrition.

Although the Indian economy has grown steadily over the last two decades, its growth has been uneven when comparing different social groups, economic groups, geographic regions, and rural and urban areas. Between 1999 and 2008, the annualized growth rates for Gujarat (8.8%), Haryana (8.7%), or Delhi (7.4%) were much higher than for Bihar (5.1%), Uttar Pradesh (4.4%), or Madhya Pradesh (3.5%). Poverty rates in rural Orissa (43%) and rural Bihar (41%) are among the world's most extreme.

Though India boasts of a high economic growth, it is shameful that there is still large scale poverty in India. Poverty in India can be defined as a situation when a certain section of people are unable to fulfill their basic needs. India has the world's largest number of poor people living in a single country. Out of its total population of more than 1 billion, 350 to 400 million people are living below the poverty line. Nearly 75% of the poor people are in rural areas, most of them are daily wagers, landless laborers and self employed house holders. There are a number of reasons for poverty in India. Poverty in India can be classified into two categories namely rural poverty and urban poverty.

Poverty in India is reducing but it is still a major issue. Rural Indians depend on unpredictable agriculture incomes, while urban Indians rely on jobs that are, at best, scarce. Since its independence, the issue of poverty within India has remained a prevalent concern. According to the common definition of poverty, when a person finds it difficult to meet the minimum requirement of acceptable living standards, he or she is considered poor.

CONTENTS

1

Introduction

Poverty in India is widespread with the nation estimated to have a third of the world's poor. According to a 2005 World Bank estimate, 42% of India's falls below the international poverty line of $1.25 a day (PPP, in nominal terms Rs. 21.6 a day in urban areas and Rs 14.3 in rural areas); having reduced from 60% in 1980. According to the criterion used by the Planning Commission of India 27.5% of the population was living below the poverty line in 2004–2005, down from 51.3% in 1977–1978, and 36% in 1993-1994. Among the causes ascribed for the high level poverty in India are its history under British rule, large population, and low literacy.

Also important is India's social structure, including the caste system in India, and the role of women in Indian society. Economic growth has in the past been dampened by a dependence upon agriculture, and the economic policies adopted after its independence. Since the 1950s, the Indian government and non-governmental organisations have initiated several programmes to alleviate poverty, including subsidizing food and other necessities, increased access to loans, improving agricultural techniques and price supports, and promoting education and family planning. These measures have helped eliminate famines, cut absolute poverty levels by more than half, and reduced illiteracy and malnutrition.

The government has initiated, sustained, and refined many programmes since independence to help the poor attain self sufficiency in food production. Probably the most important initiative has been the supply of basic commodities, particularly food at controlled prices, available throughout the country. The poor spend about 80 per cent of their income on food while the rest of the population spends more than 60 per cent. The price of food is a major determinant of wage scales. Often when food prices rise sharply, rioting and looting follow.

Until the late 1970s, the government frequently had difficulty obtaining adequate grain supplies in years of poor harvests. During those times, states with surpluses of grain were cordoned off to force partial sales to public agencies and to keep private traders from shipping grain to deficit areas to secure very high prices; state governments in surplus-grain areas were often less than cooperative. After the late 1970s, the central government, by holding reserve stocks and importing grain adequately and early, maintained sufficient supplies to meet the increased demand during drought years. It also provided more remunerative prices to farmers.

INDIA POVERTY

In rural areas, the government has undertaken programmes to mitigate the worst effects of adverse monsoon rainfall, which affects not only farmers but village artisans and traders when the price of grain rises. The government has supplied water by financing well digging and, since the early 1980s, by power-assisted well drilling; rescinded land taxes for drought areas; tried to maintain stable food prices; and provided food through a food-for-work programme.

The actual work accomplished through food-for-work programmes is often a secondary consideration, but useful projects sometimes result. Employment is offered at a low daily wage, usually paid in grain, the rationale being that only the truly needy will take jobs at such low pay. In the 1980s and early 1990s, Indian government programmes attempted to provide basic needs at stable, low prices; to increase income through pricing and regulations, such as supplying water from irrigation works, fertilizer, and other inputs; to foster location of industry in backward areas; to increase access to basic social services, such as education, health, and potable water supply; and to help needy groups and deprived areas.

The total money spent on such programmes for the poor was not discernible from the budget data, but probably exceeded 10 per cent of planned budget outlays. India has had a number of antipoverty programmes since the early 1960s. These include, among others, the National Rural Employment Programme and the Rural Landless Employment Guarantee Programme.

The National Rural Employment Programme evolved in Financial Year 1980 from the earlier Food for Work Programme to use unemployed and underemployed workers to build productive community assets. The Rural Landless Employment Guarantee Programme was instituted in Financial Year 1983 to address the plight of the hard-core rural poor by expanding employment opportunities and building the rural infrastructure as a means of encouraging rapid economic growth. There were many problems with the implementation of these and otherschemes, but observers credit them with helping reduce poverty.

To improve the effectiveness of the National Rural Employment Programme, in 1989 it was combined with the Rural Landless Employment Guarantee Programme and renamed Jawahar Rozgar Yojana, or Jawahar Employment Plan. State governments are important participants in antipoverty programmes. The constitution assigns responsibility to the states in a number of matters, including ownership, redistribution, improvement, and taxation of land. State governments implement most central government programmes concerned with land reform and the situation of small landless farmers.

The central government tries to establish programmes and norms among the states and union territories, but implementation has often remained at the lower bureaucratic levels. In some matters concerning subsoil rights and irrigation projects, the central government exerts political and financial leverage to obtain its objectives, but the states sometimes modify or retard the impact of central government policies and programmes.

DEVELOPMENT PLANNING

Planning in India dates back to the 1930s and even before independence, the colonial government had established a planning board that lasted from 1944 to 1946. Private industrialists and economists published three development plans in 1944. India's leaders adopted the principle of formal economic planning soon after independence as an effective way to intervene in the economy to foster growth and social justice. The Planning Commission was established in 1950. Responsible only to the prime minister, the commission is independent of the cabinet.

The prime minister is chairperson of the commission, and the minister of state with independent charge for planning and programme implementation serves as deputy chairperson. A staff drafts national plans under the guidance of the commission; draft plans are presented for approval to the National Development Council, which consists of the Planning Commission and the chief ministers of the states. The council can make changes in the draft plan. After council approval, the draft is presented to the cabinet and subsequently to Parliament, whose approval makes the plan an operating document for central and state governments.

The First Five-Year Plan (Financial Years 1951-55) attempted to stimulate balanced economic development while correcting imbalances caused by World War II and partition. Agriculture, including projects that combined irrigation and power generation, received priority. By contrast, the Second

Five-Year Plan (Financial Years 1956-60) emphasized industrialisation, particularly basic, heavy industries in the public sector, and improvement of the economic infrastructure.

The plan also stressed social goals, such as more equal distribution of income and extension of the benefits of economic development to the large number of disadvantaged people. The Third Five-Year Plan (Financial Years 1961-65) aimed at a substantial rise in national and per capita income while expanding the industrial base and rectifying the neglect of agriculture in the previous plan. The third plan called for national income to grow at a rate of more than 5 per cent a year; self-sufficiency in food grains was anticipated in the mid-1960s.

Economic difficulties disrupted the planning process in the mid-1960s. In 1962, when a brief war was fought with China on the Himalayan frontier, agricultural output was stagnating, industrial production was considerably below expectations, and the economy was growing at about half of the planned rate. Defense expenditures increased sharply, and the increased foreign aid needed to maintain development expenditures eventually provided 28 per cent of public development spending. Midway through the third plan, it was clear that its goals could not be achieved.

Food prices rose in 1963, causing rioting and looting of grain warehouses in 1964. War with Pakistan in 1965 sharply reduced the foreign aid available. Successive severe droughts in 1965 and 1966 further disrupted the economy and planning. Three annual plans guided development between Financial Years 1966 and Financial Year 1968 while plan policies and strategies were reevaluated. Immediate attention centered on increasing agricultural growth, stimulating exports, and searching for efficient uses of industrial assets.

Agriculture was to be expanded, largely through the supply of inputs to take advantage of new high-yield seeds becoming available for food grains. The rupee was substantially devalued in 1966, and export incentives were adjusted to promote exports. Controls affecting industry were simplified, and greater reliance was placed on the price mechanism to achieve industrial efficiency. The Fourth Five-Year Plan (Financial Years 1969-73) called for a 24 per cent increase over the third plan in real terms of public development expenditures.

The public sector accounted for 60 per cent of plan expenditures, and foreign aid contributed 13 per cent of plan financing. Agriculture, including irrigation, received 23 per cent of public outlays; the rest was mostly spent on electric power, industry, and transportation. Although the plan projected national income growth at 5.7 per cent a year, the realized rate was only 3.3 per cent.

The Fifth Five-Year Plan (Financial Years 1974-78) was drafted in late 1973 when crude oil prices were rising rapidly; the rising prices quickly forced a series of revisions. The plan was subsequently approved in late 1976 but was terminated at the end of Financial Year 1977 because a new government wanted different priorities and programmes. The fifth plan was in effect only one year, although it provided some guidance to investments throughout the five-year period. The economy operated under annual plans in Financial Year 1978 and Financial Year 1979. The Sixth Five-Year Plan (Financial Years 1980-84) was intended to be flexible and was based on the principle of annual "rolling" plans.

It called for development expenditures of nearly Rs1.9 trillion (in Financial Year 1979 prices), of which 90 per cent would be financed from domestic sources, 57 per cent of which would come from the public sector. Public-sector development spending would be concentrated in energy (29 per cent); agriculture and irrigation (24 per cent); industry including mining (16 per cent); transportation (16 per cent); and social services (14 per cent). In practice, slightly more was spent on social services at the expense of transportation and energy.

The plan called for GDP growth to increase by 5.1 per cent a year, a target that was surpassed by 0.3 per cent. A major objective of the plan was to increase employment, especially in rural areas, in order to reduce the level of poverty. Poor people were given cows, bullock carts, and handlooms; however, subsequent studies indicated that the income of only about 10 per cent of the poor rose above the poverty level. The Seventh Five-Year Plan (Financial Years 1985-89) envisioned a greater emphasis on the allocation of resources to energy and social spending at the expense of industry and agriculture. In practice, the main increase was in transportation and communications, which took up 17 per cent of public-sector expenditure during this period.

Total spending was targeted at nearly Rs3.9 trillion, of which 94 per cent would be financed from domestic resources, including 48 per cent from the public sector. The planners assumed that public savings would increase and help finance government spending. In practice that increase did not occur; instead, the government relied on foreign borrowing for a greater share of resources than expected. The schedule for the Eighth Five-Year Plan (Financial Years 1992-96) was affected by changes of government and by growing uncertainty over what role planning could usefully perform in a more liberal economy. Two annual plans were in effect in Financial Year 1990 and Financial Year 1991. The eighth plan was finally launched in April 1992 and emphasized market-based policy reform rather than quantitative targets.

Total spending was planned at Rs8.7 trillion, of which 94 per cent would be financed from domestic resources, 45 per cent of which would come from the public sector. The eighth plan included three general goals. First, it sought to cut back the public sector by selling off failing and inessential industries while encouraging private investment in such sectors as power, steel, and transport. Second, it proposed that agriculture and rural development have priority. Third, it sought to renew the assault on illiteracy and improve other aspects of social infrastructure, such as the provision of fresh drinking water.

Government documents issued in 1992 indicated that GDP growth was expected to increase from around 5 per cent a year during the seventh plan to 5.6 per cent a year during the eighth plan. However, in 1994 economists expected annual growth to be around 4 per cent during the period of the eighth plan. Four decades of planning show that India's economy, a mix of public and private enterprise, is too large and diverse to be wholly predictable or responsive to directions of the planning authorities. Actual results usually differ in important respects from plan targets.

Major shortcomings include insufficient improvement in income distribution and alleviation of poverty, delayed completions and cost overruns on many public-sector projects, and far too small a return on many public-sector investments. Even though the plans have turned out to be less effective than expected, they help guide investment priorities, policy recommendations, and financial mobilisation poverty in India *Data 1995*.

POVERTY ESTIMATES

The World Bank estimates that 456 million Indians (42% of the total Indian population) now live under the global poverty line of $1.25 per day (PPP). This means that a third of the global poor now reside in India. However, this also represents a significant decline in poverty from 60 per cent in 1981 to 42 per cent in 2005, although the rupee has decreased in value since then, while the official standard of 538/356 rupees per month has remained the same. Income inequality in India (Gini coefficient: 32.5 in year 1999- 2000) is increasing.

On the other hand, the Planning Commission of India uses its own criteria and has estimated that 27.5% of the population was living below the poverty line in 2004–2005, down from

51.3% in 1977–1978, and 36% in 1993-1994. The source for this was the 61st round of the National Sample Survey (NSS) and the criterion used was monthly per capita consumption expenditure below Rs. 356.35 for rural areas and Rs. 538.60 for urban areas. 75% of the poor are in rural areas, most of them are daily wagers, self-employed householders and landless labourers. Although Indian economy has grown steadily over the last two decades, its growth has been uneven when comparing different social groups, economic groups, geographic regions, and rural and urban areas.

Between 1999 and 2008, the annualized growth rates for Gujarat (8.8%), Haryana (8.7%), or Delhi (7.4%) were much higher than for Bihar (5.1%), Uttar Pradesh (4.4%), or Madhya Pradesh (3.5%). Poverty rates in rural Orissa (43%) and rural Bihar (41%) are among the world's most extreme. India has a higher rate of malnutrition among children under the age of three (46% in year 2007) than any other country in the world. Despite significant economic progress, 1/4 of the nation's population earns less than the government-specified poverty threshold of 12 rupees per day (approximately USD $0.25).

Official figures estimate that 27.5% of Indians lived below the national poverty line in 2004-2005. A 2007 report by the state-run National Commission for Enterprises in the Unorganised Sector (NCEUS) found that 77% of Indians, or 836 million people, lived on less than 20 rupees (approximately USD $0.50 nominal; $2 PPP) per day. As per the 2001 census, 35.5% of Indian households availed of banking services, 35.1% owned a radio or transistor, 31.6% a television, 9.1% a phone, 43.7% a bicycle, 11.7% a scooter, motorcycle or a moped, and 2.5% a car, jeep or van; 34.5% of the households had none of these assets.

According to Department of Telecommunications of India the phone density has reached 33.23% by Dec 2008 and has an annual growth of 40%. The proportion of India's population below the poverty line has fluctuated widely in the past, but the overall trend has been downward. However, there have been roughly three periods of trends in income poverty.

1950 to mid-1970s: Income poverty reduction shows no discernible trend. In 1951, 47% of India's rural population was below the poverty line. The proportion went up to 64% in 1954-55; it came down to 45% in 1960-61 but in 1977-78, it went up again to 51%.

Mid-1970s to 1990: Income poverty declined significantly between the mid-1970s and the end of the 1980s. The decline was more pronounced between 1977-78 and 1986-87, with rural income poverty declining from 51% to 39%. It went down further to 34% by 1989-90. Urban income poverty went down from 41% in 1977-78 to 34% in 1986-87, and further to 33% in 1989-90.

After 1991: This post-economic reform period evidenced both setbacks and progress. Rural income poverty increased from 34% in 1989-90 to 43% in 1992 and then fell to 37% in 1993-94. Urban income poverty went up from 33.4% in 1989-90 to 33.7% in 1992 and declined to 32% in 1993-94 Also, NSS data for 1994-95 to 1998 show little or no poverty reduction, so that the evidence till 1999-2000 was that poverty, particularly rural poverty, had increased post-reform. However, the official estimate of poverty for 1999-2000 was 26.1%, a dramatic decline that led to much debate and analysis.

This was because for this year the NSS had adopted a new survey methodology that led to both higher estimated mean consumption and also an estimated distribution that was more equal than in past NSS surveys. The latest NSS survey for 2004-05 is fully comparable to the surveys before 1999-2000 and shows poverty at 28.3% in rural areas, 25.7% in urban areas and 27.5% for the country as a whole, using Uniform Recall Period Consumption.

The corresponding figures using the Mixed Recall Period Consumption method was 21.8%, 21.7% and 21.8%

respectively. Thus, poverty has declined after 1998, although it is still being debated whether there was any significant poverty reduction between 1989-90 and 1999-00. The latest NSS survey was so designed as to also give estimates roughly, but not fully, comparable to the 1999-2000 survey. These suggest that most of the decline in rural poverty over the period during 1993-94 to 2004-05 actually occurred after 1999-2000.

In summary, the official poverty rates recorded by NSS are:

Year	Round	Uniform Poverty Rate (%)	Mixed (%)	Poverty Reduction per year (%)	Mixed Reduction (%)
1977-78	32	51.3			
1983	38	44.5		1.3	
1987-88	43	38.9		1.2	
1993-94	50	36.0		0.5	
1999-00	55		26.9		
2004-05	61	27.5	21.8	0.8	1.0

CAUSES OF POVERTY IN INDIA

CASTE SYSTEM

A disproportionally large share of poor is lower caste Hindus. According to S. M. Michael, Dalits constitute the bulk of poor and unemployed. Many see the pan-Indian social construct of caste system as a system of exploitation of poor low-ranking groups by more prosperous high-ranking groups.

In many parts of India, land is largely held by high-ranking property owners of a particular dominant caste (Brahmanas, Kshatriya) that economically exploit low-ranking landless labourers and poor artisans, all the while degrading them with ritual emphases on their so-called god-given inferior status. According to William A. Haviland, casteism is widespread in rural areas, and continues to segregate Dalits. Others, however, have noted the steady rise and empowerment of the Dalits through social reforms and the implementation of reservations in employment and benefits.

BRITISH ERA

The reign of the Islamic dynasty of the Mughals had been an era of unprecedented prosperity in India. The Mughal era ended at about 1760. Jawaharlal Nehru claimed "A significant fact which stands out is that those parts of India which have been longest under British rule are the poorest today." The Indian economy was purposely and severely deindustrialized (especially in the areas of textiles and metal-working) through colonial privatisations, regulations, tariffs on manufactured or refined Indian goods, taxes, and direct seizures, as noted by linguist and commentator Noam Chomsky.

However, according to economist Angus Maddison, such explanation ignores the role of changes in demand and technology. In 1830, India accounted for 17.6% of industrial production against Britain's 9.5%, but by 1900 India's share was down to 1.7% against Britain's 18.5%. (The change in industrial production per capita is even more extreme due to Indian population growth). This is because Europe - particularly Britain - industrialized before the rest of the world. This view claims that British policies in India exacerbated weather conditions to lead to mass famines which, when taken together, led to between 30 to 60 million deaths from starvation in the Indian colonies.

Community grain banks were forcibly disabled; land was converted from food crops for local consumption to cotton, opium, tea, and grain for export, largely for animal feed. According to Angus Maddison, "They replaced the wasteful warlord aristocracy by a bureaucratic-military establishment, carefully designed by utilitarian technocrats, which was very efficient in maintaining law and order.

However, the pattern of consumption changed as the new upper class no longer kept harems and palaces, nor did they wear fine muslins and damascened swords. This caused some painful readjustments in the traditional handicraft sector. It seems likely that there was some increase in productive investment which must have been near zero in Moghul India: government itself carried out productive investment in railways and irrigation and as a result there was a growth in both agricultural and industrial output."

INDIA'S ECONOMIC POLICIES

In 1947, the average annual income in India was $439, compared with $619 for China, $770 for South Korea, and $936 for Taiwan. By 1999, the numbers were $1,818; $3,259; $13,317; and $15,720 (numbers are in 1990 international Maddison dollars). In other words, the average income in India was not much different from South Korea in 1947, but South Korea became a developed country by 2000s. At the same time, India was left as one of the world's poorer countries. Hindu rate of growth is an expression used to refer to the low annual growth rate of the economy of India, which stagnated around 3.5% from 1950s to 1980s, while per capita income averaged 1.3%.

At the same time, Pakistan grew by 5%, Indonesia by 6%, Thailand by 7%, Taiwan by 8%, and South Korea by 9% and . The term was coined by Indian economist Raj Kumar Krishna.

License Raj refers to the elabourate licenses, regulations and the accompanying red tape that were required to set up and run business in India between 1947 and 1990. The License Raj was a result of India's decision to have a planned economy, where all aspects of the economy are controlled by the state and licenses were given to a select few. Corruption flourished under this system.

The labyrinthine bureaucracy often led to absurd restrictions - up to 80 agencies had to be satisfied before a firm could be granted a licence to produce and the state would decide what was produced, how much, at what price and what sources of capital were used.

India had started out in the 1950s with:

- High growth rates
- Openness to trade and investment
- A promotional state
- Social expenditure awareness
- Macro stability

But ended the 1980s with:

- Low growth rates (Hindu rate of growth)
- Closure to trade and investment
- A license-obsessed, restrictive state (License Raj)
- Inability to sustain social expenditures
- Macro instability, indeed crisis.

Poverty has decreased significantly since reforms were started in the 1980s.

Also:

- Over-reliance on agriculture. There is a surplus of labour in agriculture. Farmers are a large vote bank and use their votes to resist reallocation of land for higher-income industrial projects. While services and industry have grown at double digit figures, agriculture growth rate has dropped from 4.8%

to 2%. About 60% of the population depends on agriculture whereas the contribution of agriculture to the GDP is about 18%.

- High population growth rate, although demographers generally agree that this is a symptom rather than cause of poverty.

Despite this, India currently adds 40 million people to its middle class every year. Analysts such as the founder of "Forecasting International", Marvin J. Cetron writes that an estimated 300 million Indians now belong to the middle class; one-third of them have emerged from poverty in the last ten years. At the current rate of growth, a majority of Indians will be middle-class by 2025. Literacy rates have risen from 52 per cent to 65 per cent in the same period.

NEO-LIBERAL POLICIES AND THEIR EFFECTS

Other points of view hold that the economic reforms initiated in the early 1990s are responsible for the collapse of rural economies and the agrarian crisis currently underway. As journalist and the Rural Affairs editor for The Hindu, P Sainath describes in his reports on the rural economy in India, the level of inequality has risen to extraordinary levels, when at the same time, hunger in India has reached its highest level in decades. He also points out that rural economies across India have collapsed, or on the verge of collapse due to the neo-liberal policies of the government of India since the 1990s.

The human cost of the "liberalisation" has been very high. The huge wave of farm suicides in Indian rural population from 1997 to 2007 totaled close to 200,000, according to official statistics. That number remains disputed; with some saying the true number is much higher. Commentators have faulted the policies pursued by the government which, according to Sainath, resulted in a very high portion of rural households getting into the debt cycle, resulting in a very high number of farm suicides.

As professor Utsa Patnaik, India's top economist on agriculture, has pointed out, the average poor family in 2007 has about 100 kg less food per year than it did in 1997. Government policies encouraging farmers to switch to cash crops, in place of traditional food crops, has resulted in an extraordinary increase in farm input costs, while market forces determined the price of the cash crop. Sainath points out that a disproportionately large number of affected farm suicides have occurred with cash crops, because with food crops such as rice, even if the price falls, there is food left to survive on.

He also points out that inequality has reached one of the highest rates India has ever seen. In a report by Chetan Ahya, Executive Director at Morgan Stanley, it is pointed out that there has been a wealth increase of close to $1 Trillion in the time frame of 2003-2007 in the Indian stock market, while only 4-7% of the Indian population hold any equity. During the time when Public investment in agriculture shrank to 2% of the GDP, the nation suffered the worst agrarian crisis in decades, the same time as India became the nation of second highest number of dollar billionaires.

Sainath argues that Farm incomes have collapsed. Hunger has grown very fast. Public investment in agriculture shrank to nothing a long time ago. Employment has collapsed. Non-farm employment has stagnated. (Only the National Rural Employment Guarantee Act has brought some limited relief in recent times.) Millions move towards towns and cities where, too, there are few jobs to be found. In one estimate, over 85 per cent of rural households are landless, sub-marginal, marginal or small farmers.

Nothing has happened in 15 years that has changed that situation for the better. Much has happened to make it a lot worse. Those who have taken their lives were deep in debt – peasant households in debt doubled in the first decade of the neoliberal "economic reforms," from 26 per cent of farm households to 48.6 per cent. Meanwhile, all along, India kept reducing investment in agriculture (standard neoliberal procedure). Life was being made more and more impossible for small farmers.

As of 2006, the government spends less than 0.2% of GDP on agriculture and less than 3% of GDP on education. However, some government schemes such as the mid-day meal scheme and the NREGA have been partially successful in providing a lifeline for the rural economy and curbing the further rise of poverty.

EFFORTS TO ALLEVIATE POVERTY

Since the early 1950s, govt has initiated, sustained, and refined various planning schemes to help the poor attain self sufficiency in food production. Probably the most important initiative has been the supply of basic commodities, particularly food at controlled prices, available throughout the country as poor spend about 80 per cent of their income on food.

OUTLOOK FOR POVERTY ALLEVIATION

Eradication of poverty in India is generally only considered to be a long-term goal. Poverty alleviation is expected to make better progress in the next 50 years than in the past, as a trickle-down effect of the growing middle class. Increasing stress on education, reservation of seats in government jobs and the increasing empowerment of women and the economically weaker sections of society, are also expected to contribute to the alleviation of poverty. It is incorrect to say that all poverty reduction programmes have failed.

The growth of the middle class (which was virtually non-existent when India became a free nation in August 1947) indicates that economic prosperity has indeed been very impressive in India, but the distribution of wealth is not at all even. After the liberalisation process and moving away from the socialist model, India is adding 60 to 70 million people to its middle class every year.

Analysts such as the founder of "Forecasting International", Marvin J. Cetron writes that an estimated 390 million Indians now belong to the middle class; one-third of them have emerged from poverty in the last ten years. At the current rate of growth, a majority of Indians will be middle-class by 2025. Literacy rates have risen from 52 per cent to 65 per cent during the initial decade of liberalisation (1991-2001).

CONTROVERSY OVER EXTENT OF POVERTY REDUCTION

The definition of poverty in India has been called into question by the UN World Food Programme. In its report on global hunger index, it questioned the government of India's definition of poverty saying:

The fact that calorie deprivation is increasing during a period when the proportion of rural population below the poverty line is said to be declining rapidly, highlights the increasing disconnect between official poverty estimates and calorie deprivation. While total overall poverty in India has declined, the extent of poverty reduction is often debated.

While there is a consensus that there has not been increase in poverty between 1993-94 and 2004-05, the picture is not so clear if one considers other non-pecuniary dimensions (such as health, education, crime and access to infrastructure). With the rapid economic growth that India is experiencing, it is likely that a significant fraction of the rural population will continue to migrate toward cities, making the issue of urban poverty more significant in the long run. Some, like journalist P Sainath, hold the view that while absolute poverty may not have increased India remains at an abysmal rank in the UN Human Development Index. India is positioned at 132nd place in the 2007-08 UN HDI index. It is the lowest rank for the country in over 10 years.

In 1992, India was at 122nd place in the same index. It can even be argued that the situation has become worse on critical indicators of overall well-being such as the number of people who are undernourished (India has the highest number of malnourished people, at 230 million, and is 94th of 119 in the world hunger index), and the number of malnourished children (43% of India's children under 5 are underweight (BMI<18.5), the highest in the world) as of 2008. Economist Pravin Visaria has defended the validity of many of the statistics that demonstrated the reduction in overall poverty in India, as well as the declaration made by India's former Finance Minister Yashwant Sinha that poverty in India has reduced significantly.

He insisted that the 1999-2000 survey was well designed and supervised and felt that just because they did not appear to fit preconceived notions about poverty in India, they should not be dismissed outright. Nicholas Stern, vice president of the World Bank, has published defenses of the poverty reduction statistics. He argues that increasing globalisation and investment opportunities have contributed significantly to the reduction of poverty in the country. India, together with China, has shown the clearest trends of globalisation with the accelerated rise in per-capita income.

A 2007 report by the state-run National Commission for Enterprises in the Unorganised Sector (NCEUS) found that 77% of Indians, or 836 million people, lived on less than 20 rupees per day (USD 0.50 nominal, USD 2.0 in PPP), with most working in "informal labour sector with no job or social security, living in abject poverty." A study by the McKinsey Global Institute found that in 1985, 93% of the Indian population lived on a household income of less than 90,000 rupees a year, or about a dollar per person per day; by 2005 that proportion had been cut nearly in half, to 54%.

More than 103 million people have moved out of desperate poverty in the course of one generation in urban and rural areas as well. They project that if India can achieve 7.3% annual growth over the next 20 years, 465 million more people will be lifted out of poverty. Contrary to popular perceptions, rural India has benefited from this growth: extreme rural poverty has declined from 94% in 1985 to 61% in 2005, and they project that it will drop to 26% by 2025. Report concludes that, India's economic reforms and the increased growth that has resulted have been the most successful anti-poverty programmes in the country.

PERSISTENCE OF MALNUTRITION AMONG CHILDREN

According to the *New York Times*, is estimated that about 42.5% of the children in India suffer from malnutrition. The World Bank, citing estimates made by the World Health Organisation, states "that about 49 per cent of the world's underweight children, 34 per cent of the world's stunted children and 46 per cent of the world's wasted children, live in India."

The World Bank also noted that "[w]hile poverty is often the underlying cause of malnutrition in children, the superior economic growth experienced by South Asian countries compared to those in Sub-Saharan Africa, has not translated into superior nutritional status for the South Asian child." A special commission to the Indian Supreme court has noted that the child malnutrition rate in India is twice as great as sub-Saharan Africa.

2

Poverty: Political Economic Analysis

Recent events in India, culminating with the declaration of a "state of emergency" by Prime Minister Indira Gandhi in June 1975 and the subsequent suspension of many of the civil rights previously maintained under the Indian system of parliamentary democracy, have focused renewed attention on India's massive economic problems. Increasing popular unrest over the slow pace of economic progress undoubtedly played a role in fueling the rise of the loosely organized opposition movement that Mrs. Gandhi sought to destroy with her declaration of emergency.

And, the imposition by India's political leadership of a new and more authoritarian form of rule has been defended on the grounds that it offers the only hope for solving India's economic problems. At the heart of India's economic distress is the stark fact that a vast majority of Indians live in a state of more or less continual poverty. To identify a "poverty line" which separates the poor from the non-poor is inherently a somewhat arbitrary exercise; even when such a line is defined, serious data limitations make it very difficult to determine how many Indians are below it.

Nonetheless, in recent years several studies have sought to determine the fraction of the Indian population whose expenditures were below the level required to meet a minimal subsistence standard of living. These studies suggest that in the late 1960s as much as one half of the Indian people could not meet even this minimal standard. Many more were no doubt only slightly better off. By any reasonable standard, only a small minority of Indians today can be said to be truly free of poverty. The elimination of widespread poverty, as in India, requires both rapid economic growth and greater economic equity.

In the context of a distribution of wealth which is initially very unequal, a rise in the level of per capita income without any significant improvement in its distribution will leave most people in poverty for a long period of time. And in the context of an initial level of per capita income which is close to subsistence, a redistribution of income without much economic growth offers very limited opportunities for economic improvement. Poverty in India can be overcome only by a very substantial growth of per capita income achieved in the context of a significantly more equal distribution of income. The available evidence suggests that India has experienced very little progress in either economic growth or economic equity for at least the past one hundred years.

The most thorough study on long-term growth in the preindependence period estimates that (real) per capita income in India increased at an average rate of 0.5% per year between 1860 and 1950. Other studies arrive at slightly different results, but the overall conclusion to be drawn is that per capita income increased, if at all, very slowly during the last century of British colonial rule. Unfortunately there is no reliable evidence at all on changes in the distribution of income prior to independence. However, there is little reason to believe that there could have been any significant trend toward greater equality.

On the contrary: the limited degree of economic growth that did take place in British India was quite uneven in its geographical impact, and most probably just as uneven in its distribution by social class. In the post-independence period the data permit somewhat more reliable estimates of overall economic trends. According to official government figures, (real) per capita income in India has increased at an average rate of slightly more than 1% per year between 1950 and 1974. This rate represents a definite improvement over the colonial period, but it is still rather modest by international standards.

As for trends in the distribution of income, the (much weaker) evidence suggests that there has been very little change in the high degree of inequality that characterized India at independence. Poverty in India was at least as widespread at independence as it was a century earlier and that since independence it has been alleviated at best very marginally. The persistence of the problem is underlined by the very magnitude of the recent poverty estimates cited above. At the same time, the vast inequalities of income that continue to exist in India today suggest that much greater progress could have been made in reducing poverty-if only through redistributive measures.

Moreover, there are also good grounds for believing that a faster rate of overall growth in per capita income was (and is) feasible in India. The question is thus posed: why has poverty been so persistent in India? I cannot hope to provide a complete answer here, for the question is so broad and the topic so complex that no single line of inquiry can possibly do it justice. But I believe that any effort to answer the question must be grounded in a political economic analysis of the role of class interest and power in shaping the pattern of Indian economic development. The objective in this chapter is to develop such an analysis in order to provide an essential basis for the study of the persistence of poverty in India. The primary concern will be to explain the disappointing pattern of economic development in independent India. This requires first, however, an examination of the development of the Indian economy and the evolution of the Indian class structure during the period of British colonial rule.

THE IMPACT OF COLONIAL RULE

To assess the impact of British colonial rule on economic progress in India, one must begin with a conception of the precolonial economy. From the mid-16th to the mid-18th century, much of the Indian subcontinent was under the control of the Moghul emperors. The Moghuls instituted a form of agrarian bureaucracy characterized by "a sovereign who ruled, an army that supported the throne, and a peasantry that paid for both."

The Moghul aristocracy enjoyed a standard of living that was probably more lavish than that of their European counterparts, but most of the population had little more than the necessities of life. The Indian economy under the Moghuls was predominantly agricultural, and agricultural productivity was very low. Improvements in productivity were inhibited by the rigidity of the caste-based village social structure and the oppressive degree of taxation imposed by the ruling authorities. The Moghul state was largely parasitic.

Most of the surplus extracted from the peasantry was used to enhance the consumption levels of the aristocracy and to protect their continued rule, rather than to promote any long-term economic development. However, the luxury expenditures associated with the Moghul rulers did help to promote urbanisation, commerce, and (handicraft) manufacturing. The growth of internal and external trade stimulated the development of a significant class of merchants in various regions of the subcontinent. In sum, India's pre-colonial economy was quite backward but by no means completely static.

Continued growth in the extent of trade and the power of the merchant class might possibly have created conditions favourable to capitalist industrialisation (as in Western Europe), but it is impossible to say whether these forces could have overcome the powerful forces operating to perpetuate economic stagnation under the Moghuls. In any event, the penetration of the British in the 18th and 19th centuries eliminated whatever chance there was for a self-generated transition to capitalist development in India. In the sphere of agriculture the British eliminated the power of the upper crust of Moghul landed elites and introduced new property rights which benefitted primarily a small segment of the agrarian population; from this segment there arose a new landed elite.

Rising land values-with a more or less constant tax burden-put the agricultural surplus increasingly in the hands of landlords, who had little incentive to become enterprising farmers because they could sit back and squeeze the peasantry. This squeeze was intensified by the growth of other rural intermediaries such as moneylenders, who took' advantage of the increasing monetisation of the economy and the growth of the market in land to drive many peasants into a condition of indebted dependence.

Because there were so many opportunities for feudalistic exploitation of the land, agricultural production remained very backward and the surplus was largely dissipated into unproductive expenditures. Thus the British in effect introduced into Indian agrarian society many of the worst features of capitalism (the commoditisation of land and labour, with its resultant inequality and insecurity) with very few of the better features (capitalist entrepreneurial initiative and more efficient farming techniques).

The colonial rulers allied themselves with reactionary landed elites and encouraged a parasitic form of agricultural economy. In the early phase of British involvement in India the colonialists (represented primarily by the British East India Company) did not discourage Indian manufacturing but sought primarily to gain control of India's increasingly lucrative foreign trade.

However after 1815, when British industrial interests gained more influence over the colonial administration, the Indian economy was opened up to the full economic impact of Britain under an essentially free trade regime. The subsequent inflow of British manufactures (notably cotton textiles) did great damage to the Indian urban handicraft industry and helped to convert India into an exporter of primary products and an importer of manufactures. By the middle of the nineteenth century, British investment in transportation facilities (notably the Indian railways) began to stimulate some development of modern capitalist industry in India.

Although British investors tended to dominate the field, some of the Indian merchants who had survived competition with their British rivals (usually through some form of collabouration) began to develop an indigenous modern textile industry. Indian capitalist enterprise became more diversified in the first half of the twentieth century, moving into other light industries and even iron and steel production. However, indigenous industrial development was very slow and remained a weak current in the economy because of the failure of the colonial government to protect and promote it.

In view of the lack of government support, the favoured position of British nationals, and the opportunities for profit in trade and other unproductive ventures in India's largely feudalistic economy, it is remarkable that there was any indigenous industrial development at all. The Indian national bourgeoisie which did emerge under these conditions was highly concentrated among a few families and in a few regions of the subcontinent. Indian industrial capitalism was relatively monopolistic from the beginning, and it remained weak in relation to commercial interests throughout the colonial period. As the British consolidated their control over the Indian subcontinent in the nineteenth century, they set up a colonial military and civilian bureaucracy which differed in significant respects from the earlier Moghul state.

Where the Moghul ruling aristocracy had appropriated much of the economic surplus for themselves and used it in a wasteful manner, the more efficient British colonial administration imposed a lower fiscal burden on the Indian economy. The British colonists appropriated only a fraction of the surplus, which they used to maintain their own power and to undertake a limited amount of public investment in infrastructural facilities such as the railways and irrigation systems. In effect, the colonial rulers allowed an increasing proportion of the surplus to be captured by private groups rather than the public bureaucracy.

The private beneficiaries were mainly parasitic landlords, moneylenders and merchants who used the surplus to enhance their own consumption standards and-with the exception of a small number of enterprising industrial capitalists-did not use it for capital accumulation. The economic benefits resulting from infrastructural investment by the colonial administration were limited by the relatively small scale and high cost of the investment, and by its orientation to serve British rather than Indian needs.

Furthermore, the British colonists set into motion a steady drain of funds from India to Britain in the form of "Home Charges" (the ostensible cost of colonial government borne by the Indian people), private remittances by high-salaried British officials, monopoly profits by British capitalists, etc. This drain absorbed about one quarter of the savings generated in the Indian economy and thus helped to keep down the overall rate of net investment. With respect to its overall economic impact, the colonial administration was most significant in what it failed to do.

It did not hold on to the large surplus that earlier accrued to the Moghul state; it did not carry out a great deal of investment; it did not give much protection to indigenous industry until the last phase of colonial rule in the twentieth century; and, after the initial liquidation of Moghul elites, it did not work for change in rural areas but instead helped to preserve a reactionary pre-capitalist agrarian structure. No doubt the British administrators did more to stimulate economic progress in India than the earlier Moghul rulers. But by comparison with what an Indian nationalist government could have been expected to do, at least since the latter part of the nineteenth century, the British colonial regime clearly retarded Indian economic development.

THE COLONIAL LEGACY

After several centuries of colonial penetration and rule India attained independence as one of the poorest nations in the world.

During a period when many Western nations and one Eastern nation (Japan) experienced rapidly rising standards of living, India's per capita income hardly increased at all. Moreover, the distribution of income and wealth in India at the end of the colonial period was extremely unequal, both by class and by region.

While a privileged few enjoyed quite comfortable conditions, the level of living of most Indians was close to a subsistence minimum. In a number of respects the economic conditions inherited by independent India were relatively unfavourable for economic growth. First, India was disadvantaged by a very high density and a very high growth rate of population.

Colonial rule had encouraged a demographic explosion (by the lowering of mortality rates via improved hygiene, medicine, etc.) without promoting a corresponding growth in the availability of cultivable land and other material resources. Second, more than two thirds of the Indian labour force and about one half of total output was associated with a predominantly traditional and backward agricultural sector. Third, rates of saving, investment and public expenditure (actually or potentially allocable to economic development) were very low.

And finally, the Indian economy had become dependent upon foreign sources for many needed goods and services. The colonial presence had served to stimulate demand for imported commodities and to foster dependence on foreign technology and enterprise in many spheres of economic life. In a few significant respects India's initial economic conditions were somewhat more favourable for development than in most poor countries.

The continental size of the country offered a vast potential domestic market and a considerable diversity of natural resources. India at independence had already experienced a modest degree of industrialisation-small in comparison to the size of the whole economy, but significant in absolute terms and for particular regions of the country and at the time of independence there already existed in India a considerable number of indigenous professionals and administrators with some of the skills essential to the operation of a modern economy.

These were the beneficiaries of a colonial educational policy designed to train Indians to assume many of the subordinate roles in administering the empire. Thus India emerged at independence with a very poor and in some ways handicapped economy, but with considerable potential for economic development. Simply by virtue of attaining formal political independence, India rid itself of some of the obstacles to economic progress that had been imposed by British colonial rule. In several respects independent India was in a better position to achieve rapid economic growth than colonial India.

First of all, the new national government was clearly more committed to using its authority to promote economic development than was the colonial administration. An activist government seeking to stimulate the national economy replaced a relatively passive government concerned primarily with preserving law and order and protecting the interests of foreigners. Second, the colonial drain of funds from India to England was ended and there arose new opportunities to receive substantial inflows of funds from abroad in the context of Cold War competition between the Western capitalist powers and the Soviet bloc nations.

Third, the pace of economic growth and of technological progress in the world as a whole accelerated in the postwar period; to some extent all economies could be expected to benefit from more rapidly rising world demand and from new cost-cutting technological improvements. In the light of such favourable factors, it is not surprising that per capita income has grown more rapidly in independent India than under colonial rule. What requires explanation is why the improvement in growth performance has been so limited, and why it has not been accompanied by any significant improvement in the distribution of income.

To begin to address these questions, one must examine certain aspects of the colonial heritage which could not be discarded so readily as the colonial rulers themselves. More specifically, it is necessary to understand the evolution of the

Indian class structure under colonial rule. By the end of two centuries of British hegemony on the subcontinent, traditional Indian society had been differentiated along new and significant lines. In agriculture, the introduction of new property rights and new forms of taxation by the British, as well as an increasingly rapid growth of population, had led to a complex economic stratification of agrarian society.

At the apex of a multi-layered pyramid was traditional elite of native princes and absentee landlords-cummoneylenders who owed their comfortable position entirely to the British, with whom they jointly maintained order in the countryside. Below this parasitic elite were many intermediate layers of cultivators with varying rights to land, ranging from a rather small group of farmers with large holdings of their own to a mass of peasants with some (often tenuous) claim to a plot of land barely sufficient to provide for one family.

Among the cultivating land-holders there were very few whose scale and manner of operation would warrant the label "capitalist agriculture." At the bottom of the agrarian class structure, representing roughly a quarter of the rural population was a class of landless and often serf-like agricultural labourers. In contrast to the largely pre-capitalist and very backward relations of production that characterized almost all of Indian agriculture, a limited amount of modern capitalist enterprise had emerged in industry under British rule.

Although the colonial administration consistently favoured British over Indian capital, an indigenous Indian capitalist class did begin to develop slowly in the second half of the 19th century out of some of the trading classes who had collabourated with the British. Because of the obstacles faced by Indian capital, the indigenous capitalist class remained highly concentrated (among particular families and regions of India). Furthermore, its relations with British capital were highly ambivalent; the Indians often depended upon the British for technical and managerial assistance, but they became increasingly competitive with the British in marketing their output.

In the last decades of the British Raj, Indian capitalists gained financial control over an increasing number of industries formerly dominated by the British, and by the end of World War II they had become very wealthy and powerful business elite. Although yielding in some areas, British capitalists nonetheless maintained direct or indirect control over a substantial share of the modern sector of the economy. With the growth of modern industry and related services (e.g. railways and communications) there developed in India an organized industrial working class. Because of the limited spread of industry, however, this class represented only a small fraction of non-agricultural workers.

A larger number of wage-earners were employed as white-collar workers in government services. Together, these blue-collar and whitecollar workers constituted a relatively privileged urban proletariat. The great majority of the non-agricultural working force belonged neither to the capitalist nor to the organized working class. Instead, they were either part of the independent petty bourgeoisie, self-employed in services or household industry, or part of the unorganized lumpenproletariat, irregularly employed in small enterprises of one kind or another or altogether unemployed. Finally, a very significant class to emerge from the British colonial period was educated elite of professionals and administrators. Like the Indian capitalist class, this class was characterized by highly ambivalent relations with the British.

As recipients of a British education (often in England as well as in India), they were very much oriented to Western ideas and Western culture and very much at home with their British counterparts. On the other hand, they became increasingly competitive with the British colonial rulers and, in spite of the British policy of gradual "Indianisation" of public administration; they grew more and more resentful of their subordinate status in the colonial hierarchy. The Indian nationalist movement had its origins in a moderate group of professionals-both English and Indian- who formed the Indian National Congress in 1885 to press for reforms that would improve the position of the Indian upper class within the framework of continued British rule.

Leading Indian capitalists soon began to support and participate in the organisation as their interest in promoting Indian vs. British industry coalesced with the aims of the Indian intelligentsia. But it was only after the First World War that the nationalists began to press seriously for independence from British rule and the Congress became a mass movement rather than a limited interest group. By the Second World War the Congress had gained support among the urban middle and lower classes as well as many strata of the rural peasantry.

Although the most downtrodden and the most isolated groups in Indian society were probably unaware of or indifferent to the Congress, only a few groups that were very closely linked to the British (e.g. native princes, large absentee landlords, and a few members of the urban upper class) actually opposed the independence movement. From the point of view of subsequent developments in independent India, the most important aspects of the nationalist movement were (1) that the Indian bourgeoisie and intelligentsia remained in firm command throughout the struggle for independence and (2) that the attainment of independence involved no revolutionary social upheaval, but simply a transfer of power from the retreating colonial rulers to the dominant Indian classes who controlled the nationalist movement.

As a result, Indian independence left the indigenous class structure and the distribution of political and economic power basically unchanged. The Indian nationalist movement had its origins in a moderate group of professionals-both English and Indian-who formed the Indian National Congress in 1885 to press for reforms that would improve the position of the Indian upper class within the framework of continued British rule. While it is beyond the scope of this chapter to analyze why the nationalist movement did not become a revolutionary one, a few points may be mentioned.

First of all, the British colonial rulers did not completely repress the development of modern elites in India. Rather, they permitted and to some extent fostered the growth of an Indian bourgeoisie and intelligentsia that were quite Westernized (hence not implacably hostile to their colonial rulers) and ultimately powerful enough to dominate other indigenous classes. Secondly, a number of potentially more revolutionary groups in India were won over to the Congress movement by the personal appeal of leaders such as Mahatma Gandhi and Jawaharlal Nehru. Gandhi obtained mass support among the peasantry with his commitment to the ideals of the Indian village and his promotion of certain aspects of Hindu religious philosophy.

At the same time, Nehru gained support among left-oriented workers and youth (who were ultimately represented by the Congress Socialist Party within the National Congress) by raising the banner of socialism in India. Neither Gandhi nor Nehru, however, posed any real threat to the conservative tenets of the national bourgeoisie whose financial backing was essential to the Congress. On numerous occasions during the history of the nationalist movement, Gandhi and Nehru backed away from radical measures and aligned themselves with the less visible but no less powerful conservative forces in the movement.

A lack of alternative leadership and organisation, and the continual vacillation of the Moscow-dependent Communist Party of India, prevented any effective challenge to the Congress from the left. As it turned out, the only serious challenge to the authority of the Congress leadership resulted from the religious division between Hindus and Muslims; at independence the Congress was forced to yield the territory of Pakistan to the rival Muslim League.

Finally, the fact that the British rulers were ultimately ready to negotiate compromise settlements with the Indian nationalist movement, rather than force the issue to a more violent plane, facilitated a relatively peaceful and non-revolutionary transfer of power. The only noteworthy changes in the distribution of effective political power that accompanied Indian independence involved shifts among elite classes. The power of the foreign elite was of course considerably diminished by the departure of the colonial government, but British capital maintained a significant position in the Indian economy and a corresponding degree of influence in the post-independence period.

For similar reasons, many members of the traditional rural elite who had been most heavily dependent upon the British Raj lost some-but not all-of their privileges and power. Alongside them began to rise the next layer of agrarian society, the relatively well-to-do land-holding farmers who dominated the Indian villages and who had generally worked with the nationalist movement. The biggest gainers among the elite classes were clearly the Indian business and educated elites who dominated the Congress Party that took control of the reins of government in independent India.

This distribution of political power, together with several other significant aspects, of Indian geography and colonial history, combined to influence the basic institutional framework for India's contemporary development effort. The major geographic factor was the ethnic and cultural diversity of the Indian subcontinent.

Not only did this diversity set the stage for the partition of India and Pakistan at the time of independence, but it meant that independent India itself was to be comprised of a great number of different regions whose people speak different languages and have relatively little sense of a national identity. Indeed, one of the primary strands of national unity was the English language which linked the elites of all parts of India but simultaneously set them apart from the great majority of the people in their respective regions of the country. In addition to the geographically determined diversity of the Indian population, two significant consequences of India's historical experience under British colonial rule were to affect the institutional framework of independent India.

On the one hand, the British tradition of parliamentary democracy (in spite of its very limited application in colonial India) had a profound impact on the thinking of Indian elites-particularly the Western-oriented educated elites who played the most visible role in articulating the goals of the nationalist movement. In a similar way, the Western capitalist conception of property rights, introduced into India by the British, had become a central element in the ideology of many of India's leading figures and was of course a major concern for the powerful business elites. These elements of India's geography and historical tradition, as well as the distribution of power at independence, were reflected in several important features of the India constitution that was framed in the early years of nationhood.

First of all, India adopted a parliamentary democratic system on the British model. The ideological legacy of the British was no doubt significant in this regard, but ideological predilections might well have been abandoned had they not happened to serve so well the interests of the dominant classes in India. Parliamentary democracy had the virtue of appearing to distribute fairly the political rewards of the struggle for independence.

At the same time, in the absence of any revolutionary change in India's highly inegalitarian social structure, this democratic framework in actual practice would offer plenty of opportunities for the stronger classes to dominate the weaker classes in the political arena. Secondly, the Indian constitution provided for a federal system of government in which significant limits were set on the power of the central government. Important spheres of government activity-notably the fields of agriculture, education and health-were allocated to governments of the various states that made up the Indian Union.

This diffusion of government power was in considerable part a natural accommodation to the size and diversity of the Indian subcontinent. The significance of cultural distinctions was underlined by the States Reorganisation Act of 1956 in which state boundaries were realigned to conform with linguistic divisions (over the opposition of many of India's educated elite who would have preferred a stronger central government and less homogeneous-hence weaker-states).

But regional decentralisation of power also served the interests of the dominant agrarian classes, who would meet less competition from the more Westernized business and educated elites at the level of state politics, and it may have seemed desirable to at least some of the business elites as a hedge against the possibility that educated elites would use the power of the central state apparatus against them rather than for them. The third major feature of the Indian constitution of fundamental importance for subsequent political and economic development was the commitment to respect the rights of private property.

Like the system of parliamentary democracy, the sanctity of private property was an important element of inherited ideology that conformed to the self-interest of a significant segment of India's elite classes. Both domestic and foreign capitalists, as well as pre-capitalist landed elites, could unite in defense of private property against those members of the educated elite who were more receptive to notions of state control of the means of production. Parliamentary democracy, the federal diffusion of government power, and the protection of private property were maintained more or less intact in India for several decades after independence. These elements of the Indian constitution provided the basic institutional framework within which Indian economic development took place up until the major changes ushered in by Prime Minister Gandhi's declaration of a national emergency in 1975.

THE CLASS CONTEXT OF INDIAN ECONOMIC DEVELOPMCNT

The pattern of economic development that has taken place in India from Independence to the mid-1970s can best be understood as the outcome of a variety of conflicting pressures, emanating from the conflicting interests of different classes with independent bases of power in modern India. Before turning to a more detailed analysis of India's development experience, it will be useful to review briefly the class structure of independent India and the distribution of power among the various classes.

Table: Taxonomy of Class Structure

Dominant Classcs	
1.	The traditional elite
2.	The agricultural elite
3.	The foreign elite
4.	The (indigenous) business elite
5.	The (indigenous) educated elite
Intermediate Classes	
1.	The peasantry
2.	The petty bourgeoisie
Subordinate Classes	
1.	Agricultural labourers
2.	The proletariat
3.	The lumpenproletariat

Ten separate classes arc distinguished; these ten can be divided into three broad strata according to their differing relationships to the process of production (broadly defined). The topmost stratum includes five different dominant classes, whose members share the common characteristic of employing, directing, or in some way controlling large numbers of other people in the course of making their livelihood. The middle stratum includes two intermediate classes who are self-employed or self-directed in their economic activity, but who do not employ or control large numbers of other people.

Finally, the lowest stratum includes three dependent classes who have essentially no source of livelihood other than their own labour; either they are employed, directed or controlled by others (primarily members of the elite classes) or they are altogether lacking in work opportunities. The five dominant classes include (1) the traditional elite: the (usually absentee) landowners, moneylenders, speculative traders, and traditionally privileged classes whose power rests on some form of feudalistic economic exploitation of rural dependent classes and/or on a socially dominant position in village life; (2) the agricultural elite: those landowners with sufficiently large holdings to lease land to tenants or to employ agricultural labourers, but who play an active role in directing or controlling agricultural operations rather than simply exacting tribute from the dependent classes; (3) the foreign elite: the foreigners who own or control productive assets within the country, or are seeking to do so; (4) the business elite: the indigenous owners and/or directors of large private corporate enterprises; and (5) the educated elite: the indigenous professionals and administrators who direct or control civilian government agencies and enterprises, the military services, educational institutions, etc.

The two intermediate classes are (1) the peasantry: farmers who own land, or hold secure tenurial rights to the land they cultivate, and differ from the agricultural elite in that their holdings are not large enough to allow for extensive sub-letting or employment of others; and (2) the petty bourgeoisie: owners and operators of small private enterprises and self-employed professional and service workers. It is difficult to draw a sharp line between the peasantry and the agricultural elite, or between the petty bourgeoisie and the business elite. The typical peasant and the typical petty bourgeois operate mainly with family labour, but the intermediate classes include also somewhat more well-to-do farmers and small-scale businessmen.

Finally, the subordinate classes include (1) the agricultural labourers: persons engaged in agricultural activities whose livelihood is derived mainly from working on land owned and controlled by others (including insecure tenants as well as landless labourers); (2) the proletariat: those nonagricultural employees, white-collar and blue-collar, who hold regular and reasonably secure jobs in modern public or private sector enterprises; and (3) the lumpenproletariat: all of the remaining people who work irregularly in relatively insecure jobs, sometimes engaging in marginal service activities and often simply unemployed.

The three-tiered economic hierarchy of dominant, intermediate and subordinate classes reflects very roughly the extremely inegalitarian distribution of effective power that characterized India at the time of independence. It is critical to recognize, however, that power was not highly concentrated in the hands of any single class or compatible set of classes. As a consequence, no one class or cohesive class alliance could assert its political hegemony and impart a decisive direction to government policy, much less to the development of the economy as a whole. There are several reasons for the lack of decisive class rule in India. First, each of the five different dominant classes emerged from the struggle for independence with a substantial independent basis of power.

Although the traditional and the foreign elites were weakened, the former retained a great deal of authority in many parts of rural India, and the latter retained some of their economic assets and-more important - had external financial, managerial and technological resources with which to operate.

The business elite had a major base of power in their control of a significant share of the modern corporate sector of the economy, while the educated elite commanded considerable power by virtue of their important role in the nationalist movement and the post-independence governing Congress Party.

The agricultural elite maintained a power base in their land holdings, which was enhanced by their involvement with the nationalist movement and the Congress Party. Second, both the federal diffusion of governmental authority and the political framework of bourgeois parliamentary democracy in India were significant in impeding the formation of a powerful alliance of dominant classes at the expense of all the remaining classes. The federal structure encouraged the development of regional political alliances, dividing the members of a given dominant class with different regional origins and cutting across the horizontal line between dominant and intermediate classes.

The democratic political framework provided a mechanism for some of the better organized of the intermediate and subordinate classes-e.g., elements of the urban petty bourgeoisie and the urban proletariat-to exercise a limited degree of political power. In general, the federal and bourgeois democratic structure that characterized the Indian political system up to the mid-1970s made it impossible for the national government to exercise strong rule on behalf of any class or class alliance. The conflicting interests of various classes in India with some degree of power to shape the pattern of economic development prevented the implementation of any consistent and effective strategy of economic growth.

The political economic conditions in India were clearly incompatible with the successful execution of a socialist growth strategy, in which the state would revolutionize the conditions of production, mobilize the economic surplus and invest it in growth-stimulating activities. The strength of the propertyowning classes in India (and the constitutional protection of private property) assured that private enterprise would continue to play a major role in the economy and that public or collective enterprise would be limited in scope.

Moreover, a relatively weak central government could not be expected to lead any form of social or economic revolution on a national scale. In spite of the strength of the property-owning classes, political economic conditions in India were not ideally suited for the pursuit of a capitalist strategy of economic growth either. Such a strategy requires a strong alliance of progressive pro-capitalist classes, able to resist the demands of other classes and to spur the state to carry out policies stimulating profitable and rapid central accumulation by private enterprise.

In the Indian context, this alliance would have to be built around elements of the foreign elite, the indigenous business elite, and the agricultural elite, for whom economic growth along capitalist lines could become a lucrative proposition. But in independent India both the reactionary traditional elite, as well as a segment of the educated elite, much of the petty bourgeoisie and the proletariat, stood opposed to a strategy that would benefit primarily the most wealthy capitalist elites; and these classes had sufficient power to prevent such a capitalist strategy from being effectively pursued. Thus the political economic conditions necessary for rapid economic growth-along either socialist or capitalist lines-simply did not exist in India.

At the same time, the prevailing configuration of class interest and power was inimical to significant progress toward a more equitable social and economic order. For all their conflicts of interest on economic growth strategy, the dominant classes in India shared a common interest in minimizing any redistribution of income. While some well-organized groups within other classes could bring some power to bear in their own economic interest, the vast majority of poor people-and especially the agricultural labourers and the lumpenproletariat-had virtually no effective source of power with which to press their claim for a fairer distribution of economic well-being.

INDIAN DEVELOPMENT POLICY UPTO 1975

Indian politics has been dominated ever since independence by the umbrella-like Congress Party, which grouped together most of the elements of the nationalist coalition organized by the Indian National Congress. Various smaller parties (often splitting off from the original Congress Party) have arisen on the right and on the left of the political spectrum, but the Congress Party-holding much of the middle ground-has been in firm control of the national government since independence and has only occasionally lost elections in certain states to other political parties. The broad goals and policies of economic development pursued by India have therefore reflected a consensus developed within the dominant Congress Party.

According to the rhetoric of the Congress party leaders, Indian government policy has been guided by the generalobjective of establishing a "socialistic pattern of society." While initially this term seemed to suggest a rejection of an economic system based on private enterprise, it soon became apparent that what was intended was simply an important role for the state in promoting social justice as well as economic growth within the context of an essentially capitalist economy.

The ideological commitment of Indian leaders to an equitable pattern of economic development reflected the fact that, both during the nationalist struggle and during the period of bourgeois democracy which followed the dominant classes in Indian politics had to enlist the support of many of the other classes. But the overall configuration of class interest and power in India has constrained government policy in such a way as to leave a substantial gap between the development goals enunciated by the political leadership and the development achievements of the Indian economy. I will examine several important domains of government economic policy in order to illustrate the way in which political economic forces have impeded the attainment of more rapid economic growth and greater economic equity in independent India.

AGRARIAN REFORM

Already prior to independence the Indian nationalist leaders had stressed the urgency of agrarian reform on both economic and social grounds, and the hopes of the Indian peasantry for enhanced rights to land and its produce had played a large role in gaining their adherence to the National Congress and later the Congress Party. The Indian leadership was committed to eradicating the quasi-feudal social relations and economic institutions that dominated rural India, to redistributing land to the actual cultivators, and to providing various government-funded "community development" services in an effort to promote the development of a progressive peasant-based form of capitalist agriculture.

These rural reforms were to be accomplished by legislative means within the context of the democratic political system and respect for existing property rights. The Indian Government did succeed in the early years following independence in curbing the power of some of the most parasitic elements at the top of the traditional structure of rural society. Some tenurial reforms were introduced and some land was redistributed away from large absentee owners, although substantial compensation payments were required and many large holders managed to hold on to most of their land.

Except in a few areas the land reform and redistribution efforts of the Indian Government were frustrated in their implementation at the local level and therefore failed to bring about major changes in the social and economic structure of agrarian society. Eventually a form of capitalist agriculture did begin to develop in parts of the Indian countryside, but it was limited to certain regions and-in those regions-to some of the better-off farmers. Disappointment with the pace of agricultural progress in the 1950s led to a greater commitment of government resources to agriculture and to a shift in emphasis from institutional to technological change beginning in the early 1960s.

The new approach was exemplified by the "Intensive Agricultural Districts Programme," adopted in 1960, which sought to concentrate efforts to increase productivity-via greater use of fertilizers, pesticides, improved seeds, technical assistance, etc.-in one pilot district in each of the Indian states. This programme and its successors (the Intensive Agricultural Areas Programme and the High Yielding Varieties Programme) were explicitly designed to allocate scarce agricultural resources to the better-off areas and better-off farmers in an all-out effort to increase output with little regard for the distributional consequences.

In this way the "Green Revolution" came to certain areas of India in the late 1960s, but the spread of improved agriculture was limited by the persistence in many areas of exploitative agrarian social relations, and by a pattern of pricing and controls on agricultural inputs and outputs that often limited economic incentives to increase production. In the late 1960s and early 1970s there was a renewal of government expressions of commitment to land reform and redistribution, in the wake of growing popular unrest over perceived inequalities, but in practice there was little change in the overall approach to agricultural development.

The relatively well-to-do capitalist farmer remained the primary beneficiary of government investment in agriculture and the main hope for the success of agricultural development. After 25 years some progressive capitalist agriculture had emerged in India, but a relatively backward pre-capitalist form of agriculture was still widespread in most regions and dominant in some. The failure of the Indian Government to implement an agrarian strategy more conducive to growth and to equity may be attributed in part to the limited power of the central government in the face of a task of extraordinary magnitude and complexity.

The organisational demands of restructuring agrarian institutions and administering change in 500,000 separate villages are formidable. Successful implementation of any development strategy in this sphere calls for decisive action and effective administration on the part of the state. The federal structure of Indian government and the constitutional protection of private property rights (which guaranteed compensation for any expropriation) both set limits on the ability of the political leadership to act forcefully to transform rural India. But a major factor determining the approach to agrarian change in India was clearly the distribution of effective political power.

The political strength of the traditional elite, who had much to lose by the kind of agrarian reform officially promoted by the Congress Party, thwarted efforts to promote the development of capitalist agriculture on a wide scale and an equitable basis. When some degree of capitalist agriculture was successfully stimulated in parts of India, it was the more powerful agricultural elite-rather than the peasantry or the agricultural labourers-who reaped the greatest gains. The political strength of the traditional elite, who had much to lose by the kind of agrarian reform officially promoted by the Congress Party, thwarted efforts to promote the development of capitalist agriculture on a wide scale and an equitable basis.

PUBLIC VS. PRIVATE ENTERPRISE

Indian political leaders and economic planners have always intended that the central government play a major role in promoting economic development, especially in the non-agricultural sectors of the economy. The prevailing view within the government was hostile to a purely capitalist strategy of economic growth, based on private sector capital accumulation with governmental help but limited governmental control.

Instead, the political leadership favoured a major role for public enterprise and a system of central planning with careful control and restriction of private enterprise.

Equity objectives were to be served by preventing the growth of large private business empires and by providing government support for small-scale private enterprises and traditional handicraft activities. As in the case of agriculture, there has been a considerable gap between the initially stated intentions of political leaders and the actual policies carried out by the government and to be sure, the Indian public sector has grown considerably in importance. But its growth is attributable mainly to the expansion of activities normally under public management-such as utilities, transportation, and communications-and the establishment of new public enterprises in certain key branches of modern industry-notably steel, machinery, and petroleum production.

Nationalisation has been confined to some major service enterprises (e.g., banks and insurance companies) and a very limited number of strategic industries. The private sector continues to dominate the Indian economy, and its growth has been aided by the government. To a limited extent support has been provided for small businesses, mainly in the form of subsidies to traditional handicraft industries. But government policy has been most favourable to the expansion of large-scale corporate enterprise. Big businesses have been in the best position to benefit from various forms of government stimulation of private sector development, such as the provision of infrastructural facilities and credit at implicitly subsidized rates, and the establishment of an exchange rate and tariff structure that created sellers' markets for industrial products.

Very little effort was made to restrain the growth of large business houses until the late 1960s, and measures taken since then appear to have been too little and too late to have had much impact on the concentration of private capital. Although the

Indian Government has encouraged the growth of private enterprise in many ways, it has also sought to exercise some degree of control over the private sector. This effort has involved a great variety of quantitative restrictions and regulations limiting the role of the market mechanism in allocating resources.

Investment licensing, foreign exchange rationing, price controls, etc., have been major instruments of Indian economic planning. To administer this governmental involvement in the private sector, there has arisen a massive public bureaucracy dealing with economic matters. Naturally, the most powerful private business houses have been in the best position to apply pressure on the public bureaucracy to favour their own interests.

To the extent that the Indian Government departed from a purely capitalist strategy of growth, it may actually have retarded rather than stimulated the growth of the economy. Subsidisation of traditional handicraft industry is widely recognized as very inefficient from a strictly economic point of view. Limited and sporadic efforts to curb or nationalize private businesses created uncertainties that often served to inhibit private production without bringing any of the benefits that might be realized from a reduced degree of monopoly in the private sector.

The whole system of administrative controls on the private sector no doubt favoured the stronger business houses over their smaller competitors, but it introduced a great deal of inefficiency-in the form of waste, delay, misallocated resources, etc.-into the operation of the economy as a whole. Indian public sector enterprises, impressive in scope and in certain technical achievements, have nonetheless displayed a pattern of inefficiency and mismanagement that has clearly involved significant economic costs. They have not been organized so as to stimulate higher worker morale and productivity than in the private sector.

Nor have they provided the government with an important new mechanism for mobilizing funds to finance development expenditure. Lodged within a still predominantly private enterprise economy, the public enterprises have relied upon the usual capitalist incentives to motivate workers but have not imposed the discipline of profit maximisation on management. They have therefore generated neither much efficiency nor much of an economic surplus.

Unless public enterprises form part of a total economic system in which the state has the power to mobilize resources and to plan resource allocation, and in which workers have some kind of commitment to their work other than the periodic receipt of a pay-check, they are likely to function simply as somewhat inefficient private firms. In the context of India's predominantly capitalist economy and institutions, this seems to have been the typical pattern.

The growth of public sector activities may have contributed something to greater equity by usurping some areas into which the larger business houses might otherwise have expanded. And the subsidisation of some small-scale enterprises no doubt had desirable redistributive consequences, if quite limited in scope. But for reasons suggested above, Indian government policy *vis-a-vis* private enterprise as a whole has been much more favourable to big business than to small business interests.

The pattern of Indian government policy on public and private enterprise, with its mixed success in stimulating growth and its decided failure to improve equity, can be interpreted as the outcome of conflicts between several classes with a stake in the nature of the policy and some power to affect it. Almost all these classes could agree on the desirability of a strong government effort to promote economic growth, but there were important differences with respect to the character of the government role.

Business elites (indigenous and foreign) had reason to favour limited public ownership of the means of production combined with substantial state assistance to the private sector;

from their point of view, governmental administrative controls presented both opportunities and hazards. Members of the educated elite had much to gain from substantial public ownership of the means of production as well as from administration controls over the private sector.

Among the less powerful classes, the petty bourgeoisie-as competitors in many areas with business elites-had reason to favour an active government role that would curb the power of the big business houses. And the proletariat stood to gain from the growth of state enterprise and regulation, since they could expect to have more influence on and more favourable treatment from public than from private management.

The end result of these conflicting interests was a situation in which the government played a more interventionist role than business elites would have preferred but a less significant role than many members of the educated elite would have liked; and government control was far less effective in restricting big business than the non-elite classes desired. Neither the business nor the educated elites were powerful enough to shape government policy precisely to their own liking, but they were able to bring about a somewhat uneasy compromise in which their respective interests were far better served than those of the lower classes.

FOREIGN ECONOMIC RELATIONS

The foreign economic relations of a poor country involve three principal forms of interaction between the domestic economy and foreign economies: foreign trade, foreign investment and foreign aid. In each of these areas government policy options range from an internationalist position, in which economic integration into the world economy is strongly encouraged, to a nationalist position, in which economic involvement with foreign economies is sharply limited. In its early policy pronouncements on foreign economic relations, the Indian political leadership assumed a relatively nationalistic stance.

Such a stance was hardly surprising in view of the long history of the nationalist movement during which foreigners were of course the principal enemy. The economic policy espoused by Congress Party leaders called for protective barriers to trade in order to favour the substitution of domestic industrial production for imported manufactures and to reduce dependence on exports of agricultural and agro-based products; the role of foreign capital was to be carefully circumscribed so that domestic enterprise could come into its own in all sectors of the economy; and great stress was placed on the desirability of relying on indigenous resources rather than foreign aid as a source of economic growth.

As it turned out, only with respect to foreign trade did the Indian Government pursue a fairly consistent nationalist policy. Ever since the early years of deliberate planning for economic development, Indian trade policy has favoured the growth of import-substituting over export-promoting activities. This emphasis was especially strong in the mid-1950s, when very high priority was given to the development of heavy industry on the model of the self-sufficient growth strategy of the Soviet Union.

But this drive for rapid and heavy industrialisation-in the absence of sufficient government power to mobilize the necessary resources-led in the late 1950s to a shortage of investible funds and a scarcity of foreign exchange. This forced the government, among other things, to tighten its restrictions on imports and its controls over the allocation of foreign exchange. In the 1960s the interventionist policies associated with import-substituting industrialisation came under heavy criticism from several sources, including the Western aid donor countries whose external assistance had now become more important for India's development plans.

The somewhat disappointing pace of agricultural growth compounded the pressure to liberalize trade policies and give greater emphasis to the development of agriculture and the promotion of exports. This led to some modifications in Indian trade policy in the latter half of the 1960s, but on the whole it has still remained far from the internationalist ideal. The Indian policy with respect to the role of foreign capital in economic development has been somewhat ambivalent and variable ever since independence.

The early rhetoric of the political leadership, with its strong dose of economic nationalism, created a good deal of uncertainty and hesitancy on the part of actual and potential foreign investors. In effect, Indian policy toward foreign private investment up to the late 1950s involved a general tolerance of existing holdings but discouragement of most new investment, except in a few key industries such as oil. However, the shortage of investible funds and of foreign exchange that began to develop in the late 1950s led to increasing encouragement of new foreign investment, subject only to certain restrictions and regulations imposed by the government in an effort to assure participation-if not actual control-by Indian private or public capital.

While such regulations often drew annoyed reactions from foreign capitalists and alienated many of them, foreign private capital has in fact come to play a key role in many branches of modern industry in India, providing economic, technical and managerial resources and typically operating in collabouration with Indian private or public enterprise. Since the late 1960s, there has again been a resurgence of nationalist rhetoric on the part of the government. A political rapprochement with the Soviet Union has been accompanied by growing verbal antagonism toward Western powers and Western capital, but this has as yet not substantively affected the degree of involvement of Western private capital in the Indian economy.

In the first decade after independence Indian economic planners, operating from a position of strength based on a sizeable wartime accumulation of sterling reserves and the Korean War boom, did not seek much foreign aid. They did, however, solicit and receive a considerable amount of technical assistance from both Western and Eastern industrialized nations. But the severe and continuing foreign exchange crisis beginning in the late 1950s, and the willingness of Western nations to extend large amounts of aid and loans, led to a situation in which the Indian Government was heavily dependent on foreign aid for budgetary support and resources for investment. Up until the late 1960s, foreign public capital inflows played a crucial role in India's development efforts.

The capital inflows were accompanied by continuing technical assistance and by an increasingly visible role for foreign economic advisers. By the late 1960s and early 1970s, a combination of Indian nationalist backlash, mounting debt service payments, and changing policies of the aid donors led to considerable curtailment of the net inflow of foreign public capital and the role of foreigners in India. Nationalist policies *vis-a-vis* foreign investment and foreign aid clearly involve short-run costs in terms of economic growth because the opportunity to make use of foreign resources is foregone. Nationalist foreign trade policies most probably also involve short-run costs in terms of economic growth because they run counter to efficiency considerations based upon comparative advantage.

Whether or not such policies can contribute to greater long-run growth depends on the ability of the government to undertake certain necessary complementary activities. These would include programmes to develop from indigenous sources the capital, the skills and the technology that would otherwise be obtained from abroad, and measures to help shift the long-run comparative advantage of the country toward industrial activities. For reasons suggested earlier, the Indian government was not in a position to undertake such activities on a scale necessary to make a success of a nationalist strategy. Thus it appears that India's departures from internationalism have been costly both in terms of short-run and long-run economic growth.

The consequences of economic nationalism for equity are somewhat mixed. By curtailing the economic and political role of foreigners and their indigenous associates, nationalist policies on foreign investment and foreign aid are likely to reduce some of the potential for inequity in the economy. Almost inevitably the economic impact of foreign investment and foreign aid is concentrated in particular areas and among particular groups of people, and those groups who already tend to dominate are likely to be in the best position to benefit from the foreign presence. In the case of foreign trade, however, it is not at all evident that a more nationalist policy will also tend to be more egalitarian.

Indeed, protectionist policies in a basically capitalist framework tend to provide lucrative opportunities for gain both to protected private businesses and to government officials responsible for administering the protection. And a policy which promotes industry over agriculture is likely to aggravate rather than alleviate the differential between urban and rural levels of living that characterizes most poor countries. Because India's nationalist orientation was stronger with respect to foreign trade than with respect to foreign capital inflow, it has most probably had a disequalizing rather than an equalizing effect on the distribution of income.

A combination of political and economic factors appears to account for the particular mix of policies pursued by India in its foreign economic relations. In the case of foreign aid, there was clearly no adequate basis for a sustained nationalist position. On the one hand, most of India's dominant classes stood only to gain by an inflow of aid, for it represented (at least in the short-run) a costless way for the government to raise resources and it relieved to some extent the pressure on the dominant classes to undertake major reforms to promote economic development.

Foreign elites in India were of course strongly in favour of increased aid, since it provided both direct benefits through increased opportunities for trade and investment as well as indirect benefits through increased involvement in India's economic decision-making. Even had the interests of the dominant classes not coincided so fully as they did in this case, it would have been difficult for any Indian government to forego the short-run economic advantages of external assistance in the context of a parliamentary democracy that inevitably focused much greater attention on short-run than long-run economic performance.

The political forces behind an expansion in the role of foreign private capital were not as strong as those behind foreign aid. Foreign interests were of course eager to promote foreign capital, but among indigenous business, agricultural and educated elites there were no doubt mixed views. Some businesses stood to gain by association with foreign capital; others might lose out in competition. Among educated elites many would be reluctant to see foreign private enterprise gain at the possible expense of the domestic public sector.

Still, among the powerful classes there was clearly greater potential support for than opposition to foreign investment, particularly insofar as it promised short-run economic advantages. Thus the elements of resistance to foreign capital had the effect of diluting the enthusiasm of the welcome to foreign capitalists but not inhibiting it completely. Apart from these considerations, there were some more fundamental factors inherent in the Indian situation that presaged a positive attitude toward foreign capital. Short of revolutionary change, India was constrained by its class structure to pursue some kind of a capitalist development strategy. To be successful at generating economic growth, this strategy would have to draw to a large extent on private capitalist enterprise.

In the absence of a major shift toward a different strategy emphasizing different sources of growth, any significant restrictipris on the initiative of private capital - domestic or foreign-would likely retard the growth of the economy. To circumscribe seriously the role of foreign capital in India would have meant to forego an important source of growth, and such a policy could not likely be sustained for long because economic stagnation would threaten overall political and economic stability and hence also the power of the dominant classes. The one area of foreign economic policy in which there was a coalition of interests sufficiently strong to promote a nationalist policy was foreign trade.

Import-substituting industrialisation could be supported by business and educated elites alike, for it promised considerable economic and political gains both to the protected businesses and the protecting government. Foreign business elites had mixed interests in this respect; foreign investors entering a protected market stood to gain, while foreign exporters seeking to penetrate such protection would lose.

India's agricultural elites on the whole stood to lose by a de-emphasis on exports, but the balance of power was clearly on the other side in the early stages of Indian economic planning. Thus import-substituting industrialisation was embraced in the 1950s and continued to hold considerable sway later on, although it lost some of its appeal as its economic costs became more apparent and as its opponents among agricultural and foreign elites grew stronger with time.

PUBLIC FINANCE AND EXPENDITURE

A purely capitalist strategy of growth would seek to keep government taxation and expenditure as low as would be consistent with the provision of public services essential to the profitable operation of private enterprise. Taxes would be levied primarily on the lower and middle income classes, in order both to curtail the consumption expenditure of those classes and to protect the supply of investible funds in the hands of the wealthy.

Expenditures would be concentrated on infrastructural facilities (e.g., power, irrigation, transportation, credit institutions) rather than social services (e.g., education, health, housing, welfare), and the primary beneficiaries would be those who were already in the best position to take advantage of new facilities. The economic policy statements of India's political leadership implied a substantially greater scale of government expenditure than would be consistent with such a strategy. The government was committed to extensive expenditure on infrastructural facilities and social services as well as programmes designed to increase employment opportunities as rapidly as possible.

Moreover, great stress was placed on the desirability of a progressive orientation to ensure that the benefits of government programmes would be spread widely rather than be monopolized by the more well-to-do classes. This more equitable approach need not necessarily have been costly in terms of economic growth; social service expenditures do draw resources away from alternative uses (e.g., capital accumulation), but they can contribute to growth insofar as they improve the health and skills of people at work in productive jobs.

The scope of government activity in India did increase very substantially in the decades following independence. But both the sources of government revenue and the direction of government expenditure proved to be predominantly regressive in their impact. Revenues were raised primarily from regressive indirect taxes rather than from more progressive direct taxes. Infrastructural facilities and social services were utilized disproportionately by the middle and upper classes because of the absence or failure of deliberate efforts to counter the natural advantages of the well-to-do *vis-a-vis* the poor. Administrative and military expenditures grew steadily, but public projects to increase employment received scant support.

The mix of policies that emerged was less conducive to economic growth than a pure capitalist strategy would have been. Growth was hampered by the considerable drain of government resources into programmes that served directly or indirectly to improve the living standards of the middle and upper classes without contributing to increased capital accumulation or labour productivity. The unproductive swelling of the ranks of the government bureaucracy at all levels, and the indiscriminate expansion of secondary and higher educational facilities, are cases in point.

Since governmental largesse often benefitted but rarely taxed the well-to-do and rarely benefitted but often taxed the poor, it is also arguable that inequalities were increased rather than decreased by the expansion of government activities. The character of Indian government programmes can be explained to a considerable extent by the pattern of class interest and power. The rapid expansion of the overall scope of government activities was to be expected in a situation where virtually every politically active class looked to some extent to the state for succor.

But there were naturally sharp conflicts of interest with respect to sources of government revenue and directions of government expenditure. The distribution of political power in India was clearly unfavourable to a progressive structuring of revenue and expenditure: the elite classes had both a strong interest and the necessary power to resist progressive taxation and take maximum advantage of government spending. India's parliamentary democracy did force concessions to some elements of the intermediate classes and the proletariat-particularly in urban areas-but the unorganized poor had little means of influence.

Hence the expansion of government white collar employment and various urban services proceeded apace, but efforts to provide employment for the rural poor and the marginal lumpenproletariar got virtually nowhere. The obstacles to a more progressive pattern of government revenue and expenditure were not solely attributable to the distribution of power. Direct taxes tend to be more difficult to assess and to collect than indirect taxes; hence in a poor non-socialist economy there is inevitably an administrative bias towards regressive sources of revenue. Similarly, it is a more difficult organisational task to steer the benefits of government programmes to poorer rather than to wealthier groups.

And the successful implementation of public employment projects often poses a particularly organisational problem. Political and organisational obstacles to more policies may also have been compounded by certain costs associated with the implementation of these overall Indian contexts. Steering be infrastructural facilities from larger to smaller enterprises probably results in lower short-run gains. Progressive social service expenditures may not have any significant impact on economic growth if they are not accompanied by an effective employment strategy.

And public employment creation programmes are likely to be inordinately costly if they are carried out in a social environment dominated by individual gain incentives. Since the overall Indian context offered no real alternative to individual gain incentives, promised little hope of full employment, and placed a premium on short-run rather than long-run economic gains, a more progressive pattern of government expenditure was bound to be more costly in terms of economic growth than it could be in a different institutional setting.

This cost most probably compounded the regressive effect of the other factors discussed above. The combination of development policies that have characterized the Indian approach to economic development up to the mid-1970s may best be summarized as a selectively modified capitalist strategy of development. This strategy involved very few departures from a pure capitalist strategy in a direction favourable to greater economic equity-Most programmes with significant redistributive potential-land redistribution, public employment projects, progressive taxation measures, efforts to curb the growth of large business empires-were either lacking or unsuccessful.

More fundamental institutional changes to bring about a more equitable society were never even considered. The principal departures from a pure capitalist strategy actually carried out in India were moves in the direction of a hierarchical form of socialism. But these departures were partial in two senses. On the one hand, they affected primarily industrial policy, foreign trade policy, and the pattern of government expenditure; they did not have much effect on agriculture, nor on foreign aid and investment policy, nor on the pattern of government resource mobilisation. On the other hand, the departures were only partially pursued in the areas where they did occur.

The result of this mixed pattern was that the Indian strategy did not benefit from any of the strengths of a socialist strategy, for these strengths arise largely from the ability of the state to exercise total control over the economy. Under the Indian conditions of very partial control, it was primarily the inefficiencies and inequities of such a strategy that manifested them. As a result, the minor socialist modifications of India's essentially capitalist strategy served to retard economic growth and did little or nothing to promote the achievement of greater equity.

If political economic conditions had allowed India to pursue either a completely capitalist or a completely socialist strategy of economic development, a more rapid rate of growth could have been achieved. Even within the confines of a capitalist strategy, it might have been possible to bring about a greater degree of equity-e.g., by eliminating pre-capitalist sources of economic privilege and power, and by avoiding the kind of bureaucratic controls which favour big over small capitalists. But any form of capitalist growth strategy remains inherently unequal because it has to rely on private profit incentives to stimulate saving, investment and growth.

In order to achieve rapid economic growth in the context of a substantially more equal distribution of income, there is really no alternative to a socialist strategy in which private property ownership is sharply curtailed and the state assumes most of the responsibility for resource mobilisation and capital accumulation. Such a strategy is politically feasible only when and where a coalition of anti-capitalist classes has succeeded in wresting power from property-owning elites. It is in this context that one must assess the prospects for future economic development in India, following the political changes that have taken place in the mid-1970s.

These changes should be understood as a response by India's political leadership to a crisis that had been growing in intensity during the previous decade. Up until the mid-1960s India had achieved a modest record of economic growth and very little improvement in economic equity, but there was still some popular confidence in the ability of the (Congress Party) political leadership to make good on its promises of economic and social improvement for all. After the mid-1960s a slowdown in the rate of economic growth, and increasing popular exasperation with the failure of government to reduce inequalities, contributed to a significant growth in strength of oppositional movements.

For much of the time since Mrs. Gandhi became Primer Minister in 1966, her administration has had to contend with various forms of political opposition-on both the left and the right of the political spectrum, and both within and outside the legal framework of India's parliamentary democratic system. At first Mrs. Gandhi's administration sought to counter the growing opposition with a combination of selective repression (directed against the revolutionary opposition) and measures designed to win greater popular confidence in her administration's ability to deal with India's economic difficulties-especially the plight of the poor.

These measures included a limited amount of new nationalisation of private enterprise, a somewhat more nationalistic policy *vis-a-vis* foreign aid and investment, and a closer political alignment with left-oriented political groups at home (notably the pro-Soviet Indian Communist Party) and the Soviet Union abroad. The Indian political leadership was very reluctant to abandon the overall framework of parliamentary democracy, in part because it constituted an important source of legitimacy for the governing elites.

The measures undertaken by Mrs. Gandhi's administration in the late 1960s and early 1970s amounted to a rather limited move in the direction of a bureaucratic form of socialism, reversing a trend toward a more purely capitalist development strategy which had been in evidence during most of the 1960s. As such, these measures did little to promote more rapid economic growth and greater equity. However, they did contribute to a temporary increase in popular support for Mrs. Gandhi's Congress Party and a postponement of the political crisis. But the continual lack of economic progress (accentuated by the worldwide inflationary crisis of 1972-74 which hit India, as a major importer of oil-based products, especially hard) laid the basis for a resurgence of opposition to Mrs. Gandhi's administration.

A wide variety of different oppositional groups coalesced rather loosely under the nominal leadership of J. P. Narayan, and by 1975 the "J.P. movement" posed a very serious threat to Mrs. Gandhi's personal tenure in office as well as to the continuation of Congress Party rule. This time the contradictions inherent in the Indian situation could not be resolved simply by more promises, minor reforms, and selective repression on the part of the government.

A more drastic step proved necessary: a change in the democratic rules of the game which had prevailed in India for a quarter-century, but which now seemed about to lead to shifts in the distribution of power that would threaten those who were dominant in the Congress Party and the Indian Government. Prime Minister Gandhi's declaration of a national emergency in 1975, and her subsequent moves toward more authoritarian rule, marked a significant change in the character of India's basic political institutions.

Parliamentary elections were suspended; individual civil liberties were sharply curtailed; the central government and its political leadership assumed greater power; and private property rights were rendered potentially less secure. The events of 1975 amount to the seizure of greater power by a segment of India's elite classes, i.e., those whose power is based on control of-or direct access to-the central government apparatus. This includes many members of the educated elite who actually manage the now more authoritarian state; it also includes those sections of the (indigenous and foreign) business elites and the agricultural elite who have developed-or are now able to develop-a close symbiotic relationship with the Indian Government.

The traditional elite have surely been weakened, as well as those sections of the other elite classes who are unable to benefit from an enhanced central government role in the economy. In the long-run the biggest losers are likely to be the intermediate and subordinate classes; for they have lost the bourgeois democratic framework which permitted some degree of influence to numerically large and politically well-organized groups within the system, and which limited the ability of government to repress groups operating outside the system.

To help ease the transition and consolidate its newly enhanced power with popular support, Mrs. Gandhi's administration has stepped up its promises of more rapid and more equitable economic growth, and it has announced new measures to achieve this goal. Now that some of the constraints of the democratic, federal and private-property protecting institutional framework have been removed, one can expect more decisive state action to promote economic development. Yet it remains highly questionable whether an authoritarian government in the current Indian class context can succeed in bringing about a pattern of development that involves both more rapid growth and greater equity.

The class basis for a socialist strategy of economic development still does not exist in India, for pro-capitalist elites retain substantial power. If anything, the power shifts that have taken place point to the adoption of a more purely capitalist strategy of economic development in India. This prospect is somewhat obscured by the continuing efforts of India's political leadership to gain popular support by projecting a socialistic image. However, the weakening of the traditional elite and the intermediate and subordinate classes provides an opportunity for rapid private capital accumulation, unfettered by the demands of the poor for a fairer share and less hampered by the unproductive economic role of the traditional elite.

The biggest potential obstacle to the successful implementation of a capitalist growth strategy in India is the possible conflict between bureaucratically-oriented members of the educated elite in the government administration and capitalist elites in the private sector. But to the extent that the administration seeks to restrict the operation of capitalist elites, it will tend to cause reduced private sector productivity and output. Efforts to modify a capitalist strategy of growth in a context where the government still lacks the will and power to develop an effective alternative socialist strategy will soon confront the ruling authorities with a choice between accommodating themselves to private enterprise or sacrificing any real prospect for rapid economic growth.

In the absence of significant pressure from other anti-capitalist classes, it seems most likely that the governing members of the educated elite will choose to ally themselves with indigenous and foreign capitalist elites in pursuing an essentially capitalist strategy in whose benefits both can share. This analysis suggests that more rapid economic growth may well be forthcoming in India in the near future, but that it is highly unlikely to take an equitable form. For the moment, at least, the poor in India have even less power than in the past to influence government policy in the direction of greater equity.

The government may undertake some new measures consistent with both capitalist growth and greater equity-e.g., the pursuit of "black money" hoarded by the rich and unavailable for productive investment-but the overall consequences of an essentially capitalist growth strategy cannot be very favourable to the masses of working people. Thus future economic development, if it occurs at all in India, is likely to be very uneven. Together with the political repression accompanying the new authoritarian rule, it is likely to generate growing popular opposition.

This opposition can no longer be contained with the help of a legitimizing democratic framework, as in the past; instead, the Indian Government will be forced to rely all the more heavily on repressive measures. In the short-run, the Government may well succeed in maintaining order-especially if its development strategy proves successful in accelerating the rate of economic growth. But in the long-run the situation is bound to be unstable. Sooner or later the poor people of India will succeed in organizing themselves so as to bring about the fundamental redistribution of effective power without which poverty in India will never be overcome.

3

Poverty Alleviation

A 1997 World Bank Study has rekindled the debate on whether economic growth is central to poverty alleviation in India. Invoking the main findings of a research project based on household surveys over a 40-year period, the study, India: Achievements and Challenges in Reducing Poverty, claims that "overall growth accounted for the lion's share of poverty reduction: 80 per cent of the decline in the number of households below the poverty line between 1951 and 1970, and almost 100 per cent since 1970." Further, the findings "clearly refute any presumption of immiserizing growth-that is growth that tends to marginalize or impoverish significant sections of the population-in India over this 40-year period."

The message therefore is that "it is through rapid growth that India will be able to reduce poverty and generate the resources to invest in the health and education of its people-who will in turn sustain this growth." Although the overall antipoverty strategy is similar to that advocated in the 1990 World Development Report-in as much as the main components are labour-intensive growth, human capital development and social safety nets-the former is distinguishable in its greater emphasis on growth. In the present chapter, we contest this claim. While growth matters, its contribution to poverty alleviation is much less than the World Bank claims.

The related claim that growth did not immiserize or impoverishes certain sections is inconsistent with panel evidence. In fact, there is a large core of poverty that persists despite rapid growth. The issue then is whether there are specific factors that tend to exclude the poor from participating in growth. In this chapter we will attempt to identify some key factors through an analysis of a panel survey. As noted, the primacy of growth in the World Bank strategy rests not just on its direct poverty-reducing effect, but on the generation of additional resources for poverty alleviation (interpreted broadly to include human capital development).

The latter claim is examined with state data on two major anti-poverty programmes, the Jawahar Rozgar Yojana (JRY) and the Integrated Rural Development Programme (IRDP). Finally, based on the analysis of factors that impeded participation of sections of poor households in growth, we elabourate some major components of an anti-poverty strategy. Although there is some overlap with the World Bank strategy (specifically regarding human capital formation), the emphases differ.

The present study focuses more on the design and implementation of this growth focused strategy. In this context, community initiatives have a potentially significant role. But such initiatives seldom work, as the impediments are not easy to overcome. A review of some recent field evidence on the functioning of the Panchayats (an elected body), following the implementation of the 73rd Constitutional Amendment Act in 1993, yields useful insights. Although a strong coalition of the poor would help overcome some impediments, it is not obvious how the coalition could be strengthened.

EXTENT AND SEVERITY OF POVERTY

Despite over four decades of planned development in India, a large section of the population continues to live in abject poverty. According to a National Sample Survey for 1993 and

1994, about 36.7 per cent of the rural population and 30.5 per cent of the urban population live in poverty-implying a national average of 35 per cent. Although there has been some reduction in the proportion of the poor over time-especially between the mid-1970s and late 1980s-their aggregate number has risen. From about 164 million in 1951, it rose to 312 million in 1993 to 1994.

There are also sharp regional disparities. In Bihar, for example, the proportion of poor in the rural population (64 per cent) in 1993 and 1994 was two and a half times higher than that of the combined states of Punjab and Haryana (25 per cent). Similarly, there are wide variations within states. Of the 10 poorest regions in 1987 and 1988, five were either in Bihar or Orissa. Poverty was evenly distributed across the five regions in these two states. But in Uttar Pradesh (UP)-another poor state (with about 42 per cent of the rural population classified as poor)-barely 8.4 per cent of the rural population in the Himalayan region was poor, the lowest incidence in all of India.

Classifying all of India's rural population into various groups, 68 per cent of the landless wage earners, 51 per cent of scheduled tribes/castes (STs/SCs) and 45 per cent of illiterates were poor in 1993 and 1994. Using the poverty gap index to measure depth of poverty in seven out of the 14 states for which estimates are available, the gap in rural areas ranged from a low of about 5 per cent in West Bengal to a high of well over 17 per cent in Bihar in 1993 and 1994. Given the low poverty threshold, these estimates point to the extreme poverty of large segments of the rural population in several states.

As noted earlier, the 1997 World Bank Study asserts the centrality of growth in poverty alleviation. The rate of reduction in poverty was indeed faster during periods of rapid growth (i.e., between the mid-1970s and 1980s); the average annual reduction (2.4 per cent) was three times as fast as during a period of slow growth (i.e., from 1951 to 1975). These patterns hold for both rural and urban areas. At the state level, while the centrality of growth in poverty alleviation is maintained, the study notes that human capital and infrastructure have important roles as well. However, as argued below, an effective anti-poverty strategy must have broader concerns.

IMPACT OF POLICY REFORMS

Of some concern is the impact of policy reform, initiated in India in mid-1991, on the poor. These reforms were a response to the macroeconomic crisis that erupted in early 1991. Following policy reforms, the head-count ratio for rural areas rose sharply-from 36.4 per cent in 1991 to 43.5 per cent in 1992-and dropped to 36.7 per cent in 1993 and 1994. While the 1997 World Bank Study reports that no more than one-third of the initial increase in rural poverty is attributable to policy reforms, how much of the increase is attributable to such reforms remains a debatable issue. It is plausible that some impoverishment was a result of these reforms, even if an allowance is made for (random) variability of incomes from cultivation and associated variability of wages.

Equally, the subsequent reduction in rural poverty in 1993 and 1994 should not be viewed as a result of policy reforms leading to a higher overall growth rate. In general, whatever the contribution of the policy reforms in accelerating growth in recent years, we argue below that growth alone will have a limited impact, as there are large segments of rural poverty that persist due to the inability of some sections of the population to participate in the growth process.

IMPOVERISHMENT

M. S. Ahluwalia's influential contribution to the debate on growth and poverty provoked a lively discussion on whether agricultural growth 'trickles down' to the poor. Several critiques drew attention to the impoverishment of some sections as a direct consequence of growth. Given the inequality in endowments of both physical and human capital, as well as a rigidly hierarchical social structure, it is not surprising that some sections benefit while others lose when economic opportunities expand.

Under certain extreme conditions, when inequality in the distribution of land manifests itself in an oligopsonistic labour market with few large landholders dominating through wage-setting, shifts in labour demand may have a small effect on agricultural wages relative to that in a competitive labour market. Consequently, poverty persists despite growth. Indeed, if dominance of large landholders also precludes some remunerative supplementary options (i.e., working part-time on another farm), poverty could worsen through a dampening effect on the earnings of agricultural labourers.

A recent analysis confirms that while agricultural growth reduces rural poverty, a measure of oligopsony exacerbates poverty. The 1997 World Bank Study relies on a decomposition of change in rural poverty into three components: growth, redistribution and the residual. If poverty falls over time, part of the reduction may be due to a higher average income without any change in its distribution (i.e., the growth component); some reduction may be due to a change in the distribution itself without any change in the average income (i.e., the redistributional component); while the remaining reason for reduction may be due to the interdependence between growth and distributional change (i.e., the residual).

The issue is whether the favourable effect of growth is neutralized or reinforced by income distributional change. The study found that growth accounted for 80 per cent of the decline in the head-count index over the period 1951 to 1994 and almost 100 per cent since 1978. This, however, is suspect. Two problems with this decomposition procedure suffice. One is the presumption that the growth and distributional components are separable.

In case they are not, the decomposition is ambiguous. Based on 1997 World Bank estimates, illustrates vividly that changes in mean consumption and changes in the Gini coefficient in Uttar Pradesh-one of the poorest Indian states-moved together over the period 1959 to 1994 (i.e., higher values of change in consumption were associated with higher values of change in the Gini coefficient). Another problem is that changes in consumption distribution understate income distributional changes when there is consumption smoothing. To that extent, the redistributional component would therefore be lower.

A surprising claim in the 1997 World Bank Study is that the decomposition refutes any presumption of immiserising growth over the period 1951 to 1994. All that the decomposition shows is that the growth component was the largest, implying that most of the reduction in the head-count ratio was due to growth. However, as will be demonstrated below, if a subset of the poor who cross the poverty threshold is larger than a subset of the non-poor who slip into poverty, this ratio falls. As the decomposition is confined to changes in the head-count ratio, it cannot capture changes in the composition of the poor and nonpoor over time.

The latter can only be captured through a more detailed analysis of a panel survey, as shown below. Even though income from cultivation grew rapidly during this period (about 6 per cent annually), about 27 per cent of the households became impoverished (i.e., categories 1 and 4). Among the impoverished, the poor who became poorer were the dominant group. Although both groups suffered substantial income losses, the non-poor who became poor recorded a much larger reduction (about 57 per cent versus about 25 per cent among the poor who became poorer).

The poverty threshold is 180 rupees (Rs) per capita annually. This is based on the cost of a nutritionally adequate diet. For details of how this poverty threshold was determined and its applications Gaiha in "On the Persistence of Poverty in Rural India," *Canadian Journal of Developmental Studies* (forthcoming) said, over the period in question, the head-count ratio registered a reduction-from about 53 per cent to about 47 per cent-as the poor who ceased to be poor exceeded the non-poor who became poor. However, the intensity of poverty rose slightly, as the average income of the poor fell from 118 to 113 rupees (Rs).

Of considerable interest is the subset of the poor who ceased to be poor. Their average income was well below the poverty threshold (barely 65 per cent of the latter) and it doubled in about five years, suggesting that even among the poorest there is considerable income mobility. The factors that enabled a quarter of the poor households to overcome poverty are analyzed below. This analysis has some important implications for the persistence of poverty.

PERSISTENCE OF POVERTY

If there is a large core of chronic poverty-among the sick, physically weak and disabled that are unable to participate in gainful employment-the effect of growth on poverty will be weak. A detailed analysis with the ICRISAT data yields a range of estimates of chronic poverty for the period 1975 to 1984. Three alternative measures of poverty were computed. The first is a simple head-count measure over multiple periods. It identifies households whose actual incomes fall under the poverty threshold (Rs180 per capita annually) for several years, in the extreme case, for all nine years. Such households are designated as chronically poor.

The second measure is based on expected poverty (as opposed to actual income) falling below the poverty cutoff point. The third measure is similar to the second but with the refinement of control for unobserved household fixed effects, representing ability, management and other household endowments in the estimation of the above relationship. This measure provides the most stringent measure of poverty and identifies households that are innately poor (i.e., those likely to remain poor not only in the absence of random/transitory income shocks but also if they were to have the same physical assets as the sample averages).

Table: Actual, Expected and Innate Poverty Estimates: Rural South India, ICRISAT Sample, 1975 to 1984

Year	*Poverty Estimates*		
	Actual	*Expected*	*Innate*
1975-76	70.00	74.00	69.00
1976-77	68.00	74.00	62.00
1977-78	61.00	68.00	58.00
1978-79	54.00	59.00	46.00
1979-80	56.00	59.00	44.00
1980-81	59.00	53.00	39.00
1981-82	54.00	54.00	38.00
1982-83	44.00	55.00	36.00
1983-84	51.00	58.00	36.00
All 9 years	57.00	61.00	48.00

Over the nine years, the extent of poverty based on actual income averaged 57 per cent, but with a wide range from 44 to 70 per cent. The incidence of expected poverty was somewhat higher at 61 per cent, but declined from 74 per cent in the period from 1975 to 1976 to 53 per cent in 1980 and 1981, increasing thereafter to reach a level of 58 per cent by 1983 and 1984. Finally, as anticipated, the magnitude of innate poverty, averaging 48 per cent during the sample period, was smaller than that of actual and expected poverty But it is still surprisingly large, considering that it identifies those households that would remain poor despite short-run changes in their assets and other characteristics (such as family size).

While the monotonic decline in the magnitude of innate poverty over the sample period (from a level of 69 per cent in 1975 and 1976 to 36 per cent in 1983 and 1984) is encouraging, the fact that over one-third of the sample households during the last year of the sample period were likely to remain poor despite policy interventions in the short run, is both disturbing and pessimistic. What is surprising-indeed startling-about these figures is the persistence of poverty. An overwhelming majority of sample households (87.8 per cent) were poor sometime (i.e., in at least one year) during the nine-year period.

Table: Chronic Poverty Estimates: Rural South India, ICRISAT Sample, 1975-84

No. of years in which poor	0 poverty never	1 some times	2	3	4	5	6	7	8	9 always poor
% of households poor	12.4	87.8	80.2	73.1	68.4	61.3	48.9	41.8	33.6	21.8

Slightly more than 60 per cent of households were poor roughly half of the time (i.e., during five of the nine sample years). Finally, a little more than one-fifth of the households were poor during all nine years (i.e., chronically poor).

Sixty per cent of households classified as poor on the basis of actual income and 52 per cent of expected poor were also innately poor. However, because of the stringent definition of chronic poverty (i.e., poor throughout the sample period), only a relatively small proportion of the actually, expected and innately poor households were also chronically poor (i.e., 38 per cent, 34 per cent and 33 per cent, respectively).

The varying estimates of poverty reflect the heterogeneity among the poor and demonstrate that the poor are not a monolithic group; they are composed, inter alia, of households that are poor owing to transitory shocks, households that are poor owing to low levels of owned physical assets and households that are poor owing to long-run inherited disadvantages. Growth alone may not accomplish much, as different sets of policies are needed to reach each of these disparate groups.

FACTORS

Some further insights into the persistence of poverty are obtained from an analysis of the factors that impeded (or facilitated) the movement of the poor out of poverty. This analysis is based on the ICRISAT panel survey of two villages in Maharashtra over the period 1979 to 1984, which was marked by a rapid growth of farm and non-farm activities. Income from cultivation, for example, grew by six per cent per annum. The main findings of an econometric analysis are analyzed below. That it was harder for poor households with a high dependency burden to move out of poverty over the period in question is plausible, since, in general, a larger proportion of children implies not just fewer earners but also fewer employment options for female members.

Equally relevant is the unfavourable effect of an aging household head on moving out of poverty. Given the harsh agro-climatic environment of the semi-arid tract, it is likely that earnings fall sharply with a decline in physical strength and stamina. In addition, the possibility that older age-groups tend to be risk-averse, and therefore not inclined to experiment with innovative agricultural practices or seek out new avenues for higher labour earnings, cannot be ruled out. That some poor households ceased to be poor by acquiring cultivable land is significant, especially in the context of a highly unequal distribution of land.

Since the period 1979 to 1984 witnessed expansion of both farm and non-farm activities, it is a fair presumption that poor households with higher educational achievements were better able to seize income-augmenting opportunities to get out of poverty. It might appear surprising that, independent of physical and human capital endowments and of demographic characteristics of households, the caste affiliation had a significant effect on movement out of poverty. The low caste households- the lowest in the caste hierarchy being the scheduled castes-are typically the most disadvantaged in terms of both physical and human capital. Evidence on their exchange entitlements, however, is scanty.

Why returns to physical and human capital vary with the caste rank may reflect discrimination (in various forms) against lower castes in specific markets (i.e., labour and credit markets) or their weak motivation to engage in more rewarding pursuits. To the extent that there are traces of the former, it follows that market imperfections act as an impediment. To summarize, while agricultural growth will undoubtedly make a difference, a substantial reduction in poverty is feasible only if barriers to acquisition of physical and human capital-and to their productive and remunerative use-are eliminated.

ANTI - POVERTY PROGRAMME OUTLAYS

As noted earlier, the centrality of growth in poverty alleviation rests on the strength of its direct and indirect effects. However, not only is the direct effect much weaker than claimed in the 1997 World Bank Study, but the presumption that growth generates resources for poverty alleviation programmes, including those for human capital formation, is somewhat naive, if not mistaken. Given the fiscal squeeze, some components of public expenditure are more vulnerable than others, depending to some extent on the nature of the political regime.

A positive relationship between outlays on poverty alleviation and growth is thus unlikely, as illustrated below. More importantly, given the outlays, what really matters is whether these are well-targeted. In case they are not, serious doubts arise about the efficacy of the indirect effects. As state governments contribute large shares of outlays to poverty alleviation programmes (varying from 20 to 50 per cent of the total) and variations in political regime are also more pronounced at that level, it is worthwhile to analyze state outlays on two programmes: the Integrated Rural Development Programme (IRDP) and the Jawahar Rozgar Yojana (JRY).

Changes in net state domestic product (NSDP) and IRDP outlays (IRDP) diverge over the period 1992 to 1995. In a few cases (e.g. Bihar), a positive [Delta]NSDP was associated with a negative [Delta]IRDP. The correlation coefficient is positive (0.15) but statistically not significant. Similarly, the relationship between [Delta]NSDP and [Delta]JRY is weak. Thus, increases in domestic product do not necessarily entail increases in outlays.

ANTI-POVERTY STRATEGY

As a comprehensive discussion of an anti-poverty strategy is not feasible here, we shall concentrate on a few major concerns. Given the key roles of land and education in overcoming poverty a major concern is how to enhance the access of the poor to these resources. In addition, during periods of economic stress rural public works (RPW) have an important role. Finally, the old and incapacitated warrant special protection. These concerns are addressed below.

LAND

As noted earlier, acquisition of land enabled a subset of the poor to overcome poverty over the period 1979 to 1984. Land redistribution would thus help alleviate poverty. Besides, since it is unlikely to reduce farm output, the equity-efficiency tradeoff in land redistribution would be low, if any. In fact, an econometric analysis with the ICRISAT data further strengthens the efficiency case. It suggests that redistributing land from large landowners to those owning even tiny quantities of land would raise farm output. How this redistribution may be accomplished is of course not straightforward. Land ceilings are seldom implemented. One possibility is a progressive land tax.

This may induce intensive use of land and discourage the holding of land for speculative purposes. In addition, the dismantling of input subsidies may further reduce the attractiveness of land to the rich. At the same time, and contrary to conventional wisdom, a cautious approach to regulations concerning land tenure contracts, including tenancy reforms and land rent, is necessary. In particular, restrictions on share tenancy in the absence of insurance and credit markets do not help the poor. However, the rights of leaseholders already established must be preserved and made transferable.

It is imperative that complementary policies for the provision of credit, agricultural inputs and extension services be designed appropriately for smallholders. The 1990 World Development Report (WDR) assigns a key role to education: "There can be little doubt that educating the children of the poor greatly improves their chances of escaping poverty. Since labour is the one scarce resource on which all able-bodied poor can rely, increasing the productivity of this labour is clearly the most effective way to escape poverty."

However, in its advocacy, the 1990 WDR does not go much beyond recommending a shift in the allocation of funds from "higher level services to basic health and primary education" to enable greater access of the poor to these services, "increasing the number of female teachers" and "paying parents to send their girls to school" to limit gender inequality. Drawing upon some recent work, we will concentrate on breaking the vicious circle between low quality of primary education-especially in rural areas-and weak motivation among poor families for education.

Values have an important role in both public provision of education and its utilisation. Public provision of education-especially for the benefit of lower castes-is often constrained by the perception of politicians and policymakers that education is not particularly important for them. Equally, the traditional attitude among lower castes that they can engage only in some unskilled occupations results in a neglect of schooling among their children-especially among the female children. The deprivation of the latter reflects a limited role for women.

Weak motivation and lack of incentives are inextricably linked. The opportunity cost of the time spent in school imposes a huge burden on poor families, since children play an important role in household chores and farm activities. The gender division of labour (combined with patrilineal property rights) tends to reduce the perceived benefits of female education. The norms of patrilocal residence and village exogamy (requiring a woman to settle in her husband's village), prevalent in large parts of India, further undermine the parental incentive to educate their female children.

Dowry and hypergamous marriage (i.e., a woman should "marry up" in the social scale), also prevalent in large parts of India, turn female education into a liability. The abysmal quality of school education is also a strong disincentive. Absenteeism and shirking among school teachers are rampant. Vocational content is low, if not nil. Given the permanence of posts, bureaucratic protection and the absence of a link between performance and remuneration, there is no incentive for reform from within the school system, though pressures from the outside may have desired effects.

Active public campaigns have a decisive effect on the demand for education. School meals and related incentives enhance school attendance rates by reducing the opportunity cost of attending school. Special incentives in the form of fee exemptions or scholarships for girls would have a favourable effect on their enrollment. Whether compulsory primary education is a feasible alternative is debatable, since views on the time frame, age limits, enforcement mechanisms and social security arrangements designed to obviate the need for child labour vary a great deal. Whatever the merits, compulsory education on its own will not remedy the inefficient functioning of schools in rural areas. Much depends on whether the school system is accountable to the community and whether the latter can exercise effective control.

RURAL PUBLIC WORKS

Rural public works (RPW) confer transfer and stabilisation benefits. Transfer benefits can be direct-the gross benefit to a participant less any cost he/she incurs in participating-or indirect-including the effect on agricultural wages and higher incomes through the creation of productive assets (e.g. roads) in rural areas. To the extent that an additional source of income during agricultural slack periods helps stabilize consumption and prevent costly adjustments (through, for example, liquidation of assets), RPW confer stabilisation benefits as well.

The analysis summarized below focuses on the targeting of RPW, as both transfer and stabilisation benefits depend crucially on it. Less than one-third of the households participating in the survey (about 31 per cent) were classified as poor. However, the share of poor that participated in RPW was slightly higher (5.1 per cent as against 4.1 per cent of the non-poor). As poverty and landlessness are closely associated, RPW participants were cross-classified into three landholding intervals: 0 to 0.4 hectare; 0.41 to 2 hectares; and over 2.01 hectares.

About 38 per cent of the total participating households were nearly landless (i.e., belonged to the first interval), and the majority had access to some land. In fact, about 27 per cent of the participants had access to land exceeding 2 hectares. In addition, the proportion of households participating in RPW was highest in this interval (8.2 per cent versus 3.4 per cent in the first and 4.6 per cent in the second interval). Members of the scheduled castes and scheduled tribes were among the poorest.

These two groups accounted for less than half of the participants (about 42 per cent). However, the proportion participating in RPW was higher among them (6.1 per cent as against 3.8 per cent in the rest). In sum, the presumption that a work requirement by itself would be an effective deterrent for the non-poor is not corroborated by this analysis. In fact, a substantial proportion of the total participants-if not a large majority-were non-poor. Although the 1997 World Bank Study draws attention to a few familiar design and implementation problems, it does not throw much light on the exclusion of the poor.

More revealing insights are obtained from an analysis of the Employment Guarantee Scheme (EGS). Concentrating mainly on the net benefits from the EGS, it is arguable that these were higher for the non-poor, resulting in the exclusion of the poor. Although the opportunity cost of time is not likely to vary much between the poor and non-poor during slack periods, other costs do, making it more difficult for the poor to participate in EGS due to bureaucratic red tape. Such costs relate mostly to long waiting periods between registration and work opportunities and to long distances between the residence and worksite.

On the benefit side, the actual remuneration (and not so much the wage rate) and the periodisation of payments matter. Given the piece-rate system, there is a premium on physical strength and dexterity. But piece-rates cause long delays in the payment of wages as an assessment of the quantity and quality of work done takes time. Although it is stipulated that wages must be paid once a week (or fortnight at the latest), it is not uncommon for wages to be delayed for up to eight weeks.

More seriously, wages paid are often less than the recorded amount. Given the wage rate, the actual remuneration is substantially lower for the poor because they are more likely to be physically less strong and more exposed to being cheated because of their illiteracy. Thus, the disincentives to the poor on the benefit side (i.e., delays in payment of wages) may be just as strong as those associated with long delays in offers of EGS work-especially if they are subject to a tight liquidity constraint. Given budgetary constraints, improvements in the design and implementation of the EGS would enable greater participation by the poor.

Specifically, replacement of the piece-rate contract by a time-rate one for some routine tasks is necessary. This would help reduce delays in the payment of wages. A wider dispersal of EGS projects may add to the attractiveness of this scheme to the poor, since the guarantee is effective only at the district level, requiring participants to travel distances longer than the stipulated eight-kilometer limit. Simplification of registration procedures and reduction of the waiting period between registration and work would further facilitate the participation of the poor. With these improvements, which are indeed feasible, both transfer and stabilisation benefits of the EGS to the poor would be substantially greater.

SOCIAL SECURITY

The concern for the aged and infirm- both highly prone to chronic poverty- has grown over the years as a result of the aging of the population and the weakening of traditional family and community support. Formal social security is limited largely to urban areas and the benefits are small. Particularly relevant in the present context are old age pension and subsidized life insurance, as they provide a modicum of social security to the poor. A means-tested old age pension scheme operates in all Indian states. Some states also have pension schemes for destitute widows and the physically handicapped, and some provide for survivor benefits to families when a family member dies as a result of an occupational hazard.

Recently, the central government introduced a group insurance scheme for agricultural labourers and IRDP beneficiaries. The coverage of the old-age pension scheme varies considerably among the states. The low coverage (no more than 20 per cent of the old people in poverty) is due partly to lack of information among the eligible beneficiaries, but it is mainly due to restrictive qualifying conditions relating to age, destitution, residence and ad hoc financial ceilings. Corruption and procedural delays limit effective access. The pension amount is paltry, ranging from Rs 30 to Rs 60 per month.

The coverage of voluntary insurance is considerably lower, covering barely 8 per cent of the adult population. Further, the coverage of the rural population is substantially lower than its share in the total. The survivor benefits in the group insurance for agricultural labourers are a paltry Rs 1,000, not adequate even to meet funeral expenses.

However, extension of social security to the rural poor-particularly old age pensions and survivor benefits-on a comprehensive scale is affordable, as the overall resource requirement is no more than 1 per cent of India's GNP and no more than 4 per cent of the combined resources of the central and state governments. Part of the premia could of course be financed from contributions of the insured persons. A recent initiative to strengthen social security for the poor, while laudable, is "belated redress rather than radical reform."

IMPLEMENTATION

The World Bank critique is standard: overcentralized administration, multiplicity of official agencies and hesitant devolution to the Panchayats of poverty alleviation programmes. Each of these concerns is dealt with sketchily. As devolution to the Panchayats following the 73rd Constitutional Amendment Act is in some ways a landmark, these concerns deserve a more detailed and critical review. The 73rd Constitutional Amendment provides for a uniform three-tier structure of the Panchayats-specifically at the district, block and village levels-mandatory elections after five years, proportional representation of the scheduled castes/scheduled tribes, a quota for women, periodic auditing of accounts and specification of areas of responsibility of the Panchayats.

As a definitive assessment of this structure is not feasible for lack of detailed data, the focus is restricted to a few aspects of the devolution. A major concern is the implementation of two anti-poverty programmes for which the Village Panchayats are responsible: the Jawahar Rozgar Yojana (JRY) and the Integrated Rural Development Programme (IRDP). Drawing largely upon the fieldwork carried out by researchers at the

National Institute of Rural Development (NIRD), in Uttar Pradesh and Karnataka, as well as from our own survey in selected villages of Uttar Pradesh (UP), some useful insights are obtained. Briefly, far from empowering the poor, the Panchayats have not even smoothed their formal participation.

PARTICIPATION

There were delays in holding the 1995 Panchayat elections, partly because of political uncertainty, but mostly because of social resistance to quotas. In general, chairpersons and deputy chairpersons-especially at the block and district levels-tend to be from relatively affluent sections and often manipulate elections, thereby reducing the Panchayat meetings to a mere formality. Decisions taken by the chairpersons are formally approved by the members present. But even if the chairperson belongs to the SCs/ STs and other reserved categories, the dominance of the affluent sections means that the outcomes are often similar.

Quotas for the poor have mixed effects. The possibility that they divide or weaken the poor cannot be ruled out. Also, as noted above, to the extent that the local power structure is deeply rooted, those elected typically serve the interests of locally powerful groups. On the other hand, quotas may legitimize power sharing over a period of time. On balance, therefore, the impact on the poor may be favourable but limited.

DEVOLUTION

Both the UP and Karnataka case studies point to serious aberrations regarding local governance and these aberrations took different forms: arbitrary reassignment of areas of responsibility, shortfalls in financial allocations and lack of administrative and other forms of support. These are considered in turn. Out of all areas assigned to the Panchayats in the UP Act, only rural sanitation was in fact devolved to them. All other areas remained under the overall control and supervision of district/ state agencies.

That the bureaucracy or official agencies could overextend their domain in violation of the provisions in the State Acts had a lot to do with an unstable coalition (between the Samajvadi Janta Party and the Bharatiya Janta Party) and unsettled conditions in the hill areas. The Karnataka case points to other sources of aberrations: relative bargaining strength and skills of the Panchayats at different levels. Given a relatively stable political environment and a properly carved-out role for the bureaucracy, the battlefield shifted to the Panchayats.

Most of the major schemes were monopolized either by the Zilla/District Panchayats or the Taluk/ Block Panchayats, with a minimal role for the Gram Panchayats. The Karnataka case study also underscores the ambiguity in the roles of some key functionaries (e.g., executive officers of Taluk Panchayats) and absence of support staff. As a result, the Panchayats have not functioned well.

Our own survey in UP revealed that the long absence of the village development officer-a key link between official agencies and Village Panchayats-delayed and/or disrupted implementation of some important programmes. Some field evidence from the Rae Bareli district in UP points to larger underutilisation of JRY and IRDP outlays following the installation of the new Panchayat system. It is difficult, however, to ascertain whether it was the need for greater transparency or general unfamiliarity with the new procedures that resulted in delays in utilisation of funds.

ANTI-POVERTY PROGRAMMES

Jawahar Rozgar Yojana

Some glaring shortcomings in the implementation of the JRY came to light in our survey of villages in UP. The amounts received by a Gram Panchayat ranged between Rs16,000 and Rs 18,000 in 1996 and 1997, and these were utilized mostly for making brick roads. The chairpersons claimed that 200 to

250 persons participated in this activity for 7 to 10 days. Some of the participants denied receiving wages, but admitted contributing free labour to prevent water-logging in residential areas. The number of participants reported seems grossly inflated also because the wage rate implied was well below the official JRY wage.

That the whole operation was masterminded by the chairpersons, Panchayat secretaries and village development officers for their personal benefit is further corroborated by the fact that none of the Panchayat members knew anything about the scheme-the financial outlays, the nature of activities or the number of participants. In fact, in one case, it was discovered that the bricklaying activity was completed well before the JRY grant was received. Whether the poor benefited at all from this scheme seems doubtful.

Integrated Rural Development Programme

IRDP was a dismal failure as well. Instead of the Gram Sabha identifying the beneficiaries, the chairpersons of the Gram Panchayats selected them. In one case, it was widely known that the chairman exacted hefty fees. Following complaints, he absconded. Even under the new chairperson, little seems to have changed. Lack of awareness of the scheme and weak accountability mechanisms in the village community tend to perpetuate the status quo.

OTHER RELATED PROGRAMMES

The role of the Gram Panchayat in other rural development schemes, including village hygiene and sanitation, literacy, consolidation of holdings (chakbandi) and land transfers, reflected gross negligence or the unmistakable influence of a few dominant groups. Few Panchayat members (including the chairpersons) seemed concerned about lack of access to drinking water, primary health care facilities, nonfunctioning schools, unhygienic conditions, etc.

When their attention was drawn to some of these concerns, they blamed the district agencies for the meagerness of the outlays. Several instances of chakbandi favouring a few influential/wealthy individuals came to light. For example, the chairpersons, in connivance with a few village officials, assigned them large plots near the main road for a "fee." Equally, land transfers-specifically the leasing out of Panchayat land-invariably benefited a few influential individuals, when the beneficiaries were supposed to be exclusively SC/ST families.

Reforms

Since the Panchayats are expected to play a key role in implementing poverty alleviation programmes, some recommendations for reform are sketched below.(98) Given that the Panchayats are ill-equipped to carry out the responsibilities assigned to them, there is a strong case for selectivity. A small cluster of responsibilities could be identified through a systematic application of some economic considerations. Economies of scale and inter-jurisdictional externalities favour responsibilities assigned to the higher levels, while need for local information and accountability favour assignment to the Gram Panchayats.

Areas of responsibility that complement one another may also favour joint provision. Simultaneous involvement of more than one level of the Panchayat in an area may be necessary when each level has specific comparative advantages. Consider, for instance, primary education: the buildings could be constructed by the district or Block Panchayat while the responsibility for running the schools could be vested in a Gram Panchayat. Incentive incompatibility between the Panchayats and official agencies raises a serious concern.

This results in delays in the disbursal and utilisation of funds-especially at the Gram Panchayat level. A similar incompatibility exists between the Panchayats and support staff drawn mainly from state government departments, often delaying implementation of the schemes. Although there is considerable emphasis in the State Acts on accountability of the Panchayats to higher authorities, it is not matched by a concern for accountability of the Gram Panchayat to the Gram Sabha. There are, in fact, some glaring lacunae in the existing provisions.

Although the Gram Panchayat is required to place the statement of accounts, budgets and other proposals before the Gram Sabha, its approval is not binding. Nor does the Gram Sabha have the power to dissolve the Gram Panchayat in case there is deliberate default (e.g. embezzlement of funds). There is thus a case for broadening the functions and powers of the Gram Sabha and for making its approval mandatory with a view to preventing the "capture" of the Gram Panchayat by locally influential groups. But these reforms by themselves may not guarantee that the interests of the poor will be better protected or promoted.

A strong coalition of the poor could make a difference. Greater awareness among them of their collective strength, combined with more "voice" given to them in the Panchayats, may help develop a collective identity. As pointed out by Bardhan, "changing the local political structure in the village gives more 'voice' to the poor and induces them to get involved in local self-governing institutions and management of local public goods."

Over time, this would facilitate a more active and decisive role of the poor *vis-a-vis* locally powerful groups. From this perspective, the forging of closer links among the Panchayats, cooperatives and labour unions is thus imperative. As emphasized in the 1997 World Bank Study; the primacy of growth in poverty alleviation efforts rests on its strong direct and indirect effects. But as shown in this chapter, both the direct effect of growth on poverty alleviation and the indirect effect through the generation of resources for poverty alleviation programmes are weaker than claimed.

Poverty tends to persist among those who are old, lack physical and human capital and/or belong to lower castes. Growth alone will not make a significant difference unless combined with specific interventions. These include land reforms through a market-mediated mechanism, the provision of school education of higher quality-especially at the primary level-and social safety nets (rural public works and social security).

Community involvement has considerable potential for making such interventions effective, but as our analysis of the restructuring of the Panchayats following the 73rd Constitutional Amendment Act emphasizes, there are serious functional aberrations. In a politically unstable environment, official agencies maintained their domination, while in another there was a reallocation of responsibilities among different levels of the Panchayats. In either case, contrary to the state's objectives, the Gram Panchayats were left with a minimal role.

More seriously, other evidence points to the "capture" of the Gram Panchayats by a few influential persons resulting in large-scale diversion of JRY and IRDP funds. Delineating a few proposals for reforms-selectivity in assigning responsibilities at different levels of the Panchayats; incentive compatibility between the Panchayats and official agencies; and greater accountability of the Gram Panchayats to the Gram Sabhas-we emphasized that these must be accompanied by efforts to strengthen coalitions among the poor.

Greater awareness among them of their collective strength together with their increased "voice" in the Panchayats may make a difference. In conclusion, it is not so much lack of growth as the exclusion of some sections of the poor from growth that perpetuates their poverty. Growth alone will not accomplish much unless it is combined with measures designed to promote the participation of the poor. Community initiatives in the implementation of such measures, backed with a strong coalition of the poor, could make a significant difference.

4

Identity and Work

To generalize about work in India is virtually impossible. But it would be wrong to ignore such an immensely significant nation, one so intensely alive and essentially industrious, certain assertions to the contrary notwithstanding. Obviously, this chapter cannot hope to define, or even touch upon, all the forms of work found in India, but at least certain leads can be offered to the reader. In many respects the foundations of work as it exists in India today were laid during the two centuries of European colonisation.

That was a period which saw economic liberalism coexisting with monopolies, enormous wealth with famine, peace in the Empire with communal rioting. These are pieces in an age-old puzzle which has still not been solved. Industrial development around poles or in clusters, one of the enduring legacies of the British Raj to independent India, took place on a modest but significant scale and ahead of its time. The Congress Party, which won Independence in 1947, opted for a semi-planned and protectionist form of development between 1946 and 1977.

Many of the policies initiated at that time are still far from being implemented. Major economic infrastructures were established, and the spectre of famine receded, but poverty remained. The years since 1985 appear to have broken with this recent past as regards economic development, with the emphasis now being put on private enterprise, though this is scarcely a widespread trend. Large areas in the west, south and centre of India are becoming industrialized, while the old industrial centres are crumbling. Any consideration of the notion of work in India must start by accepting that, however difficult to understand, the caste system is a fact of life. Caste is not synonymous with a division of labour; rather it encompasses and relativizes those divisions.

The traditional prescriptive and theoretical hierarchy of the four varnas (priests, warriors, merchants and others) vaguely reminiscent of the medieval European "orders" - should not be confused with the caste system that endures and proliferates today. The practice of everyday "caste" (jati) is related but different. The de facto caste system infiltrates everywhere, even among the Muslims. Despite its notorious rigidities, it is flexible and adaptable. It confers status and a sense of belonging; it defines category and rank, identity and its negation; it permits monopoly (endogamy) and rules (internal) competition; it is a system based on loyalty and yet a potential challenge to all allegiances.

These innumerable aspects of the sacred yet commonplace de facto caste system long constituted a system or ensemble of local systems, a universe where social relationships were more important than action. At least, this was what the collective consciousness or the discourse of the Great Ones wished. In very many situations, therefore, tasks were dissociated from labour. They were, and still are in some cases, an interpretation in status terms of the act of production. We are far removed from the much-flaunted and prized European concept of the work ethic, but still not so far, basically, from the realities that marked it.

We need only recall the guilds. Caste is sometimes explicitly set against the order of the varnas, and bhakti is even less inclined to accord a central place to work than is "Brahminism", the conception of a universal order that sustains the spirit of caste hierarchy. Bhakti is one of the essential pillars of religion, whose language and system of social relations pervaded precolonial societies. Even today, working people in India still hold to that vision of the world.

Admittedly, Kabir, the fifteenth-century weaver, and other saintly figures revered by the people used metaphors borrowed from the experience of labour. They did so, however, to open up what they conceived of as paths towards liberation (from work, from a contemptible world, from one's allotted fate) through religious fervour. In many other fields besides, labour as understood at the International Labour Organization, in the form handed down to us by the post-medieval European consciousness, seems a rare or marginal category.

Little scope is left for the expression of labour after the passage of such dominant influences as astrologers' control of individual destinies, a self-referential cult of texts and of knowledge for its own sake; a culture of bodily satisfaction, of sophisticated emotions and pleasures; a world of rivalries, betrayals and secrets; problems of liberation and renunciation, of discipline and dominion; an obsession with war and power, closely or loosely associated with religion; the tiny, insular, but very ostentatious worlds of courtly magnificence, of interminable discussions; a world of landowners' power and domination through countless intermediaries.

For centuries, for work to gain respect as a factor of identity, it had to be carried out within the family, and the task performed had to be clean or virtually untainted. The work of low castes, of the Untouchables (now "Scheduled Castes") and a majority of Muslims (who often previously belonged to low castes) was almost always a form of manual work. Sweat was considered "dirty", violence degrading - and work was conceived of as violence. While craftsmen differed in their practices, their discourse and aspirations differed far less.

Even the Untouchables (15 per cent of the population) insist on their own caste system. Did colonisation destroy a universe of product sophistication and quality, where labour, proficiency and skill were recognized? Or did it just debase a state of affairs which had long remained structurally stable? Certainly, in the eighteenth century India was the world's largest exporter of textiles, but its producers' loyalties lay with caste, sect and family, they identified only secondarily with the work they did.

As in our age of "globalisation", their "economic opening-up" in no way prevented their "closedness" with regard to the concept of work and even more so to the idea of producer autonomy. And yet, there has long been a negotiated labour market in southern Asia. There are labour markets, migration for economic reasons, changes in economic activity, with the particular harshness brought to these processes by a shortage economy and low productivity.

For centuries there have been strategies and tactics in connection with economic activity: the pace of work - which was often more important than earnings - the recognition of trades and occupations in local hierarchies, etc. These situations also display contradictions, for example, status is one of the elements in labour costs (the case of the lower castes is particularly revealing on this question). The foregoing has referred to the structure of Indian society but it would be inappropriate to contrast that with history.

As in Europe, realities are so complex, so interwoven that it is difficult to define what was contributed by colonisation, with the trauma it caused and the compromises it brought, to the establishment of a legal status of labour, to work discipline, mass production and unemployment. One thing is certain: it is simplistic to contrast a pre-wage-labour feudal society with its "Europeanized" opposites. Right from the start, indentured labour and dependent employment were at the centre of the labour question, both within and outside the transitional areas surrounding wage labour. One has only to recall the servant class in the wealthy households, the farm labourers and the sharecroppers, the hierarchically organized family societies.

Well before Plassey, which opened the gates of India to the British colonizers in 1757, the dependent worker considered him- or herself to be an "extension" of the master. With the coming of European domination began a long period of prostration by such workers, a period aptly termed the "culture of silence". The imposition of the concept of private property and new legal standards deprived these workers of their power of negotiation, their mobility and their sense of perspective. They were always the first to suffer famines and police beatings.

The courageous amongst them became bandits. Manual work in factories came about unconsciously, without recognition. The small dark native, "feminine and passive", to use the terms of the nineteenth-century orientalists, became the typical manual worker, the coolie of colonial terminology. Introduced around 1850, manual work in factories was to be the fate of the lower castes and the Muslims. These workers, however, very soon became conscious of issues of honour dividing them, and of little economic tactics, which seldom served to unite them.

The craft 6lite was often by-passed and the peasant labourer, alternating between country and city, came to predominate in most sectors. The scarcity of readily available workers lasted for more than half a century. But such workers were to gain little from their rarity value as they were far from being free. The figure of the recruiting agent, the guarantor of morality and the link in the hierarchical chain, dominated large factories right up to the 1940s, and has by no means disappeared. Providing the crucial link between the sahib (colonial master) and the profit which he sought, the recruiting agent was often a skilled worker who relied rather on his way with people, his "social skills".

There were innumerable ways of avoiding work in India and the recruiter's glib talk was one of them. However, as they increased in number, manual workers dreamed more of security than of work. Though employers continued to display paternalism, this had its limits. Managing agencies ran most companies according to speculative principles. When Taylorism appeared, it quickly aroused the opposition of employers and workers alike.

The employer considered the worker to be either rebellious or apathetic. He did not yet profess any interest in the workers' motivation. The labour movement developed from a somewhat chance encounter between the aspirations of non-citizen wage-earners and the keen rivalry exhibited by different political tendencies in the middle class. Philanthropists and teachers preceded the rebellious workers into the class struggle, but it was a number of young Brahmins educated by the British who founded communism in India in the 1920s. Intermediaries then multiplied on the backs of the workers.

They it was who controlled the mob silenced the voiceless because, though feared for his rebelliousness, the worker was first subdued. Though initially fragmented, these "wage relation mediators" were the masters in an exploitative, violent world, an area of savage competition which they managed on a fairly rational basis. They devised and organized a new relationship with the State based on cash demands and the need for stability.

Workers' sense of being exploited, keenly felt at local level, was sustained by utopian dreams of redistributive justice. From the 1920s onward, the general strike was a familiar spectre, or symbol, in certain sectors. Trade unions soon displayed their emblems and fashioned their jargon, composed of loan words and neologisms: proletariat, working class, white-collar workers. But only the figure of the white-collar worker was to acquire a massive following.

WORK, THE LAW AND THE STATE

The State is always behind the law, and this is also true of labour law. Relations with the State condition relations in the legal sphere. A basic relationship crystallized during colonial rule: the State was something both to be avoided and to be held responsible. It was, as it were, the "father and mother of its subjects", to which, however, one owed nothing, a notion containing parallel but contradictory perceptions, a sort of shameful but necessary stain spreading everywhere.

It took a long historical process for these peasant concepts and these Brahmin ideas to change. In many places and at many times, the changes were barely perceptible. Older "layers" of relationships with the State, from the days before the ideology of the contract, from before the notion of nationhood, still lay just below the surface. They are still present even under the existing Welfare State, the rule of law, the State as protector of minorities.

This conception is itself now being challenged by the affluent classes and modern ideologues, who consider the "State at the service of all" to be too costly, cumbersome and antiquated. As a direct result of its complex origins and its unfinished projects, other aspects and tendencies of state power are now emerging: for example, authoritarian, hygiene-obsessed, utilitarian tendencies, a fantasized state liberalism, the power of the judge and the expert, aspects of the military or police state... However, is it true that Indian labour law was a by-product of competition? Colonisation certainly brought in a great deal of money and that was the primary and continuing source of its legitimacy.

This was the framework in the mid-nineteenth century for the establishment of the rule of law as a coercive force, as the embodiment of domination, as a machine for making profit. The manufacturer in Manchester demanded it, for his part, if he was to continue selling his goods in the face of the low wages and infernal working conditions prevailing in India. Finally, colonial labour law can also be considered as a manifestation of the power of intermediaries and middlemen in a world where most people have no rights. Non-citizenship and extreme inequality were the norm for most Indians until Independence.

This comment applies even more to the people who had work. Drawing its inspiration from the Congress Party, Indian labour law developed from the 1930s onward, seeking sometimes to address the interests of employers and workers simultaneously, despite its awareness of the yawning inequality between them. Though freedom of association was granted fairly early on, the right to strike was withheld. Even today, though strikes occur, there is no right to strike. In the labour world, the alliance of law with violence is not fortuitous. There at the beginning, its influence is still felt. Despite sporadic and localized attempts by government and trade unions, the workers have never made up for lost time as regards mastering rules that they did not formulate, and in which they rarely saw their interests reflected.

Major laws were enacted during the period from 1946 to 1952, and again in the 1960s. More legislation piled up in the 1970s and 1980s. But attempts to standardize and simplify labour law have repeatedly failed. The language of mass disputes is different. India is a country of strikes and lockouts, and this tendency is fuelled, though not engendered, by the competitive nature of the numerous trade unions. Entire regions have been marked by sporadic but fierce confrontations: in 1958, 1962, 1967, 1974, 1977-78, 198283, 1989. Contemporary labour law serves both to protect workers, an aim which today's employers find unacceptable, and as a means of dispossession.

It is a law written in English, and still often reflects its origins in British law. The concepts it invokes are not widely understood and are often foreign to the daily realities of workers' lives. This is what permits its universalisation. ILO Conventions are ratified and international categories recognized. However, at other levels, it is a class law, it protects narrow interests which purport to represent Indian society's destiny, to be its driving force.

This is reflected in a number of ways: in its power to control, protect and repress. However, industrialists, and still less the ruling class, do not speak with one voice. Industrial tribunals date from 1956. At first the judges on these tribunals were respected, but they found themselves increasingly challenged by the workers, especially during the confrontations of the early 1980s. Nevertheless they prevailed and, with their increasing influence, a new type of intermediary has begun to dominate the world of labour: tens of thousands of lawsuits are pending and it takes ten years or more to settle them.

Finally, the law functions as an exclusionary force, a determinant of identities. Labour law never applies to everyone, usually only to a small minority. Large parts of the labour force are thus left subject to community or customary law, if not to the law of the strongest. In India, only criminal law is universal. The development of an organized modern system was a slow legal and historical process. Originating in the wide gap separating the sahib from his servants, and intensified by the development that followed Independence, the organized sector was the only domain in which labour law fully applied.

Is the organized sector therefore a community of the elect, a form of corporatist power, a sign of continuing colonial domination, a class of "privileged subjects" of the State? A little of all this, undoubtedly. Yet a bastion of law, of individual and union protection did emerge and, in a remarkable series of contradictions, managed both to express and to sublimate class difference. Working within its framework are those who profess to abolish the sway of customary and community law.

There is a tendency to brush aside as belonging merely to the unorganized sector all communal links and traditions, which are thus constantly confronted with a rational, well-organized model of society, a superior force beyond democracy and the Constitution. Invoking the needs of modern organisation, the law required the collection of statistics, influenced the language of economics, and shaped the prospects for development.

The division between formal and informal sectors is one of identity. It also provides a reference point, a vocabulary determining ordinary people's attitudes to employment and social advancement. The peasantry who flocked to the towns but retained many of their traditional attitudes devised ways of recreating and perpetuating their inherited means of livelihood, to ensure stability for the next generation.

During the 1960s, when large-scale employers were starting to protest against labour protection, employment in the public sector became the universal aspiration of the working class. In 1996, this is still the key issue around which to mobilize groups of all kinds, but the optimism of the 1950s has faded. Organized employment and its accompanying rhetoric finally prevent workers and work itself from assuming an independent identity. Organized employment amounts to more than work, non-organized employment to less.

THE PRESENT

Never has wage employment been as important in India as it is today, though it still engages only a minority of the labour force. It is almost always associated with other situations, other sources of income. Yet, despite its unprecedented scale, never has wage employment attracted so little attention. Neo-liberal discourse tends to blame protected employment for all the woes of the economy and the country. None the less, either because of state intervention or despite the State's best endeavours to prevent such practices, sinecures and favours continues to be handed out to friends, relatives or benefactors.

Employers and their "liberal" mouthpieces rant against the "privileges" of bus drivers and factory workers and express their dislike of the second-rate and restrictive social security system. They profess to abhor the corrupting factor of influential connections, but they have made profitable, lifelong use of their old, private networks. Is this the hypocrisy of a schizophrenic society? Undoubtedly, but it also echoes the profoundly held conviction that capital should no longer be protected, that it should also be entrusted with the management of society.

Investment and development may sometimes ensue, but another, more sinister result is the drift into organized crime, that epitome of the alliance between hierarchy and the profit principle. The economic liberalism of today's 6lites is not only a reflection of the social forces which made the higher castes convinced upholders of the ideology of individual merit. Nor is it confined to considerations of dominant financial interests. And yet, in the name of economic liberalism, workingclass movements are thrown out of the "organized sector". Elsewhere, one celebrates the end of the class struggle; here it rears its head.

The principles and practices of organisation are shaped by the social imperatives which created the Welfare State, by pressure from rural notables, militant urban progressives and "enlightened" feudal leaders. New wealthy neighbourhoods with armed guards and security systems are being built, there is a heightened obsession with security, and the ideology of development is being reformulated for the benefit of a minority of consumers. Such arguments are to be heard, such practices put into place as soon as the questions of lay-offs, automation and relocation of factories appear on the agenda.

Though the State remains a pillar of society, like work, it is ignored or denounced. Where large firms employ a stable or decreasing staff, workers are becoming polarized. The technicians of the organized sector are joining the workers of the precarious unorganized sector. Modern bosses dream of a worker-free factory, and all that stands between them and their dream seems to be the hated politician class and ... the high price of robots. Workers in the new factory are divided into two polarized groups and hardly know each other.

There is a spiralling increase in precarious casual employment, often on a daily basis, and in the subcontracting of certain types of work through recruiters. The employment of skilled workers on precarious conditions is becoming common, stable employees are a dying species. On the other hand, managers and executives are becoming more numerous and assertive, and in the best-protected workplaces everyone aspires to management status.

Outside the large enterprises, employment in small mechanized workshops is on the increase, but the number employed is variable, fluctuating with the moods of the economy. Like sub-contracting to workshops, home-based work is expanding at an unprecedented rate in the mass production sectors. A new working class is silently emerging, far from the factories, or just alongside. Though it comprises the largest number of persons, it is of course neither recognized nor represented. Unmarried girls, widows and children, workers who do not exist in any legal sense, are ideal fodder for an aborted form of Taylorism and its postFordian excesses.

There has been a shift from the culture of silence to the sweat-shop system, to the world of sub-contracting at both local and international levels. This is where products are copied and brands are pirated. A shoddy little world where trained technicians produce computer software but are considered unskilled. There has been a rapid spread of workplaces where dehumanizing conditions reign supreme. Free trade zones are beginning to appear, in an updated version of the colonial trading posts. Trade unions and community protection have no place in these places.

Are these examples of monstrous, unequal development evidence of totalitarian forces at work in the midst of a world governed by economic liberalism? Meanwhile, work relationships based on dependence flourish nearby, whether within the family or the caste, or in a modernized form, for example, in the vast worlds of domestic service and arduous work where essential services are so discreetly performed by workers unable to defend themselves in the language of production and organisation. For decades the frugal, reliable office clerk provided the universal role model of the humble and honest worker, and continues to do so today.

His figure represented the meeting ground between peasants escaping from shortages of every kind and exploitative entrepreneurs in quest of stability and low labour costs. This model has undergone countless modifications and its latest incarnation is to be found in the modern urban environment: the bank clerk in his spotless shirt, a union member sometimes several times over and a pillar of respectability. And yet, this reassuring figure lives under the threat of redundancy and competition from computers.

Though still alive and active, he is beginning to topple and crack. But there is no new conception of the worker and of work to take his place, merely a void - one that the pretence of a middle class will not fill. This pretend middle class is a fundamental element. Despite its selfconfidence, it remains intangible - for what is a "middle class" that comprises only 10 per cent of the population? Consider its extravagant and wasteful lifestyle, which is presented as the only valid model to shanty-town and village dwellers.

This new model is invading the popular imagination through its constant representation by the increasingly uncontrolled mass media. Work has no place in these contemporary dreams, even though each "middle-class" household still has its industrious domestic servants, its selfeffacing workers. The scramble to get rich is causing a shift from the dream of supervised harmony, where the elder or the symbolic father controlled the wishes of the masses, towards a world where the poor are forgotten, invisible.

There is no question here of democratic debate. There is a slide away from the paternalism of the State, from the monopolistic firms and notables of an authoritarian system marked by bitter mutinies, towards mobile and far more implacable categories. Masters and rulers hide behind the "invisible hand of the market", whilst yuppies believe they alone represent the nation. To be sure, most people remain far removed from these extreme models. Nostalgia for the tiny pension, the popularity of running one's own little business, and the resistance of family and neighbourhood networks hamper the realisation of the dreams of transparence nurtured by the promoters of a self-regulating market.

Has the destruction of working environments been less traumatic in India than in Europe? Certainly it has been aggravated by a prevailing puritanical atmosphere and by inter-communal strife. But the family still insists on (good) marriages, therefore jobs, and assertion of status requires money, therefore resources. While the working classes may still believe in the humble and honest worker, in actuality various hated but unavoidable forms of trafficking and getting by are increasingly the source of livelihoods and self-contempt. In such a context, the idea of respect for work is pure nostalgia.

Not everyone is marching to this tune. There are still sectarian, no doubt rearguard, and attempts to reinforce the pride of the working man. But they are ambivalent in nature: the last defenders of the anticolonial svadeshi (believers in "do-it-yourself") rub shoulders with non-governmental organisations subsidized by the goodwill of post-Christian Europe. For decades, with the blessing of tools at major religious festivals, the worker has briefly been recognized as an actor in the urban setting.

At festivals which draw thousands, the conservative nationalist Hindu party tries to persuade workers in large factories to identify themselves with the builders of Shiva's chariot. Hindu nationalism, which talks of pride in one's work and the need for production but refuses to oppose employers and workers, lies just below the surface in many parts of the trade union world. For certain backwardlooking minorities, work are still perceived as a means of acquiring national power, just another form of war. Other depictions of work often fail even to mention the term, despite the slogan "there is no substitute for hard work" plastered on the walls of rural railway-stations, in places where nobody can understand English.

Reference is often made to the usefulness of putting people to work, to an ideal society freed from trade unions and caste pressure groups, to the abundance of a universe developed for and by those who consider themselves to be "middle class", or to the prestige of imported or copied consumer goods. But these visions nearly all emanate from the ruling class. Practically all categories of manual workers have given up or are giving up any attempt to express what they stand for. Important union leaders failed dismally, around 1980, in their attempts to create a less paternalistic worker movement.

Must one conclude that the impact of reason and order which so marked eighteenth-century Europe has been exceptionally short-lived and superficial in India? Poverty is old news. For thousands of years the great majority of human beings have lived and laboured at a low material standard of living. In the first hunter-gatherer societies that emerged on the savannahs of Africa, in the agrarian villages that later appeared in the highlands of the fertile crescent, in the great agricultural empires that arose in Mesopotamia, the Mediterranean area, India, and China, most people were very poor. This iron fact of life prevailed in all human societies until quite recently. Despite universal material deprivation, human societies evolved cultures and social structures that permitted people to live and reproduce in relative peace.

Social order was possible in conditions of pervasive poverty because of one fundamental condition: The deprivation existed at low geographic densities. Under this circumstance, the socially disruptive correlates of poverty occurred infrequently and could be managed, more or less, through informal means; and because the poverty-stricken masses rarely came into contact with the tiny elite, they did not perceive the full extent of their relative deprivation.

The one place where rich and poor families came into direct contact was in cities, but preindustrial urban centers were few in number and never contained more than a tiny fraction of the human population. In premodern cities, moreover, the wealthy were constantly exposed to the poor and their privations, because preindustrial technologies permitted neither the separation of work from residence nor the segregation of the elite from the masses. Class integrity was maintained largely through social means, not physical separation. Indeed, the coexistence of poverty and wealth at high densities created problems of social order, as any student of ancient Rome can attest.

The industrial revolution of the nineteenth century upset the apple cart by creating and distributing wealth on a grand scale, enabling affluence and poverty to become geographically concentrated for the first time. Through urbanisation, the rich and the poor both came to inhabit large urban areas. Within cities new transportation and communication technologies allowed the affluent to distance themselves spatially as well as socially from the poor, causing a rise in the levels of class segregation and a new concentration of affluence and poverty.

For a short time after World War II, mass social mobility temporarily halted the relentless geographic concentration of affluence and poverty in developed countries. The postwar economic boom that swept Europe, Japan, and the United States created a numerically dominant middle class that mixed residentially with both the upper and the lower classes. After 1970, however, the promise of mass social mobility evaporated and inequality returned with a vengeance, ushering in a new era in which the privileges of the rich and the disadvantages of the poor were compounded increasingly through geographic means.

In the coming century, the fundamental condition that enabled social order to be maintained in the past-the occurrence of affluence and poverty at low geographic densitieswill no longer hold. In the future, most of the world's impoverished people will live in urban areas, and within these places they will inhabit neighbourhoods characterized by extreme poverty. A small stratum of rich families meanwhile will cluster in enclaves of affluence, creating an unprecedented spatial intensification of both privilege and poverty.

As a result of this fundamental change in the geographic structure of inequality, the means by which the undesirable correlates of poverty were managed in the past will break down. The juxtaposition of geographically concentrated wealth and poverty will cause an acute sense of relative deprivation among the poor and heightened fears among the rich, resulting in a rising social tension and a growing conflict between the haves and the have-nots. We have entered a new age of inequality in which class lines will grow more rigid as they are amplified and reinforced by a powerful process of geographic concentration.

THE SPATIAL CONCENTRATION OF POVERTY

Poverty is notoriously difficult to define; statistics on its incidence are unreliable and difficult to acquire, especially in the developing world. Tabatabai and Fouad conducted a survey of poverty estimates in developing countries for the International Labour Office and found that most regions lacked statistics dating back more than a few years. In Latin America, however, they were able to assemble reasonably accurate estimates of poverty rates beginning in 1970. To illustrate trends in the geographic concentration of poverty in developing countries, I apply rates of rural and urban poverty estimated by Tabatabai and Fouad for Latin America to rural and urban populations estimated for this region by the United Nations.

In 1970 most of Latin America's poor-nearly twothirds-lived in the countryside, typically in isolated farming communities, small agrarian villages, and tiny rural hamlets. In the ensuing two decades, however, the poor urbanized rapidly. By 1980 the balance of rural and urban poverty was approaching parity, and by 1990 a substantial majority (60%) of Latin America's poor lived in urban areas. This transformation of the geographic structure of human deprivation was so quick that the ratio of rural-to-urban poverty in 1990 was almost precisely opposite the ratio that had prevailed only 20 years earlier.

Therefore, in this hemisphere, poverty is already well on the way to complete urbanisation. The typical poor Latin American of the twenty-first century will not live in a village or town but in a city, and most likely a very large one. Although data limitations prevent me from demonstrating this fact for other regions of the developing world, projected trends in urbanisation suggest that a majority of the world's poor will soon live in cities. The urban concentration of poverty is already well advanced in developed countries. By 1970 U.S. poverty was already predominantly urban; 56% of all poor persons lived either in central cities or in suburbs.

Nonetheless, a large plurality of the poor (44%) lived in nonmetropolitan areas only two decades ago. Over the next 20 years, however, the percentage of poor people living in nonmetropolitan areas dropped steadily, to 31% in 1980 and to 28% in 1990; thus by the early 1990s, 72% of America's poor lived in urban areas. Not only was poverty becoming more urbanized, however; it was also becoming more highly concentrated in the urban core.

The proportion of poor people who lived in central cities stood at 34% in 1970, but the figure rose to 39% in 1980 and to 43% in 1990. Meanwhile the percentage of the poor living in suburbs, after rising during the 1970s, fell slightly during the 1980s and reached 29% in 1990. While American poverty was becoming more concentrated in central cities, it was also concentrating in alreadypoor urban neighbourhoods. John Kasarda recently computed the share of poor persons living in poor and very poor neighbourhoods at different points in time.

He defined a poor neighbourhood as one with a tract poverty rate from 20% to 40%, and a very poor neighbourhood as one with a tract poverty rate of more than 40%; nonpoor neighbourhoods had a tract poverty rate below 20%. In 1970, 45% of central-city poor people lived in a neighbourhood that was not poor, whereas 55% lived in a poor or very poor neighbourhood (38% in the former and 17% in the latter). Over the next two decades, however, the concentration of poor people in poor places increased sharply.

From 1970 to 1990, the percentage of central-city poor people living in nonpoor areas declined from 45% to 31%, while the percentage living in poor neighbourhoods increased from 38% to 41%. Meanwhile the share living in very poor neighbourhoods grew markedly, from 17% to 28%. As of 1990, more than two-thirds of all central-city poor people lived in poor or very poor neighbourhoods. Elsewhere Mitchell Eggers and I argue that the P* isolation index popularized by Stanley Lieberson provides a reliable and accurate summary measure of poverty concentration. This index gives the rate of poverty in the neighbourhood of the average poor person.

Over the past two decades, class isolation among the poor has risen steadily, growing by 21% between 1970 and 1990. As of 1990, the average poor resident of the nation's largest metropolitan areas lived in a neighbourhood where roughly one-quarter of his or her neighbours were also poor. Analyses performed by Abramson and colleagues show that this geographic concentration of human poverty was remarkably widespread, and in some metropolitan areas reached extreme levels. By 1990 the average poor person in New York, Chicago, and Detroit lived in a neighbourhood where 29% of the people were poor; the typical poor resident of New Orleans lived in a neighbourhood where the poverty rate was a remarkable 35%. Over the past two decades, the social environment of the poor shifted to higher and higher densities of poverty.

THE SPATIAL CONCENTRATION OF AFFLUENCE

Despite a substantial and growing effort to study concentrated poverty, remarkably little attention has been given to the concentration of affluence. Since the dawn of urbanism, however, the elite have always clustered in cities for purposes of command and control. Indeed, in pre-industrial times they tended to settle in and around the city center. Because communications were rudimentary, effective administration required face-to-face interaction that could be achieved only through physical propinquity. Moreover, because transportation technologies were limited, goods and services required by the elite had to be produced, distributed, and sold near their places of residence.

The core of preindustrial cities thus tended to house a variety of social classes, generating considerable face-to-face interaction across class lines. Although the rich may have been centralized, they were not separated physically from the masses, and although a wide social gulf separated them from the poor, affluence itself was not spatially concentrated. This residential status quo was terminated in the nineteenth century by improvements in technology.

Advances in transportation, communication, and construction led to an increase in density at the urban core, a separation of work from residence, and new possibilities for physical separation between the classes. Especially in the United States, the middle and upper classes began to leave central cities for affluent suburbs on the urban periphery early in the twentieth century, first axially along rail lines and then, as the automobile became more widely available, concentrically throughout a wide hinterland. Although we have no direct measure of income segregation before 1940, we know that ethnic segregation increased substantially during the late nineteenth and early twentieth centuries in response to the changed ecological structure of the city.

It is reasonable to surmise that class segregation also increased. After the World War II, however, both class and ethnic segregation clearly declined, fueled by an ongoing process of generational succession, social assimilation, and mass economic mobility unleashed by the postwar boom. As shown in seminal work by Blau and Duncan and Featherman and Hauser, a remarkably fluid and open stratification system emerged in the United States during the years World War II. Socioeconomic status came to depend less on one's social origins than on one's achievements; the result was a sustained decline in income inequality and an unprecedented rise in living standards.

From 1947 to 1973, U.S. families doubled their incomes, while inequality declined by 5%. According to James Smith (1988), the share of families with middle-class incomes grew from a minority of 40% of the population in 1940 to twothirds of the population in 1970, while the poverty rate fell from 34% to 11%. In only 25 years the United States became a middle-class society structured meritocratically. This broader trend toward socioeconomic equality was expressed spatially, as the degree of residential segregation between the upper and the lower classes was reduced sharply.

According to calculations by Albert Simkus, residential dissimilarity between high- and low-status workers declined markedly between 1960 and 1970. In the metropolitan areas he studied, the average dissimilarity index between professionals and labourers decreased by 19% from 1960 to 1970, while that between managers and service workers decreased by 17%. At the same time, residential dissimilarity between managers and labourers dropped by 23%, and that between managers and service workers by 17%.

Therefore, during the 1960s, people located at the extremes of the American occupational structure were moving rapidly together in residential terms, and observers at the time thought class segregation was on the wane. Sometime during the mid-1970s, however, this pattern was reversed, and the classes once again began to pull apart socially and spatially. Just as we observe an increase in the concentration of poverty between 1970 and 1990, we also encounter a remarkable increase in the concentration of affluence. This index gives the proportion affluent in the neighbourhood of the average affluent person. Affluence is even more highly concentrated spatially than poverty.

Whereas the average poor person lived in a neighbourhood that was 19% poor in 1970, the typical affluent person lived in a neighbourhood that was 39% affluent. In the ensuing years, this already high concentration of affluence became even more intense: The isolation index increased to 43 in 1980 and to 52 in 1990. By the beginning of the present decade, in other words, the typical affluent person lived in a neighbourhood where more than half the residents were also rich; the outcome was a social environment that was far more homogeneously privileged than at any time in the previous 20 years. In their daily lives, affluent residents of U.S. urban areas were increasingly likely to interact only with other affluent people, and progressively less likely to interact with other classes, especially the poor.

THE NEW WORLD ORDER

The hallmark of the emerging spatial order of the twentyfirst century will be a geographic concentration of affluence and of poverty. Throughout the world, poverty will shift from a rural to an urban base; within urban areas poor people will be confined increasingly to poor neighbourhoods, yielding a density of material deprivation that is historically unique and unprecedented. As poverty grows more geographically concentrated over time, its harmful by-products also will become more highly concentrated, intensifying social problems that the affluent will naturally seek to escape.

Class segregation will increase, ratcheting up the concentration of affluence and poverty in self-reinforcing fashion. This new ecological structure stems from deep and powerful forces operating in the world today. Simply put, concentrated poverty follows from any process that gathers poor people together in space and then inpedes their socioeconomic and residential mobility.

At the end of the twentieth century, poor people are being assembled geographically through an ongoing process of urbanisation that is already well advanced. Their social mobility is blocked by the emergence of a global economic structure characterized by stagnant mean incomes, rising inequality, and growing class rigidity; and their spatial mobility is stymied by a rising tide of class segregation that is exacerbated, in many places, by an ongoing pattern of deliberate racial and ethnic exclusion. Welcome to the new world order.

THE URBANISATION OF POVERTY

In a world where the great majority of people live in cities, poverty perforce will be urbanized. Obviously most inhabitants of developed countries already live in urban areas: The proportion urban in the developed world was 74% in 1990 and is projected to reach 82% by 2020; in the United States the respective figures are 75% and 84%. Therefore, among developed nations, poverty already is highly urbanized, and this concentration will increase slowly but steadily in the coming decades. The potential for change is considerably greater in the developing world. As late as 1970, only one-quarter of its population was urban; in 1990 the figure was only 35%.

The path of urbanisation, however, generally follows a logistic curve, beginning slowly and then accelerating rapidly for a time before leveling off and gradually approaching an upper asymptote. Developing countries are now in that segment of the logistic curve characterized by rapid growth; the percentage urban is projected to rise rapidly in the next two decades, reaching 41% by the turn of the century and 47% in 2010.

Sometime between 2010 and 2020 the developing world as a whole will cross a significant dividing line: For the first time, a majority of its population will live in cities. Because the great majority of these new urbanites will be impoverished by any standard, this event implies that poverty also will become concentrated in urban areas. Therefore, early in the next century, the typical poor citizen of Planet Earth will cease to inhabit a small town or rural village, and instead will live in a large city. Because there is no precedent for a reversal of urbanisation once it has begun, the future of human poverty almost certainly lies in cities. Barring a catastrophe that wipes out much of the world's urban population, poverty will become progressively urbanized during the next century, and nobody can do much to change this fundamental fact.

THE RETURN OF INEQUALITY

Urbanisation stems entirely from rural-urban migration rather than from natural increase within cities. Historically much of this urbanizing population movement was internal, with peasants leaving rural areas for cities in their own countries, but a substantial part has always been directed to urban destinations overseas. Such was the case in Europe as it underwent development in the nineteenth century; much the same is occurring in developing nations today. When they arrived in cities, rural in-migrants of the past took advantage of numerous ladders of mobility to climb out of poverty and into the working, middle, and even upper classes.

Through the mid-1970s a pattern of widespread social mobility prevailed for in-migrants to cities, not only in developed countries such as the United States but also in developing societies such as Mexico. In the future, however, poor migrants who arrive in the world's burgeoning metropolises will be more likely to stay poor. Industrial growth and development from 1870 to 1970 produced a wholesale upgrading of the occupational structure to create a diamond-shaped status distribution that supported mass upward mobility, rising income, and declining inequality; in contrast, the postindustrial transformation since 1973 has produced an hourglass economic structure of high-paying jobs for the well-educated, a dwindling number of middle-income jobs for the modestly schooled, and many, many poorly paid jobs for those with little schooling.

Such a structure creates few opportunities for mobility and carries great potential for inequality. We are thus in an era of high and rising inequality. Gini indices measuring income inequality in selected developed nations in 1980 and 1990, During the 1980s, inequality increased most sharply in Anglophone countries such as Australia, Ireland, Britain, and the United States, where the Gini rose from 33 to 36.

The index also rose in Scandinavia (Finland, Norway, and Sweden) and Western Europe (Austria, Belgium, Germany, and the Netherlands). Only the relatively poor countries of southern Europe-Italy, Spain, and Portugal, where incomes were lower and inequality was greater to begin with-opposed the trend toward greater inequality. The shifts in Gini coefficients may appear modest, but they conceal a rather profound transformation in underlying economic structure. The nature of this transformation may be discerned by a closer look at trends in the United States during two contrasting eras: 1949-1969 and 1973-1991.

During the earlier period, median family income doubled in real terms; this increase was shared by families throughout the income distribution. When Sheldon Danziger and Peter Gottschalk (1995) divided family incomes by the poverty line and observed changes between 1949 and 1969, they found that relative incomes in the bottom quintile increased by 457%, while those in the next lowest quintile increased by 169%. In the two highest quintiles, meanwhile, relative incomes grew respectively by 102% and 93%. Therefore, in the postwar economy that prevailed through the early 1970s, everyone did betterthe poor as well as the rich.

A rising tide lifted all boats, and the poverty rate dropped from 40% to 14% while the Gini index fell from 38 to 35. After 1973, however, the median family income stagnated in real terms, ending only 6% higher in 1991. This stagnation in average income was produced by divergent trends at the extremes of the distribution. From 1973 to 1991, relative incomes for families in the two bottom quintiles declined by 19% and 8% respectively, whereas those for families in the two top quintiles increased by 21% and 22%.

Rather than a rising tide that lifted all boats, after 1973 Danziger and Gottschalk found uneven tides that elevated the yachts of the rich but beached the dinghies of the poor. As a result of these contrasting trends, the shape of the income distribution changed gradually. As Martina Morris and her colleagues have shown, the middle categories shrank while the extremes expanded. After 1973 the poverty rate stopped falling in the United States, and the Gini index for family income rose from 35 to 40 by 1991.

This 14% increase in inequality over the course of 18 years wiped out the entire postwar decline, and by 1991 had produced a more skewed distribution of income than existed in 1947! Similar trends were occurring elsewhere in the developed world. Except for Australia and the United Kingdom, however, they were less dramatic than in the United States. In continental Europe, the new economic order was expressed more strongly as stagnating employment than as a decline in real wages.

Income inequality rose slightly in European countries during the 1970s and 1980s, but unemployment increased fivefold between 1973 and 1985. Despite population growth, European employment fell in absolute terms between 1973 and 1985, yielding a jobless rate whose degree and permanence were unprecedented in the postwar era. It is much more difficult to make factual statements about trends in inequality in developing countries. Certainly in Mexico, the one developing country prospects for socioeconomic mobility seem bleak.

From 1980 to 1989, the real minimum wage declined by 47%, GDP per capita declined by 9%, and the percentage of families earning less than twice the minimum wage, a rough indicator of poverty, rose to include 60% of the population. According to conservative estimates, 48% of all Mexicans lived in poverty by 1989; by 1996 Mexican wages had lost 68% of their 1982 value. Over the course of the 1980s, Mexico's standard of living fell to levels last seen in the 1960s. In just five years, from 1984 to 1989, income inequality increased enough to cancel out half of the decline achieved over the two previous decades; it would have increased even more if not for the massive entry of additional household workers into the informal workforce.

Rates of occupational mobility increased during the 1980s, but most of the movement was downward. Therefore, whether they stay in Mexico or come to the United States, therefore, poor Mexicans migrating from rural communities will face dim prospects for social mobility wherever they go, be it Los Angeles or Guadalajara. On both sides of the border, rural-urban migrants will confront a socioeconomic structure that offers few ladders of mobility, little access to high-wage employment, and, for those without education, the strong possibility of an enduring place at the bottom of the income distribution.

These trends are not likely to moderate soon. Although the causes of the new inequality are under debate, my own reading of the literature suggests that the transformation stems from three broad, interrelated trends that are rooted deeply in the postindustrial economic order: the computerisation of production, the globalisation of capital and labour markets, and the fragmentation of consumer markets. The cybernetic revolution has profoundly altered the nature and the social organisation of human production. During the 1970s and early 1980s, computerisation swept through manufacturing.

Older manufacturing plants that employed thousands of well-paid, unionized workers were replaced by new, capital-intensive facilities where a few workers operated mechanized, continuous-flow production lines controlled by computers and staffed by robots. Manufacturing productivity soared, and those plants that could not compete either closed their doors or relocated to low-wage areas overseas. Employment in manufacturing plummeted, especially in older urban areas; as manufacturing employment dwindled, so did union membership.

Between 1969 and 1989 the share of nonagricultural workers in unions dropped from 29% to 16%; in the private sector the level of unionisation reached 12%, a figure last seen in the 1920s. While manufacturing bore the brunt of the cybernetics revolution during the 1970s and early 1980s, the moment of truth came for the service sector during the late 1980s and early 1990s. Large bureaucratic organisations loaded with mid-level white-collar workers gave way to reengineered, downsized, and flattened organisations that were "lean and mean".

Making use of new, ultrafast computer chips and fiber optics, Programmers wrote software that routinized human expertise within canned algorithms that had user-friendly interfaces. Armed with these new cybernetic tools, one modestly trained operative could perform all of the tasks formerly carried out by scores of expensive white-collar workers, often in a fraction of the time. During the 1990s, the gray flannel suit gave way to the pink slip as corporations shed midlevel bureaucrats by the thousands. While computers were transforming productivity in manufacturing and services, they were also facilitating a revolution in the geographic reach of factor markets.

Over the past two decades markets for capital and labour have globalized, causing a worldwide competition for funds and workers. Capital now roams the world incessantly, seeking companies and countries that offer high returns and low risks, while labour finds itself in a global hiring hall where high-wage workers in developed nations compete directly with millions of desperately poor workers throughout the developing world. This globalisation of factor markets was facilitated by the rising speed of communications, the declining costs of transportation, the increasing ease of international movement, the growing prevalence of smaller and lighter consumer products, and the rising importance of knowledge in the productive process.

If the owners of capital find more attractive prospects in one venue, or dislike developments in another, they can shift billions of dollars across international borders in a nanosecond, as Mexico learned to its dismay in December 1994. Likewise, if producers based in developed nations need to reduce their labour costs, they can easily relocate factories to low-wage areas overseas, or they can simply wait for immigrants from these areas to appear at their factory gates. The third development of the postindustrial era has been the fragmentation of consumer markets. From 1870 to 1970, nations in general and the United States in particular prospered because companies were able to manufacture standardized goods and sell them to a growing mass market of middleclass consumers who exhibited similar needs and tastes.

Products became more affordable because economies of scale reduced their price; consumer markets grew because mass production required armies of well-paid, unionized workers to staff the manufacturing apparatus and legions of salaried white-collar workers to administer it. Since 1970, international competition, technological innovation, and demographic shifts have fragmented these mass markets. In response, firms have developed new strategies to cater to small, specialized market niches that rely on new techniques of flexible production, just-in-time delivery, outsourcing, and continuous-flow production.

Under the old industrial regime, companies were large, hierarchies were deep, authority was rigid, markets were massive and homogeneous, and firms were slow to respond to shifts in consumer demand. In the new postindustrial order, companies are lean, hierarchies are flattened, authority is flexible, markets are fragmented and diverse, and successful firms move quickly to anticipate shifting demand. The end result is a further segmentation of labour markets in developed countries and additional downward pressure on salaries and wages.

The forces of computerisation, globalisation, and fragmentation have operated simultaneously over the past two decades in mutually reinforcing fashion; it is fruitless to ask which came first or which is most important. Rather, the three processes have fed off one another to cause a marked and seemingly permanent change in the economic structure of nations and the world. The abruptness of the discontinuity is suggested by the disappearance of numerous well-established empirical regularities that characterized economic life in the United States through 1970.

In contrast to the industrial regime of the past, wages in the new postindustrial economy are not related to trends in productivity; poverty is not correlated with the business cyle; corporate pay is not tied to the company's profitability; and there is no longer an association between workers' wages and managers' salaries. Clearly we are in a new era, and there is no going back. Computers cannot be disinvented; instantaneous telecommunications cannot be undone; transportation cannot become slower and more expensive; the globalisation of factor markets will not be reversed; and the homogeneous mass consumer markets of the postwar era will not return soon. If anything, the pace of technological change will quicken to reinforce the structural changes that have already occurred. The age of economic inequality is upon us.

CLASS SEGREGATION

Not only have the rich and the poor been pulling apart economically through a transformation of the income distribution; since 1970 they have also been separating spatially through a resurgence of class segregation. In the United States, the geographic barriers between rich and poor have increased steadily, resulting in a significant rise in residential segregation by income. The left-hand bars show the degree of residential dissimilarity between poor and nonpoor persons in 1970, 1980, and 1990 in the 10 largest metropolitan areas of the United States.

The middle bars show the extent of residential dissimilarity between affluent and poor families; figures for 1970 and 1980 come from Massey and Eggers (1993), and those for 1990 from Nancy Denton. Both series reveal a steady rise in the degree of segregation between the haves and the have-nots in U.S. society. The poor-nonpoor index rose from 37 in 1970 to 40 in 1980 to 41 in 1990, while the poor-affluent index rose from 49 to 52 to 56 over the same period. In a forthcoming chapter, Paul Jargowsky shows that the use of dissimilarity indices to measure class segregation confounds changes in the spatial distribution of income groups with changes in the shape of the income distribution itself, thereby understating the degree of class segregation.

To control for this bias, he proposes an alternative "class sorting index" based on the correlation ratio. This index increases from 37 to 45 between 1970 and 1990, a confirmation that earlier trends based on the index of dissimilarity were not merely methodological artifacts. Detailed analyses conducted by Jargowsky and by Abramson et al. show that increasing class segregation was remarkably widespread among regions and population groups. Whether one looks south, north, east, or west, or at whites, blacks, Hispanics, or Asians, America became a more class-segregated society during the 1970s and 1980s.

Because of an absence of data, once again it is difficult to assess whether comparable trends are occurring elsewhere in the developed world, or whether U.S. trends can be generalized to developing regions. Certainly in Mexico, the evidence suggests a long-standing pattern of residential segregation between high- and low-income groups in metropolitan areas, an ecological gulf that widened significantly during the 1980s.

RACIAL AND ETHNIC SEGREGATION

Given a high and rising level of urbanisation, growing income inequality, and rising class segregation, an increase in the geographic concentration of affluence and poverty is all but inevitable. These spatial processes are magnified, however, when they occur in a group that is also segregated on the basis of an ascribed characteristic such as race; and no feature of our national life has proved to be as enduring as the residential color line separating black from white America. Because of a history of discrimination in the real estate and banking industries, the persistence of white racial prejudice, and a legacy of racially biased public policies, blacks continue to be the most residentially segregated group in the United States.

As a result, when black poverty rates rose during the 1970s and 1980s, the increased poverty was absorbed by a small set of racially homogeneous, geographically isolated, densely settled neighbourhoods packed tightly around the urban core; and because class segregation was increasing as well, a disproportionate share of the economic pain was absorbed by neighbourhoods that were not only black but also poor. As a result, broader trends toward income inequality and class segregation in the United States isolated poor blacks far more severely than poor whites.

By 1990, according to John Kasarda, 41% of poor blacks in U.S. central cities lived in poor neighbourhoods, and 42% lived in very poor neighbourhoods, figures well above the comparable levels for whites (32% and 11% respectively). Computations performed by Lauren Krivo and colleagues (1996) show that the extent of poverty concentration was 50% higher among central-city blacks in 1990 than among central-city whites (with an isolation index of 32 for the former and 21 for the latter).

Focusing on central cities, however, understates the black-white contrast. When Mitchell Eggers, Andrew Gross, and I examined the 50 largest metropolitan areas in 1980, we found that 64% of poor blacks lived in neighbourhoods with a poverty rate over 20%, compared with just 13% of poor whites. The isolation indices we computed revealed that the level of poverty concentration for poor blacks was four times that of poor whites. To a great extent, then, increases in the concentration of poverty observed during the 1970s and 1980s in U.S. urban areas reflect rising inequality caused by racial rather than class segregation.

At any given level of income segregation, poverty is concentrated most strongly in cities that are also racially segregated; and when for the degree of class segregation is controlled, racial segregation exerts a powerful independent effect on the extent of poverty concentration. Were black-white segregation to be eliminated, a principal force behind the spatial concentration of poverty in the United States would disappear. Unfortunately, although Reynolds Farley and William Frey have detected "small steps toward an integrated society," we are not yet able to debate whether the glass is half empty or half full.

At this point the glass is about 80% empty and 20% full. Although black-white dissimilarity declined by 10% in the two decades after 1970, it still stood at a remarkable 73 in 1990.

This figure is higher than even the most extreme scores observed for other groups, such as Hispanics and Asians. A glance at the isolation indices yields an even more pessimistic picture: During the 1980s the small declines of the 1970s were arrested and reversed. Over the 20-year period, average black isolation decreased from 69 to 65 and then rose again to 67. The sad fact is that African Americans were virtually as isolated in 1990 as on the day when Congress passed the Fair Housing Act in 1968.

The two areas that missed the threshold did so by a trivial amount, and all areas that were hypersegregated in 1980 showed an increase on at least one dimension of segregation by 1990. Thus, metropolitan areas that were hypersegregated in 1980 generally remained so in 1990, and we found little trend away from this extreme pattern of racial isolation. On the contrary, hypersegregation spread to new urban areas during the 1980s. Of the 44 nonhypersegregated metropolitan areas examined in 1980, six met the criteria in 1990, bringing the total number to 20. Taken together, these areas contain 11 million African Americans, who together constitute 36% of the black population of the United States.

Thus it is quite clear that racial segregation will not disappear from U.S. urban areas soon, and that its poverty-concentrating effects will be with us for the foreseeable future. Although trends in racial and ethnic segregation are documented less clearly in other countries, we know that racial and ethnic minorities are rapidly growing throughout Europe, Australia, and Japan as a result of international migration, and that these growing populations have aroused racist sentiments in many countries. Insofar as these sentiments are translated into residential segregation, broader trends toward concentrated affluence and poverty will be exacerbated.

THE POLITICAL ECOLOGY OF INEQUALITY

Unless there is a radical departure from recent trends, poverty and affluence are almost certain to become geographically concentrated at high levels throughout the world early in the next century. Increasingly the poor and the rich will inhabit large urban areas, and within these places they will concentrate in separate neighbourhoods. This ecological structure constitutes a radical departure from the past, and creates the potential for a new geopolitical order capable of compounding the benefits and liabilities of class by superimposing administrative segmentation on economic segregation.

Whether or not this potential is realized depends on how political districts are constructed. Insofar as the boundaries of local governmental units can be arranged to approximate the geographic contours of concentrated affluence and poverty, and insofar as the financing and delivery of public services can be shifted down the political hierarchy, the potential for reinforcing class advantages and disadvantages will be maximized. In a society where most people live in small towns and villages, rich and poor families must mix socially, share the same public services, and inhabit the same political units.

In such a geopolitical structure, the poor benefit from public institutions to which the rich are committed by reason of selfinterest. When poverty and affluence become urbanized and geographically concentrated, however, the affluent acquire a means to separate themselves politically from the poor through the judicious drawing of political lines in space. If they can create separate governmental and administrative districts that encompass concentrations of poverty, and if they can force these poor districts to supply and pay for their own services, then the affluent will be able to insulate themselves from the economic costs imposed on society by the poor.

In the United States, the poor are isolated politically by the segmentation of metropolitan regions into a patchwork of separate municipalities. The concentration of affluence in certain suburbs generates high real estate values that allow the affluent to tax themselves at low rates while offering generous, even lavish municipal services. The concentration of poverty in central cities and some inner suburbs generates a high demand for services but yields low property values; thus, higher tax rates are required to support generally inferior services.

The end result is a vicious cycle whereby city taxes are raised to maintain deficient services; consequently families with means are driven out; property values then decline further; the result is more tax increases and additional middle-class flight, which further exacerbate the concentration of poverty. Under an ecological regime of concentrated affluence and poverty, efforts to decentralize government and shift the financing and provision of services to local government represent a means of enhancing the social and economic wellbeing of the rich at the expense of the poor.

Political decentralisation is progressive and democratic only in a world where all classes live together in small communities; this antiquated model of society no longer prevails, however, although it appears frequently in the writings of conservative thinkers. In today's world of dense, urban agglomerations characterized by pronounced income inequality and increasing class segregation, political decentralisation is punitive and regressive, forcing the poor to bear most of the cost of their own disadvantage.

In a world of small towns and modest communities, political decentralisation yields the social world of Andy Hardy; in a class-segregated world of large urban areas it produces the bleak vision of the Blade Runner. Many mechanisms compound class advantages and disadvantages in the new ecology of inequality, but perhaps the most significant occurs through schools. Education is the most important single resource presently traded on global labour markets: In recent years workers with college and postgraduate degrees have seen their earnings rise, while high school graduates' and dropouts' wages have fallen.

Access to high-quality education thus has become the crucial factor determining one's position in the postindustrial pecking order. Because the emerging ecological structure concentrates the best-prepared students in areas of resource abundance while gathering the least well-prepared students in areas of resource scarcity, it necessarily exacerbates class inequities and promotes a more rigid stratification of society.

Students from low-income families with poorly educated parents, little experience with books or reading, and multiple social problems attend schools with the fewest resources to help them learn, while students from affluent families with well-educated parents, extensive experience with books and reading, and few social problems attend well-funded schools that are most able to promote learning. The spatial concentration of affluence and poverty thus raises the odds that affluent children will receive a superior education while poor children will get inferior schooling.

THE CULTURAL ECOLOGY OF INEQUALITY

Until recently, poverty, though endemic, was spread uniformly in space and rarely occurred at high densities. Most impoverished families lived in small rural communities where the range of material well-being was limited. The few affluent families that were present locally were not especially affluent, and they tended to be closely related to others in the community. Truly wealthy families in the governing elite lived far away; the prevalent atmosphere in most places was one of collective poverty and shared deprivation. In such settings, proclivities toward violence, crime, and other maladies exacerbated by material deprivation could be held in check by informal means.

In small rural communities, as generations of cultural anthropologists have shown, everyone knows everyone else, either directly through personal experience or indirectly through ties of kinship or friendship. Through social networks, rewards and punishments are meted out to reinforce and maintain accepted standards of behavior. Age-old devices such as gossip, ridicule, shame, and ostracism, backed occasionally by physical discipline, are employed to punish public departures from accepted behavior, whereas praise, esteem, and prestige are accorded to those who conform.

As observed by theorists from Emile Durkheim to Edward Banfield, these informal mechanisms of social control which prevail in small towns and villages produce a repressive moral code that preserves public order and maintains social stability at the cost of individuality, innovation, and change. Louis Wirth, however, noted in his classic 1938 essay that these informal mechanisms break down in large, densely settled, &nd diverse urban populations. Great size confers anonymity and certain immunity from social interference by friends and relatives.

In a city, rural migrants are freed from the constraints of tradition to pursue their own individual interests and tastes, conducting activities that might have been discouraged or even punished in their communities of origin. Wirth was disturbed by the implications of urbanism; he viewed it as breeding impersonality, isolation, alienation, anomie, and a proliferation of vice and deviance, a collection of maladies he generically labeled urban malaise.

Certainly there was plenty of malaise in his own time and place, Chicago in the 1930s, which by any standard exhibited high rates of violence, alcoholism, prostitution, drug abuse, and intergroup conflict. All of this was documented extensively by Wirth's students and colleagues at the University of Chicago. In subsequent years, however, key postulates of Wirth's theory were not sustained by research, and his ideas fell into disrepute. Although correlations between urbanism and various forms of social deviance endured over time, urban sociologists such as Claude Fischer did not find that urban dwellers were isolated, alienated, or anomic. Indeed, inhabitants of large cities were connected to other people just as fully as inhabitants of small towns.

Although the networks they built were composed more of friends than of family, their social circles were about the same size and they were just as satisfied with their lives. It is clear that Wirth failed because he looked at the social world of Chicago in the 1930s and made the wrong inference. He saw high rates of unconventional and antisocial behavior, and attributed these outcomes to urbanism that what actually saw in depression-era Chicago were the consequences of concentrated poverty. Louis Wirth was the first social scientist to note a connection between the geographic concentration of poverty and the proliferation of socially destructive behavior, although he didn't quite recognize it at the time.

The social malaise observed by Wirth did not stem from urbanism per se, but from the concentration of poverty during the Great Depression. A few years after Wirth wrote his essay, St. Clair Drake and Horace Cayton published a map showing the percentage of families on relief in various Chicago neighbourhoods in 1934. This map is almost identical to a map published 40 years later by William Julius Wilson. In the 1980s, as in the 1930s, the spatial concentration of material deprivation stemmed from the same underlying causes: rising income inequality and growing class segregation amplified by racial segregation.

Drake and Cayton's maps clearly revealed the close connection between high concentrations of poverty and various social problems such as unwed childbearing, delinquency, and disease. The importance of these empirical connections was soon forgotten, however, as mass socioeconomic and residential mobility during the 1950s and 1960s weakened the ecological correlations underlying Wirth's theory and discredited his ideas. A series of detailed ethnographic studies also showed that poor urbanites were anything but socially disengaged and alienated. In 1975 Claude Fischer proposed a theory to account for the connection between urbanism and unconventionality without resorting to concepts such as alienation, anomie, and malaise.

His analysis provides a way of understanding the cultural consequences of concentrated affluence and poverty.

In essence, Fischer argued that cities create fertile conditions for the emergence and perpetuation of urban subcultures. Under conditions of geographic concentration, subcultures emerge and intensify to produce high rates of unconventional behavior. Apparent deviance within cities occurs not because urbanites are alienated or anomic, but because they are deeply embedded in intense, socially cohesive subcultures that sustain and reinforce attitudes and behaviors which the wider public finds exotic, foreign, or deviant. According to Fischer, "subcultural theory seems really to be a theory of group concentration...[and] subcultural processes are revealed to be fundamentally about intragroup accessibility.

Spatial agglomeration is...one way group members gain access to one another [and] in the end, [it]...is largely about the ability of subcultural members to communicate, to create 'moral density'...it is not necessarily about cities per se" (emphasis in original). The geographic agglomeration, through urbanisation, of people with similar traits gives rise to distinct subcultures that reflect the characteristics of the people who are concentrated in space. In this sense, the advent of geographically concentrated affluence and poverty as the dominant spatial structure of the twenty-first century has profound implications for the nature of social life.

Not only will the informal means by which past societies preserved public order break down and ultimately disappear under the onslaught of urbanisation; they will be replaced by new cultural forms rooted in the ecological order of concentrated affluence and poverty. Just as poverty is concentrated spatially, anything correlated with poverty is also concentrated. Therefore, as the density of poverty increases in cities throughout the world, so will the density of joblessness, crime, family dissolution, drug abuse, alcoholism, disease, and violence.

Not only will the poor have to grapple with the manifold problems due to their own lack of income; increasingly they also will have to confront the social effects of living in an environment where most of their neighbours are also poor. At the same time, the concentration of affluence will create a social environment for the rich that is opposite in every respect from that of the poor. The affluent will experience the personal benefits of high income; in addition, they will profit increasingly from the fact that most of their neighbours possess these advantages as well.

Therefore, in the emerging ecology of inequality, the social worlds of the poor and the rich will diverge to yield distinct, opposing subcultures. Among those at the low end of the income distribution, the spatial concentration of poverty will create a harsh and destructive environment perpetuating values, attitudes, and behaviors that are adaptive within a geographic niche of intense poverty but harmful to society at large and destructive of the poor themselves. At the other end of the hierarchy, a contrasting subculture of privilege will emerge from the spatial niche of concentrated affluence to confer additional advantages on the rich, thereby consolidating their social and economic dominance.

Perhaps no consequence of concentrated poverty is as destructive as the proliferation of crime and violence. Criminal behavior is associated strongly with income deprivation; thus the geographic concentration of poverty will cause a concentration of criminal violence in poor neighbourhoods. According to estimates developed for Philadelphia, every one-point increase in the neighbourhood poverty rate raises the major crime rate by 0.8 point. Krivo and Peterson (forthcoming) use data from Columbus, Ohio to show that moving from a neighbourhood where the poverty rate is under 20% to a neighbourhood where it is over 40% increases the rate of violent crime more than threefold, from around 7 per thousand to about 23 per thousand.

How will the poor adapt to an environment where violence is endemic and the risk of victimisation great? At the individual level, a logical adaptation is to become violent oneself. As my colleague Elijah Anderson has discovered through his ethnographic fieldwork, one can deter potential criminals and increase the odds of survival by adopting a threatening demeanor, cultivating a reputation for the use of force, and backing that reputation with selective violence.

In a social world characterized by endemic violence, an obsessive concern with respect becomes a viable adaptive strategy. Therefore, given the progressive concentration of violence, some poor people certainly will adopt violent attitudes and behavior as survival strategies. As more people adopt more violent strategies for self-preservation, the average level of violence in poor neighbourhoods will rise, leading others to adopt still more violent behavior.

As the average level of violence rises over time, more people will adopt increasingly violent strategies to protect themselves from the growing threat of victimisation, and ultimately will produce a self-perpetuating upward spiral of violence. The fundamental need to adapt to structurally embedded conditions of endemic violence leads to the emergence of a "code of the streets" that encourages and promotes the use of force. Asking residents of poor neighbourhoods to choose a less violent path or to "just say no" to the temptation of violence is absurd in view of the threatening character of the ecological niche they inhabit.

To survive in such areas, one must learn and (to a significant extent) internalize the code of violence described by Anderson. In this way, aggression is passed from person to person in a self-feeding, escalating fashion. Recent brain research suggests that this internalisation of violence is more than a socially learned reaction that one can set aside whenever the situation warrants. Repeated exposure to high levels of danger and physical violence wire emotional predispositions to rage and violence directly into the brain and make them an organic part of a person's makeup.

Research has shown that perceptions of danger are channeled directly to a small mass of neural cells known as the amygdala, which sits above the brain stem near the bottom of the limbic ring. The amygdala is capable of generating an emotional response that triggers aggressive, violent behavior without passing through the neocortex, the center of rational thought. Emotional responses developed through the limbic system are learned, but they are unconscious and automatic.

Perceptions of danger may be signaled not only by physical threats but also by symbolic injuries to self-esteem or dignity. The threat triggers the amygdala to produce a limbic surge, which releases catecholamines to generate a quick rush of energy lasting minutes. At the same time, the amygdala activates the adrenocortical system to produce a general state of readiness that lasts for hours or even days. Adrenocortical arousal, in turn, lowers the subsequent threshold for anger and increases the intensity of emotions, raising the odds that the rational centers of the brain will be overwhelmed by powerful emotions beyond the control of the neocortex.

By dramatically increasing the exposure of the poor to violence from a very early age, the new ecological order will maximize the number of people with hair-trigger tempers and elevated predispositions to violence. These emotional reactions, moreover, will not be turned on and off easily and rationally in response to shifting social contexts. People who grow up in areas of concentrated poverty and violence will experience profound spillover effects in other areas of life: Disagreements with bosses, spouses, and children will be more likely to turn violent, and thus the odds of successful employment, marriage, and childrearing will be diminished.

Concentrated poverty is a stronger predictor of violent crime than of property crime, and of violence between people known to one another than between strangers. The contrasting ecologies of affluence and poverty will also breed opposing peer subcultures among rich and poor youths. As affluence grows more concentrated, the children of the privileged will socialize increasingly with other children of well-educated and successful parents. Knowledge of what one does to prepare for college and an appreciation of the connection between schooling and socioeconomic success will be widespread in the schools of the affluent.

Students will arrive in the classroom well prepared and ready to learn. School officials need only build on this base of knowledge and motivation by using their ample resources to hire well-informed guidance counselors and enthusiastic, talented teachers. Meanwhile, the children of the poor increasingly will attend schools with children from other poor families, who themselves are beset by multiple difficulties stemming from a lack of income. Parents will be poorly educated and will lack adequate knowledge about how to prepare for college.

Children will not fully appreciate the connection between education and later success. Supervision and monitoring of students will be difficult because so many come from singleparent families and the schools will be unable to offset this deficit because of funding limitations. Students will arrive in the classroom poorly prepared, and neither the dispirited guidance counselors nor the overworked, underpaid teachers will expect much from the students. In such settings an alternative status system is almost certain to develop. Under circumstances where it is difficult to succeed according to conventional standards, the usual criteria for success typically are inverted to create an oppositional identity.

Children formulate oppositional identities to preserve self-esteem when expectations are low and when failure by conventional standards is likely. Thus, in areas of concentrated poverty, students from poor families will legitimize their educational failures by attaching positive value and meaning to outcomes that affluent children label deviant and unworthy. In adapting to the environment created by concentrated poverty, success in school will be devalued, hard work will be regarded as selling out, and any display of learning will be viewed as uncool.

Oppositional subcultures already have become entrenched in many black inner-city areas of the United States, where high levels of racial segregation have produced unusually high concentrations of poverty and educational distress. Once such a subculture becomes established, it acquires a life of its own that contributes independently to the perpetuation of educational failure the reproduction of poverty, and the cultural transmission of low socioeconomic status from person to person, family to family, and group to group.

INTO THE AGE OF EXTREMES

Thus a new age of extremes is upon us. In the social ecology now being created around the globe, affluent people increasingly will live and interact with other affluent people, while the poor increasingly will live and interact with other poor people. The social worlds of the rich and the poor will diverge, creating the potential for radical differences in thought, action, values, tastes, and feelings, and for the construction of a new political geography that divorces the interests of the rich from the welfare of the poor. For the first time in human history, the advantages and disadvantages of one's class position in society will be compounded and reinforced by a systematic process of geographic concentration.

Describing the forces that produce geographically concentrated affluence and poverty and outlining the consequences of these trends without reference to a specific racial or ethnic group. I believe that social scientists in the United States have focused too narrowly on the problems of African Americans in urban ghettos, and thus have mistakenly racialized processes that are much broader and more general than most observers realize.

The effects of ongoing urbanisation, rising income inequality, and growing class segregation are exacerbated by racial segregation so that the effects are most salient and most visible among African Americans, but the basic processes are sweeping the world and concentrating poverty everywhere. Our obsessive interest in the generation and reproduction of class is rarely focused on the affluent. Scores of ethnographers descend on the homes, bars, and street corners of the poor to chronicle their attitudes and behavior; few attempt to infiltrate the mansions, clubs, and boutiques of the wealthy to document the means by which they maintain and reproduce their affluence.

The concentration of affluence and poverty means that the social lives of the rich and the poor increasingly will transpire in different venues; we must study both in order to fully comprehend the newly emerged system of stratification and a few of the ecological mechanisms by which inequality will be created and reproduced in the postindustrial society of the twenty-first century, my list is not exhaustive.

A great deal remains to be said, written, and researched. Although limitations of time and space do not permit me to go into detail that the concentration of poverty is a primary force behind the spread of new diseases such as AIDS and the resurgence of old ones such as tuberculosis; it also stands behind the creation and perpetuation of joblessness and the decline of marriage among the poor. It is implicated as well in the increase in unwed childbearing, and it contributes to the spread of homelessness around the United States and the world. No doubt concentrated poverty also can be implicated in a variety of other social and economic phenomena in ways that have yet to be discovered.

Confronting the new ecology of inequality is particularly difficult because concentrated poverty creates an unstable and unattractive social environment that is at once a cause and a consequence of class segregation. The social chaos stemming from concentrated poverty propels the affluent further into geographic and social withdrawal, and their departure further isolates the poor and stokes the fires of social disorder. Insofar as racial and ethnic segregation perpetuate concentrated poverty and its consequences in minority communities, the proliferation of antisocial behaviors will fuel pejorative stereotypes and intensify prejudice, making political solutions so much more difficult.

Addressing serious issues such as increasing income inequality, growing class segregation, racial prejudice, and the geographic concentration of poverty will inevitably require sacrifice, and the immediate course of least resistance for affluent people will always be to raise the walls of social, economic, and geographic segregation higher in order to protect themselves from the rising tide of social pathology and violence. If the status quo indeed is the most likely outcome, inequality will continue to increase and racial divisions will grow, creating a volatile and unstable political economy.

As class tensions rise, urban areas will experience escalating crime and violence punctuated by sporadic riots and increased terrorism as class tensions rise. The poor will become disenfranchised and alienated from mainstream political and economic institutions, while the middle classes will grow more angry, more frustrated, and more politically mobilized. The affluent will continue to withdraw socially and spatially from the rest of society, and will seek to placate the middle classes' anger with quick fixes and demagogic excesses that do not change the underlying structure responsible for their problems.

5

The Impact of Economic Reform

1997 is the 50th year of India's independence, an appropriate time to critically assess the social, cultural and economic condition and independence of the country. Viewed from the wide boulevards of its cities, India seems to be thriving. There is an undisputed increase in GDP and the growth rate of the economy and the urban markets appear to be flourishing. Not, however, with the vast diversity of available indigenous products, but increasingly with a plethora of middle class consumables-from kitchen gadgets and washing machines to the latest stereo systems and cars.

Over 20 channels of television with a staggering array of national and international prcgrammes are beamed into millions of homes. Cellular phones and domestically-assembled Mercedes-Benz cars have become the new status symbols. Behind the facade of these superficial symbols of consumption, however, lies a story of increasing disparities: a rise in under- and unemployment; a deterioration in the livelihoods of a majority of the population; an increase in critical poverty; a decline in the membership of trade unions; and a phenomenal increase in the number of workers in the informal sectors of the economy and in the extent of the irregular employment.

Additionally, there has been an intensification of rampant corruption, particularly by political and economic elites; a staggering increase in environmental degradation in both urban and rural areas; loss of genetic bio-diversity; and growing social unrest arising largely out of greater immiseration. At the same time, there has been an increase in dependence upon international capital and multilateral and transnational institutions, resulting in a critical loss of control-not just by producers, but by the country itself.

This chapter explores this dualism by looking critically at the impacts of the new package of economic reforms on India's social and ecological diversity, on the livelihoods and lifestyles of a majority of the people, on the political trends that seek a more rapid "integration" into the global marketplace and on the capacity of the country to build a pattern of social and economic development that is in consonance with the deepening of democracy; the widening of social justice and the sustainability of the environment.

INDUSTRIALISM, PLANNING AND EQUITY

For almost four decades after independence in 1947, India managed to keep largely out of a debt trap, although this post-independence period arguably witnessed the planting of the seeds of economic dependency and debt through industrialisation, militarisation and a move to a chemical input-based agriculture.

After the prolonged struggle for freedom throughout the late 19th and early 20th centuries, widespread aspirations for social and economic justice impelled a constitutional and planning process that initiated a series of dramatic social reforms during the 1940s and 1950s-the abolition of zamindari (landlordism), the introduction of the reservations system (affirmative action) for scheduled castes and tribes and investment in telecommunications, basic industries and infrastructure.

Unfortunately, the colonial structures of administrative control were left relatively intact, as were the structures of private property. Even the educational system retained its colonial legacy. Dramatic social reform policies thus went hand in hand with structures and institutions that perpetuated power and privilege. For example, in keeping with the government's formal commitment to greater social and economic welfare, the first Five Year Plan initiated by the first independent government in 1950 retained a strong dimension of equality with an emphasis on agriculture and on cottage, small- and medium-sized industries.

At that political and economic juncture, the policy of achieving self-reliance through import substitution and through appropriate trade barriers to protect domestic production from being swamped by powerful foreign and corporate interests seemed to be a prudent and judicious strategy. By the second Plan, however, the former Finance Minister P.C. Mahalanobis shifted the policy emphasis toward achieving "commanding heights" in industry and agriculture-a strategy that, while stressing the importance of agriculture in attaining self-sufficiency also saw the first significant food imports.

By 1957, Mahalanobis admitted that this growth poiicy would, in the short run, lead to an increase in inequality. There is no escape from the fact that these strategies heralded a system that favoured the corporate sector more than the mass of people and that it laid flesh foundations of uneven and unequal development. The basic endemic causes of inequality and poverty-grossly inequitable ownership of land and productive resources, entrenched caste hierarchies, and natural resource-intensive industrialism that caused the impoverishment of millions dependent upon resources for subsistence-were only marginally addressed by the development plans of the early governments.

As the intensification of industrialism and "green revolution" agriculture began to favour the middle and upper classes, the patterns of economic development began to gradually push equity and justice considerations into the background. It is not that the planning process neglected the rights and aspirations of the poor. Numerous poverty alleviation programmes were designed and much of development planning was justified in the name of the poor. By the 1970s, however, most of the top-down programmes yielded, at best, marginal benefits. It was at this juncture that the then prime minister, Indira Gandhi, was facing a major political challenge from politically mobile middle-caste groups as well as the lobbies of the wealthy classes.

Anticipating widespread popular agitation and responding to the decline in support for her ruling Congress party, she announced a new populist thrust-the Garibi Hatao (Abolish Poverty) programme. Gandhi promised to focus fresh attention on the bottom third of the population and institute policies that would curb the power of the wealthy (i.e. bank nationalisation and the abolition of privy purses-special monetary and other privileges-to erstwhile rulers).

However, these programmes ran into a wall of endemic social and cultural barriers, most of which were obvious and should have been addressed. The barriers included: entrenched political and economic interests; complex patron-client relations based on ties of kinship, caste, linguistic or religious affinity; official graft; inefficiency; and reluctance by those in power to grant the historically underprivileged classes an equal share in the country's productive base. From the fifth Five Year Plan initiated in 1970 onwards, top-down efforts to eradicate, abolish or temper poverty reinforced dependency and corruption rather than leading to widespread asset creation and control by historically underprivileged and marginalized peoples over the industrial and natural means of production.'

What vitiated against even minimal success at the national level was the bureaucratic model of implementing "socialist" objectives. A bureaucratic stranglehold on this process and the failure of the ruling Congress party to, on the basis of a well-organized party with strong representation of lower caste and class groups, forge a polity that would have succeeded in implementing and institutionalizing more egalitarian, redistributive policies assured the failure of these programmes.

Despite socialist overtones, the problems of an essentially elitist and colonial administrative system coupled with entrenched political and economic elites with links into the upper echelons of social and cultural hierarchies in rural and urban India remained the most serious limiting factors in the successful planning and implementation of an egalitarian post-independence development model. As a consequence, there was a critical neglect of education for the less privileged, of redistribution of productive resources, of the introduction of land reform.

In the end, islands of prosperity were created by the imposition of an economic model that retained its socialist principles without ever seriously challenging the hegemony of pre-existing powerful feudal and capitalist lobbies. Undoubtedly, as the economy expanded in the years after independence, many people from poorer classes and castes were able to benefit from increased opportunities. Their numbers, however, were marginal in comparison to the overall population in the country.

Instead, the license-permit raj became the means through which small groups of businesspeople, landed farmers and politicians were able to accumulate wealth at the expense of the majority. Even more important was the nexus that developed between state officials and businesspeople, as well as between the state officials and the landed interests in the hinterland. Some researchers have argued that this system lowered productivity and "dampened the possible multiplier effects on employment and incomes from expanded production, thereby denying the underprivileged sections of society opportunities to improve their economic and social conditions."

While some trickle down effects did take place, the basic causes of poverty, deprivation and discrimination remained largely untouched. The policy of reservations helped make some jobs available to those in the scheduled castes and tribes, but the expansion of employment in government relied heavily upon access to influential persons through patron-client relations. Patronage was also extended by local political leaders, who used poverty alleviation programmes and infrastructural development monies to advance their patronage networks.

In the process, most programmes sustained dependency of the recipient on the donor rather than creating wider social and economic security. The experience of the first 40 years of independence thus highlight the fact that despite the idealism and the stated commitment to the establishment of an egalitarian order-sentiments that were so pervasive in the post-colonial period-those with power and privilege in urban and rural areas contributed little to the establishment of a dynamic and decentralized society and economy.

In fact, the government became increasingly dependent upon internal and external borrowing, while programmes to transfer land and resources to the deprived and excluded populations were weakly executed. It must be acknowledged that post-independence idealism as well as a diversity of progressive and radical political parties and other representative bodies at the national and state level led to the adoption of several major welfare measures. Progressive labour legislation, limited land legislation, the public distribution system, the public health system and subsidies to farmers became major programmes of successive governments.

Yet, except in a few notable cases, most of these schemes were unable to significantly address the reality of social and cultural exclusion and economic marginalisation. During this 40-year period, given the thrust of industrial and agricultural development, a slow and limited policy of opening up to international finance began to unfold. With the first major International Monetary Fund loan of $3.5 billion in 1981, selective economic liberalisation was introduced.

Bureaucratic regulations were diluted and state intervention reduced so that market forces could play a "freer" role in steering the economy. What is more important, however, and not often acknowledged, is this programme also introduced increasingly indiscriminate borrowing practices, creating a situation that brought India into a sustained, debilitating and subservient relationship with international institutions, corporations and capital markets.

1991: THE UNFOLDING OF GLOBALISATION

Nothing was as dramatic, however, as the introduction of the International Monetary Fund (IMF)/World Bank/Trans-National Corporation inspired New Economic Policy of 1991 that heralded the present phase of globalisation, represented by the Structural Adjustment Programme/Loan (SAP/SAL) from the World Bank. India also applied for and secured a loan of $5.3 billion from the IMF. The new package was outlined in a memorandum presented by the World Bank to the Indian government in 1990.

The immediate justification was the serious balance of payments crisis and the critical fiscal situation in the country. Since then, the government has initiated sweeping changes in economic policy, and the speed and penetration of some of these reforms have created an impression that many of them are irreversible. Significant shifts have taken place in the structure and ownership pattern of business enterprises, and there has been an unprecedented entry of transnational corporations and policy reforms to encourage foreign capital.

What is significant here are the political and re-colonizing impacts of the conditions imposed by the IMF and the World Bank in the context of their loans, as well as the social consequences of those requirements? It is these changes that have defined the latest phase of globalisation and economic reform, and it is to these that we now turn.

ECONOMIC AND POLITICAL CONSEQUENCES

THE NEW PHASE AND THE POLITICS OF ADJUSTMENT

The main thrust of the 1991 reforms was to allow for the operation of a so-called free market, where the forces of demand and supply could freely compete and the local and the national economy could be integrated into the global economy By dismantling the elabourate structure of licenses, controls and regulations that had evolved during the four decades of independence, it was thus hoped that not only would production increase, but that prices would decline due to an increase in efficiency and demand.

At the suggestion of the IMF and the World Bank, import restrictions were relaxed and the Indian Rupee was devalued and made partially convertible. The SAP also included targets for concrete steps toward the liberalisation of foreign trade and investments, a severe reduction in custom duties, an increase in the pace of privatisation and a progressively increasing bundle of incentives and policy changes to attract foreign capital.

These changes heralded a virtual explosion in the import of capital goods with three main consequences: a widening of the gap between imports and exports; a crisis in the capital goods industry in the public sector; and a more rapid export of primary resources, which led to a further deterioration in the living standards of millions of people. The following six years saw most of the imports and fresh investments in the productive economy oriented not toward meeting the basic needs of a majority, but primarily toward satisfying the consumption patterns of the elite.

A wide array of foreign cars, televisions, washing machines, air-conditioners, processed foods, perfumes, fancy toiletries and the like became freely available and has become symbolic of the new status-conscious climate. The stimulus for the recovery of industrial production has come primarily from these demands.

It is not cereals, beans, fish and other protein sources, improved access and control over productive resources, low-cost and decentralized energy sources, or sustainable water harvesting systems that have come of the new programme, but rather products and services that are mostly beyond the means of the majority.

For instance, a little more than 1 per cent of households own cars, and almost half of these are in 23 cities. Only 6 per cent of households have a refrigerator. Elitist policies favouring the more affluent sections of the society have also contributed to the compounding of the balance of payments situation-from 17 billion Rupees ($470 million) in 1981 to over 100 billion Rupees ($2.7 billion) in 1996.

THE DEBT TRAP

In addition to the balance of payments problem, India's external debt trebled from about 1 trillion Rupees ($27 billion) in 1990 to 3.3 trillion Rupees ($92.2 billion) in March 1997, giving it the distinction of being the world's third-most indebted country. According to estimates presented to Parliament in February 1996, the total annual debt repayment liability in 1996/97 was 1.3 trillion Rupees ($35 billion)-almost 99.6 per cent of the expected revenue receipts. Equally pressing but rarely acknowledged is the size of the internal debt, which at the end of March 1995 stood at 4.8 trillion Rupees ($134 billion).

The burden of external debt thus amounts to 3,800 Rupees ($105) per capita and of the internal debt to 5,400 Rupees ($150) per capita. The critical extent of India's vulnerability and dependency is evident in these figures, since even for current administrative expenses, let alone any development expenditure, the government will have to borrow more. In a recent article on India's macroeconomic situation, Indian economist Arun Ghosh stated that, "like the proverbial Indian cultivator, mortgaging all his assets (and his future labour) to the indigenous money lender, the Indian state is indebted to the hilt, its entire revenue being earmarked for debt repayment."

India's level of debt is making it imperative for the government to grant insulting concessions and dilute protective legislation in the name of attracting foreign capital and continued loans from the IMF and the World Bank. As Ghosh once commented, "The management of the economy over July 1991 to December 1995 appears to have increased the country's economic vulnerability and significantly reduced future policy options and maneuverability."

EXTENDING CORPORATE HEGEMONY

Despite these measures, foreign investors and transnational corporations have been reticent to make long-term investments in India, highlighting how global capital is mostly moving to gain control over profitable state-owned enterprises or to invest in the stock market under new reforms that require no lock-in period. Trends so far suggest very little investment in productive activity except in light industrial sectors such as food processing, medicines, soft drinks, seeds and assembly of electronic goods-all of which ensure a rapid and secure return.

Similarly, other sectors that have seen significant investment are the banking sector (including the speculative market) and the insurance sector, in which the latest budget has proposed permitting foreign interests. In this undoubtedly reckless process, there seems to be little concern that the country is being made dependent on highly volatile short-term capital flows. This may sound extreme, given the confidence exuded by planners and the media.

Yet, one of the most important sources of economic instability is coming from the portfolio capital inflows from foreign institutional investors and non-resident Indians who see the emerging Indian market as a source of both speculative capital gain and cheap productive assets. Most of these investors not only have little or no stake in the country beyond private accumulation, but also have no concern whatsoever for the social and ecological impacts of their investment.

Over 75 per cent of the capital that has entered the Indian market has been in the form of portfolio investment, and its role has been to claim a share of the profits made by Indian enterprises. A major study by three economists of the Florida International University concluded that the scale of the capital flight from India to the United States alone was a staggering $15.7 billion, primarily achieved through the over-invoicing of imports and under-invoicing of exports. Other estimates place the annual capital outflow to the OECD countries at 400 billion Rupees ($12 billion).

Other foreign inflows have been aimed at the privatisation process, in which several socially detrimental trends have emerged. The euphemism of efficiency and profitability is leading to the closure of many public services, causing higher rates for health services, education, electricity, etc. This means that an increasing number of people are losing access to these social services. There is also increasing pressure to abandon or dilute public education programmes and the policy of reservations in education and public sector jobs, which had provided a way to combat the structural disadvantage that less privileged sectors of Indian society have historically suffered.

However, privatisation has brought a whole range of new subsidies to the private sector, including concessions in the provision and price of electricity and infrastructure, concessions on the purchase of land, easier credit and profit guarantees, even as profitable state-owned enterprises (SOEs) are habitually undervalued when sold. The wholly reprehensible effort by the government to divest shares of profit-making SOEs when over 200,000 private sector enterprises are "sick" only reinforces the belief that governments are under pressure from an alliance of domestic and transnational capital to privatize profitable companies so that private accumulation can be furthered.

Rather than address the problems of loss-making SOEs and the need to give these companies greater autonomy, a comprehensive plan for the closure and disinvestment of many SOEs has been implemented by the government. These reforms are clearly not leading to the reduction of graft or to more egalitarian interventions. Indeed, what is of concern is that these kind of economic interventions further centralize economic power, with fewer people benefiting from the economic intervention.

Left alone, many SOEs like the Bharat Heavy Electricals Limited and Steel Authority of India have upgraded their technology, expanded and remained competitive. Indigenous production need not mean stagnation, as there is adequate innovation and creativity among the workforce in India. The growing influence of transnational corporations is also beginning to affect the rural areas, since transnationals are becoming a dominant factor in building major infrastructure projects and in the international trade in food, seeds and inputs.

Infrastructure construction, including hydroelectric and irrigation projects, mines (particularly open cast mines), super-thermal and nuclear power plants, industrial complexes, military installations, weapons testing grounds and superhighways cause an annual displacement of over 500,000 people. If the numbers of adversely affected artisan communities and other self-employed people were added to this, we would have close to a million people forcibly uprooted every year from their habitats and sources of livelihood. The development process is profoundly stacked against the capacities of these marginalized people to subsist, since the industrial system is itself in recession or is incapable of providing a secure job to those who are displaced.

As for agriculture itself, the growing commodification and commercialisation of natural resources is creating a serious crisis for hundreds of millions of people whose lives are critically dependent upon the availability and sustainability of these resources. Their capacities to negotiate a relationship with the market and make decisions regarding their choice of resource use and social organisation are all linked to this symbiotic relationship. However, with liberalisation and the entry of transnational corporations, there has not only been a more rapacious exploitation of national natural resources, there has also been a loss of commons, an increase in the pollution of life sustaining bodies and increasing focus on export-bound cash crop production.

The government is now considering passing a grossly inequitable international property rights regime supported by transnational corporations that would undoubtedly allow these corporations access to what domestic farmers can grow, as long as it is competitive in the international market. Trends suggest that, by and large, this measure will devalue and eventually marginalize traditional knowledge systems, which would particularly affect the women who have been socialized for generations into traditional systems.

However, what is of particular concern it is not just the loss of these interdependent human-nature relationships, but also how women are increasingly being rendered obsolete and unwanted in the new agrarian structure as a result of the new definition of property rights. The argument that they will benefit by the intensification of agriculture controlled by large farmers or transnational corporations belies the experience of the past 30 years.

There will undoubtedly be some exceptions, but there is little evidence in the past six years to suggest that women, particularly those belonging to the less-privileged Dalit and tribal communities, benefit from the changes that liberalisation has brought into agriculture. Also, given that 76 per cent of women workers are in the agricultural sector, the overwhelming proportion of whom are vulnerable to small shifts in productivity, wages and climate, the new vulnerabilities brought by economic reform are distinctly felt.

A wide range of traditional occupations have a higher component of female labour-handloom, handicrafts, cashew and coir-are in crisis. The domestic silk industry has been adversely hit by a policy decision to free imports of silk, directly affecting women. It must be acknowledged that new agricultural technologies do improve some employment opportunities for women, but given the national scale of impoverishment and displacement, these gains are probably minuscule.

The argument here is not only about the diversification of what is produced, but rather about whose interests are served by these changes in property and production relations in the agrarian sector, who controls the diversification, who benefits and whether it is ecologically sustainable. As long as the demand is for land consolidation and handing over control to agro-processing and food processing companies, small, marginal and landless and particularly women among them will be severely affected. Whether in the age of colonisation or the unfolding age of globalisation, India seems to have been unable to prevent its economy from becoming a subservient actor in the global economy.

BLACK MONEY, SCARES AND CORRUPTION

The 1991 reforms, besides affecting production, have also had a definite impact on the way business is transacted. Arguably the most important reason for the continuing inflation (7 per cent to 11 per cent) and increasing internal and external debt is the sustenance and increasing scale of the "black," unregulated economy. Evidence that illegal activity is steadily finding its way into the public domain is suggested by a dramatic increase in tax evasion, graft and financial speculation, as well as an increase in the illegal traffic in weapons and drugs. Black money is used extensively for political patronage and economic gains.

It is spirited abroad through the havala markets, where foreign currency is exchanged for Rupees at higher than the official rates, and is also cleared through the under-invoicing of exports and over-invoicing of imports. Some black money becomes legitimate through amnesty schemes announced periodically by the government to attract black money. Much of it, however, is used to purchase gold, arms, drugs, electronic goods and gems, which are smuggled into the country and purchased by others flush with black money.

The actions of smugglers, havala market racketeers and import-export manipulators are leading to an estimated loss of about $10 to $15 billion annually, contributing to the serious balance of payments situation. Black incomes are estimated to make up a staggering 20 per cent to 25 per cent of the national income. Obviously, some of this is not the consequence of SAP, but rather part of an elite-oriented process of economic development. The Indian economic scene was never truly oriented toward people but was all along dualistic with major benefits going to the rich.

The SAP only takes that process much further and introduces a totally new element of foreign exploitation. Undoubtedly, many who acquired vested economic interests under the regimes of licenses and controls will lose privilege, patronage and influence if these regimes are reformed. Advantages and privileges historically enjoyed by domestic capital and landed farmers will also be challenged. However, the system that is taking the place of the earlier regime is not leading toward greater decentralisation and accountability, but rather legitimizing new structures of centralized power. This point is crucial.

As a result of the SAP policies, we are now witnessing a continuation of the accentuation of poverty among those who had succeeded under state sponsored development, depriving them of the ability to remain politically active and pressurize those at the top. This translates into a significant loss by the majority over the gains of increasing productivity, however skewed initially, and of sovereignty. The systematic violation of laws and regulations that perpetuates black money has partially been made possible by a grand symbiosis between businesspeople, politicians and bureaucrats who have entrenched themselves in the political system.

The Joint Parliamentary Committee investigating irregularities in securities and banking transactions from July 1991 to May 1992, which amounted to a staggering $1.3 billion, exposed the involvement of a large number of public agencies, big industrial houses and the highest levels of government in illegal transactions. The all-party Committee was categorical in stating that the irregularities it uncovered were a result of liberalisation without adequate safeguards.

These safeguards have not yet been put into place, and the country continues to rock with regular exposes of massive scams, diversion of funds from public sources into private hands, flight of capital and endemic corruption. It is true that the blame for all this cannot be placed on the doors of the liberalisation programme, but as numerous deals with foreign corporations' progress, the practice has been further reinforced and institutionalized.

Indian Institute for Public Administration economist Kamal Narayan Kabra summarizes: "The capital market liberalisation contributed in a variety of ways to the perpetration of the worst and the most complex bank fraud committed since independence. Without these policy changes and a permissive growth-at-any-cost environment of business associated with liberalisation, neither the motor power, nor the amounts involved nor the stock market's wild bull run would have been available to the scamsters."

RISING PRICES AND THE CONSEQUENCES OF INFLATION

India's economic health has also been affected by the 1991 reforms, and not always in the way policymakers had envisioned. For example, the restructuring has led to spiraling price rises, particularly in the case of essential commodities. Within a year of the New Economic Policy, grain prices increased by 96 per cent and those of coarse cereals by over 50 per cent.

Between 1991 and 1994, the issue price of the common variety of rice increased 85.8 per cent and of wheat 71.8 per cent. During the same period, the wholesale price index increased 44.4 per cent. Between 1990/91 and 1994/95, the consumer price index for agricultural labourers increased 53.1 per cent. The cuts in social spending, hikes in food prices supplied through Fair Price shops, steep increases in public transport fares, increases in fees for public services and growing unemployment seriously hit workers in the informal sector as well as agricultural labourers.

Government data graphically illustrate this point. In 1990/91, the general price level represented by the wholesale price index was 185 (1980/81 = 100). It increased to approximately 300 by the end of 1995, an increase of over 60 per cent. Similarly, the price of food items increased from 201 to 340, an increase of almost 70 per cent. It follows that an extremely small percentage of people have not been affected by inflation, since a minuscule slice of the population have had their earnings rise by that amount.

While the rate of inflation may have come down somewhat in 1997, prices have soared alarmingly high and continue to rise, especially those of essential commodities that directly affect the livelihoods of the most vulnerable people. Studies of the smallscale sector, which accounts for a substantial quantity of goods and provides significant employment, have shown that this sector has been adversely affected by the new economic policies. As one report noted regarding economic strategy, "The present policies are oblivious to the problems of small farmers and other primary producers, especially in the semi-arid regions."

SOCIAL IMPACT

EMPLOYMENT UNDER LIBERALISATION

In 1991, when the New Economic Policy began, India already had a massive unemployment burden of about 11 million people. Without the SAP, it was expected to rise to 15 million by 1994. However, with the SAP, the number of unemployed people is increasing more rapidly because of the decline in the rate of new recruitment due to curtailment in development expenditure, withdrawal of budgetary support for state-owned enterprises, decline in industrial production due to import liberalisation, the speeding up the computerisation plans in the name of efficiency, privatisation and the closure of state-owned enterprises.

It maybe argued that six years is not enough to assess the consequences of the new package of SAP reforms. Yet, some visible impacts can be highlighted. A comprehensive survey of employment in the post-1991 phase suggests, counter to the claims in the government's Economic Survey of 1995, that this period has been one of "jobless growth," and that whatever employment has been generated has been through poverty alleviation programmes, which have little impact on either asset creation for the poor or on aggregate economic growth.

Simultaneously, there has also been a reduction in (real) public investment and government expenditures on health, education and welfare. For those who depend on a daily wage to survive, these trends have had disastrous consequences. Undoubtedly, a few will adapt to find new or better-paying employment and others will find alternative, often nonlegal ways to earn a living. The overall unemployment trend, however, suggests a net adverse impact on access and control over productive resources.

One estimate suggests that restructuring the economy through privatisation, import liberalisation and deflationary fiscal policy will lead to an increase in unemployment by at least several million people per year over the next two years. Another study states that there will also be growing unemployment in the organized sector, owing to increasing capital intensity that will push workers into the informal and agricultural sectors.

Over the past five years, employment in the organized sector has in fact increased by 1.2 million people (0.5 million in the private sector and 0.7 million in the public sector.) However, compared to the 35 million added to the labour stock in this period, the extent of the crisis in employment is obvious. The decline in private sector employment has come despite growth in production, partially due to computerisation plans that are being accelerated in the name of efficiency and profits. The employment situation also has deteriorated due to the retrenchment, privatisation and closure of SOEs.

Several estimates indicate that, with a decline in the number of salaried persons with salaries/wages protected partially against inflation, there will be a sharp fall in the demand for consumer goods and services, which in turn will result in a fall in the employment opportunities in the informal sector. The expected number of unemployed would therefore be 30 million by 1997, an addition of over 10 million people due to the SAP.

Meanwhile, the unorganized sector which provides employment to 90 per cent of workers has seen its share in the national income decline from 70 per cent in 1981 to 63 per cent in 1991. Among the communities most adversely affected are artisans and handloom weavers, who suffer the gravest consequences from SAP-induced inflation and squeeze in credit supply.

A significant percentage of the almost 20 million handloom weavers across the country have been affected by the export of raw cotton and cotton yarn, which has resulted in a shortage of yarn and a rise in its domestic price. For those living in a fragile subsistence economy, this changes-in some cases reducing incomes by as much as 50 per cent-can means hunger and starvation. There seems to be little concern that with each death, a slice of India's unique heritage of remarkable textile tradition inches towards extinction.

The situation also affects the young, as available evidence suggests that the rise in unemployment is driving young people into underworld activities in larger and larger numbers, including young girls engaging in prostitution. AIDS is spreading in India and it might be assumed that epidemic proportions of prostitution, drug trafficking and crime will grow as expected as a consequence of the compounding of unemployment and increasingly materialist values under the SAP regime.

The plight of India's children has also received little attention from policymakers. Estimates of the number of child workers range from 70 million to 100 million with India having the distinction of having half the world's child workers. The past six years have generated little change for child welfare in India. In fact, growing impoverishment and displacement has only increased the vulnerability and insecurity of children.

Current data show that expenditures on social sectors-particularly health and education for the lower half of society including child welfare-is stagnant or in decline. According to the U.N. Development Programme, India spends a lower share of public expenditure on health and education than nine of the least developed countries, most of which have per capita incomes much lower than India's. Unemployment in the rural areas is also a problem. C.H. Hanumantha Rao, who as chairperson of the National Commission on Rural Labour gathered extensive evidence on conditions in rural India, unambiguously made the linkage between SAP and the deterioration of livelihoods of rural labour.

According to Rao, SAP measures affect rural labour through the reduction of public investment in both agriculture and social sectors, including primary education, health care and drinking water. Since investments in agriculture, rural development, irrigation and social sectors are basically financed by state revenues, these have become the first victims of the new economic measures. Although central outlays on poverty alleviation programmes have by and large been protected, Rao argues that since the resources of states have been eroded, expenditures on essential outlays for agriculture have declined, with adverse consequences for the social sector and rural employment.

Second, Rao holds that the increase in the prices of essential commodities like food grains is a consequence of the SAP, and that this has substantially impacted the poor. For instance, if the National Commission on Rural Labour had recommended a daily minimum agricultural wage of 20 Rupees at mid-1991 prices, within two years it had to recommend a 40 per cent increase in order for wages to accommodate the rising cost of basic needs.

POVERTY AND THE POLARISATION OF WEALTH

A relatively conservative scholar concluded that "... while economic liberalisation may have accentuated economic disparities, sharpened caste divisions and promoted patriarchy and fundamentalism, it is important to note that the market has released undercurrents which may eventually suppress and overwhelm the divisive forces."

Unfortunately, here the author has not carried the honesty of an acknowledgment of the massive social, cultural and economic disarray the New Economic Policy has caused forward into an analysis of the structural root causes. Instead, the author uses a convenient escape route in the hope of a possible reversal at some unspecified period in the future. However, the poverty line in India is fixed at such a low level that crossing it by no means ensures dignified living conditions for a household.

The contentious debate over the number of people below the poverty line was somewhat stilled by a startling yet sobering comprehensive survey by the National Council of Applied Economic Research released by the deputy chairman of the Planning Commission in January 1997. The survey showed that over 40 per cent of India's people were still below the poverty line and that another 30 per cent are just above it. Thus, according to the criterion under which citizens are guaranteed the right to live in dignity, an overwhelming majority would be classified as belonging to the category of those whose right to life is being violated.

A social scientist, commenting on the seemingly endless preoccupation with "poverty studies" said ".... it is a tragedy of human efforts that, despite an enormous investment in social capital on the creation of equitable conditions of existence, we continue to be involved in developing cognitive tools for understanding distress." The debates and studies on poverty are marked by a distancing from any engagement with the need for political change to positively alter the conditions of the poor.

Witness the continuing dependence among planners and donors on technical fixes, despite 50 years of evidence that they are, at best, superficial and, at worst, an insult to the poor. The past four decades of developmental planning and poverty alleviation programmes suggest that not only is trickle down not working, but that economic growth does not yield a deeper process of democratisation, the realisation of more egalitarian control or access to natural and financial productive resources.

The abandoning of any serious equity thrust is reflected not just in statistics showing that income disparities between the poorest 20 per cent of the population and the wealthiest 20 per cent have doubled in India in the last 30 years, but also in a country where many salaries in the corporate sector exceed $300,000. In a national situation where the minimum daily wage is less than $2 and half the working population does not even earn that much, serious ethical and political issues arise.

In 1995, the then-ruling Congress party responded to growing unrest over poverty issues in an election year by announcing a wide range of welfare and rural development programmes and financial allocations in the yearly budget. These safety nets were designed to mitigate only the short-term effects of stabilisation and structural adjustment, without consideration of the long-term adverse impacts of economic reforms on the rural areas and the rural poor.

One of the much-touted safety nets is the Public Distribution System, which is aimed at providing food security for the poor. Evidence suggests, however, that this is far from the case. Not only has there been a net decline in the purchasing power of the bottom 40 per cent of the population, but recent data suggest that only 2 per cent of the poor population in rural Bihar, Uttar Pradesh, Orissa and Punjab are able to obtain supplies.

In the urban areas of eight states, less than 10 per cent of the people buy from the Fair Price Shops (outlets for food from the Public Distribution System) and 88 per cent of the people covered by the survey reported that they do not get supplies when they need them. Persistent undernutrition and malnutrition, as well as an increase in starvation deaths compounded by growing under- and unemployment and rising food prices, are inexcusable when the country food buffers are overflowing.

Recently, a more targeted programme has been proposed to halve the prices that are charged to those below the poverty line. Given the experience of the past several decades, unless concomitant institutional reforms are also put into place with appropriate mechanisms for accountability and monitoring, even this effort will fail to even partially alleviate the poor's access to affordable food.

All this should not be construed as a critique of the Public Distribution System organisation itself, since there continues to be a critical need to provide subsidized food in the short run to those who are really poor, but rather a recognition that centralized storage and distribution systems are not a substitute for a four-pronged strategy that includes the following:

i. Improving the productivity and availability of enough food locally;
ii. Recovering and restoring the productivity of degraded agricultural lands and distributing them to the poor;

iii. Creating conditions for the democratisation of access and control over productive natural resources; and
iv. Increasing incomes of the bottom 40-50 per cent of the population.

Likewise, it is not enough to blame the corporate world or the SAP regime for engendering unethical practices and for legitimizing the polarisation of wealth. The Fifth Pay Commission has recommended massive increases in the salaries of bureaucrats and elected representatives. In the past few years, NGOs are also being increasingly corporatized and commercialized, with little accountability and commitment to challenge entrenched economic and political interests.

To the contrary, they have become increasingly pliable agents for the priorities and programmes of bilateral and multilateral donors and in the perpetuation of fragmentation and competition in what needs to be a truly "voluntary spirit." In this way, a multiplicity of actors and sectors of society are responsible for perpetuating poverty and the stratification of wealth.

A relationship between liberalisation, corrupt lifestyles, and the criminalisation of the poor, growing civil strife including caste "wars," commercialisation of expectations and the resultant cultural disarray and breakdown of civil society is slowly becoming clear. The task of concerned researchers and activists is in making this intermeshing clearer as the dominant; top-down doctrine of globalisation and liberalisation-cum-marketisation unfolds itself.

EXPORTS AND ENVIRONMENTAL DEGRADATION

In addition to the unsustainability of capital-intensive methods of agriculture and natural resource extraction, globalisation has also brought about an increase in the exploitation of natural resources that are the basis of subsistence for nomads, artisans, fisher folk and agricultural labourers-mostly in the name of boosting exports. The past six years have witnessed an intensification of unsustainable practices on the land, in rivers, in oceans and in forests with a consequent erosion of the country's bio-genetic diversity.

In keeping with the thrust of the economic reforms, the past three years has seen growing pressure on the government to reverse existing land reform legislation and lift or relax laws that place a ceiling on rural and urban land holding. Various businesses and their associations, as well as editors of financial newspapers, have been at the forefront of this demand to relax ceiling laws and grant long-term leases so as to encourage agro-industries on large captive farms.

A related demand is that oil palm, cashew, mango and pineapple be classified as plantation crops so that entrepreneurs can grow these crops on a large scale without concern about various land legislation. Large businesses have also demanded increased access to forest land in order to promote agro-forestry and horticulture. Capitulation to these types of demands, however, inevitably causes severe environmental and economic damage.

In one case, the government from 1991 to 1994 gave 82 companies clearance for joint (foreign and Indian) venture marine fisheries, which meant the introduction of 255 deep sea fishing trawlers. Consequently, exports of fish and fish products increased from 159,000 tons (9.6 billion Rupees, or $266 million) in 1990/91 to 321,000 tons (35.4 billion Rupees, or $1 billion), in 1994/95. The trawling joint ventures were predominantly export-oriented, and what motivated the government in granting the licenses was not the long-term sustainability of the fish stocks nor the rights of millions of traditional fisherfolk to their only source of protein, but rather the prospect of one more source of foreign exchange.

Defenders of trawling claim that they fish in waters where the traditional fishworker does not fish. Unfortunately, past experience has shown that trawlers violate this boundary and undertake practices that destroy the sustainability of diverse fish stocks. Fortunately, there has been massive sustained resistance from traditional fisherfolk to trawling (mobilized nationally under the banner of the National Fishworkers Federation), which resulted in a dramatic decision by the Indian government in March 1997 to suspend and eventually phase out all joint venture fishing licenses.

Cash cropping for exports has also generated severe ecological vulnerability. The popular argument in favour of cash cropping is that the practice will bring more surplus revenue to local farmers, who would then be able to exercise more economic and consumption options. Some activists from women's movements have also pointed out that this value addition would give women greater capacity to become economically independent.

Unfortunately, the experience so far suggests that cash cropping places greater emphasis on maximizing production with little consideration for ecological sustainability or equity. As a result, more chemical and water-intensive methods are used and a shift in cropping from food crops to non-food crops (floriculture, tea, tobacco, sugarcane, etc.) takes place with the benefits accruing primarily to middle-class and wealthy farmers. The process of displacement of smaller farmers and in some cases of agricultural labour is compounded.

Another example of the threat to India's future posed by the focus on exports is the explosion of aquaculture on India's coasts. Intensive prawn and shrimp farming ventures have disrupted the delicate salinity balance of coastal areas, caused pollution, depleted the groundwater and led to a reduction in rice production. Coastal farmers and traditional fishing families have been displaced by aquaculture production, which has provided less than half the employment that farming previously did.

Yet, both the private and public sectors have drawn up ambitious plans to expand aquaculture in the country. According to a recent article, the head of the Aqua Foundation of India was quoted as projecting a jump in shrimp exports from 70,000 tons at present to 2,000,000 tons by 2000, and stating that "the world is looking to India to meet its shrimp requirements." The Gujarat Fisheries Development Corporation and other agencies have signed an agreement to develop 250,000 acres of the state's coasts for aquaculture.

Both these strategies have therefore made millions of farmers and fisherfolk, as well as their ecosystems, more vulnerable. The introduction of the demands of an international agricultural market is also increasing ecological vulnerability through a loss of genetic diversity as India's indigenous products are standardized and made uniform.

As Ashish Kothari notes, a single variety of Basmati rice, favoured by foreign consumers, has replaced dozens, possibly hundreds of other local varieties of rice. Pepsi's subsidiary, Pepsi Foods, has reportedly encouraged farmers to grow one particular variety of tomato, which is suited to its production process. Kentucky Fried Chicken is reported to have delayed the start of its operation in India because it wants maize-fed chicken, which it will introduce to replace the local Indian breeds of poultry.

POLITICAL IMPACT UNDERMINING DEMOCRACY

As we have seen, economic policy making is becoming more and more centralized and secretive, which has resulted in the undermining of democratic institutions and the democratic process itself. Most agreements with transnational corporations have shown complete disregard for environmental impact assessments; consultations with communities likely to be affected by project plans and public accountability about these projects are lacking.

In fact, when communities in Maharashta peacefully sought more public debate about the proposed Enron power project, they were brutally attacked by the police and hundreds (including women and children) were jailed. Another instance of backtracking on the democratic process occurred when the national budget for 1992/93 and the Eight Plan documents were first revealed to the World Bank before they were presented in the Indian Parliament.

Similarly, the GATT agreement was signed with not only little consultation with the states and with elected representatives, but with almost no popular debate on its consequences for a wide range of sectors as well as on the sovereignty of the country itself. In fact, since 1991, most economic policy changes have been adopted without any public debate or any effort by the state and central governments to explain the social, ecological and cultural implications and consequences of the Structural Adustment Programme.

Another critical failure of the reform package that has a bearing on the question of democratisation is the persistence of a growing and grossly inequitable society in which there continues to be even greater mystification of economic policies and instruments. A reflection of the unrepresentative and infirm democracy in India may be seen in the following statement of former Prime Minister Rao in the context of a comprehensive social audit of the economic policy changes since 1991.

According to a report in the newspaper, Rao began his speech by "delineating the social structures into three segments. The crust, according to him, consists of about six crore (1 crore= 10 million) people, who do not need to be canvassed about economic reforms. The next layer contains 25-30 crore people belonging to the middle classes, who are beginning to appreciate the benefits of liberalisation. It is the next segment, of 55-60 crore of lower income and poor people who remain unappreciative of the changes in the economy."

Even if the reforms were improving the lives of a majority, it is indeed a sad commentary of our times and of the actions of our policymakers that dramatic economic changes are cynically heralded by bypassing a majority in the citizenry. Taking a majority for granted in the design and imposition of the reform package is one of the most profound failures of the reforms.

Most of this majority is comprised of those who are engaged in primary production, whether in the field, factory or household. Tribal members, traditional fisherfolk, artisans, and marginal and small peasants comprise these millions who are so callously expected to either survive on crumbs or to fend for them. In fact, it is no longer that the poor are being taken for granted, but rather deliberately excluded and considered dispensable under a political and economic regime that legitimizes poverty and destitution.

Can we be so arrogant, so insensitive to the plight of a majority who are scattered across the country and who cannot have their voices heard in the shallow and faulty representative electoral processes in the country? Can they be discarded or bypassed as necessary "social costs" of the liberalisation process, in much the same way as millions have been displaced in the name of "national interest" and "progress?"

In this context, it is surely callous and immoral to confine analysis to aggregate gains in growth, GDP, foreign exchange reserves, stockpiles of food and the like. It should be reprehensible to promote elitist consumption when so much of the country suffers from malnourishment, inequity and discrimination. This itself is reflective of a critical lack of democratic process in the defining economic policy.

ALTERNATIVES TO THE 1991 REFORMS

In many ways, the question of whether there are any alternatives to the present package of reforms is moot. Given the social, cultural and ecological impacts of these reforms and their contribution to making the country more economically dependent, alternatives will have to be defined; howsoever marginal they may seem in the present climate of superficially consensual, elite-led development. In numerous sites across the country, often despite overwhelming odds, those who have been neglected or excluded by dominant policies are attempting to define small incremental changes that can give greater meaning to their lives.

From asserting control over systems of governance and productive resources to organizing public hearings and resisting destructive developmental projects, people all over the country are becoming part of a democratic stirring from the bottom up. Grassroot campaigns against economic reforms have so far been scattered and in most cases not sustained. It is also true that the formal political space to critique the New Economic Policy is shrinking as political parties across the ideological spectrum have reached a tacit consensus on seeing the reforms through.

In the early years of reform, several important strikes by workers as well as other initiatives such as the preparation of an Alternative Budget took place, but in the past two years debates on the Structural Adjustment Programme have increasingly been confined along sectional or single issue lines. Even so, organisations like the Association of Rural Poor in Tamil Nadu have been successful in waging struggles against moves to deprive peasants of land and to protect tenants and make them owners of land.

Several crucial actions against specific transnational corporations such as Kentucky Fried Chicken, DuPont and Cargill or against specific projects supported by bilateral and multilateral organisations like British Overseas Development Agency or the World Bank have witnessed significant mobilisation. While Kentucky Fried Chicken was forced to considerably scale down its operations, Cargill and DuPont had to cancel or relocate their activities. Recent initiatives like the National Alliance of Peoples Movement or the National Forum for Tribal Self-Rule or the much older National Fishworkers Federation have launched sustained agitations against undemocratic and unjust development interventions that have come in the wake of liberalisation.

Their campaigns point to the need to widen approaches and sensitize peasants against seed imperialism, cultural imperialism and the short-term interests pursued by the political and economic elites, be they foreign or domestic. The National Alliance of Women and other women's groups have also played a significant role in defining a progressive plan of action that has been included in a preliminary approach paper for the government's ninth Five-Year Plan, and complex strategies are being forged to pursue its implementation.

Grassroots organisations are also underscoring the need for a coordinated platform to build awareness regarding the alternatives for a production system that nurtures cultural pluralism and fulfills the diverse needs of a majority of people. There are modest efforts underway to build strategies to gain equitable control over productive resources through an alliance among workers, peasants, scientists, intellectuals and women across the country.

These movements also point to the need to respect the growing support for further democratisation. The content of these movements may seem utopian given the "triumphalism" that pervades the new package of reforms. Nevertheless, in a slow but ever expanding rumble, grassroots efforts are spreading to a wider range of locales. Growing demands for autonomy and the formation of autonomous councils in several regions as well as the resurgence of sub-nationalist movements are all reflective of the growing frustration with centralized control that legitimizes wealth accumulation by a minority at the expense of a majority.

MANAGING DISSENT

Simultaneously, of course, political and economic regimes are either becoming more sophisticated in their management of consent and dissent-or in their capacities to suppress dissent-by labeling opposing groups as "corrupt," "anti-development," or even "anti-national." Numerous anti-democratic laws like the Maintenance of Internal Security Act and the Terrorist and Disruptive Activities Act, as well as the colonial Official Secrets Act, have been used to control the activities and protests of trade unions, farmers' organisations and grassroots movements.

Thus, while the democratic space of upper- and the middle-classes has expanded with growing wealth and influence, there has simultaneously been a definite shrinking in the democratic space of those victimized by the New Economic Policy. Witness the significant expansion in the security forces to "deal" with internal dissent or to facilitate domestic capital or foreign exchange-bearing entrepreneurs. In fact, increasingly business interests have become associated with national interests, while social and cultural interests are relegated to a secondary position if not sacrificed altogether.

One former finance minister, echoing this spirit of policy focus, stated recently that power should increasingly move from the state to the boardroom. Worse still, a recent official announcement stated that the Indian police would be trained by Western security experts to protect the "life and property of foreign investors." This growing convergence between the state and the market to promote narrow interests is one of the unfolding and unfortunate outcomes of the New Economic Policy. Much of the discussion of alternatives to the present patterns of economic liberalisation and reform are either labeled as being utopian or dismissed as a package of romantic Gandhian or socialist ideas.

The argument from those on the side of democratic and egalitarian development is that the values of justice and equality can no longer be neglected at the altar of national security and these patterns of development. Millions who have been historically subjugated or marginalized by caste or class oppression are today, in increasing numbers, demanding justice from and within an inequitable system. In many ways, these sentiments are more crucial than the scattered campaigns and fragmented "movements" or a bunch of policy alternatives.

Various "Andolans" (social and political movements), socialists, radical Gandhians and other concerned people can contribute to the potential changes by giving focus to these stirrings, by sounding warning signals when the oppressed get divided and fight among themselves and by providing ideological and intellectual inputs. The success of the struggles of the poor to act as equal citizens may seem more difficult at the present juncture than ever, given the mystification, centralisation and power of economic institutions nationally. It is therefore an even more profound challenge not to abandon the struggle for justice and equity

Political parties will have to contend increasingly with this emerging sense of self-confidence among the poorer classes and castes as they assert their rights to greater dignity. The party system has so far contributed to raising awareness, but has largely failed to address the endemic root causes of economic subservience and impoverishment. With this failure of elites to address real economic and social problems, the only hope of a resolution lies in the further strengthening of grassroots democracy. Dreze and Sen reflect a similar sensibility when they argue that:

It is in terms of these broader egalitarian concerns that India's record has been most disappointing and that the scope for action may be particularly extensive. The importance of local democracy is not confined, of course, to this issue of public services, or other instrumental roles of intrinsic value for the quality of life. Indeed being able to do something not only for oneself is one of the elementary freedoms which people have reason to value. The popular appeal of many social movements in India confirms that this basic capability is highly valued even among people who had very deprived lives in material terms.

Given the fact that we live on a finite planet and that our needs should not expand beyond what can be sustainably provided by the natural cycles of regeneration, any continuation of an ethic of satisfying unlimited wants will only continue to justify the exploitation of resources as well as those dependent upon these resources for their subsistence. This argument should not be considered anti-market, but rather pose the important questions of: Which market? Who controls the market? And at what cost? Democratisation is important in this context.

While the democratisation of regional and global institutions and economic and political processes is imperative, the primary struggle is within India with follow-up support in the globalisation of resistance. The enemy within-what has been called the "Resident non-Indians"-has to be confronted and challenged. This internal political process must not be neglected, particularly in a climate of depoliticisation brought about by economic developmentalists and a majority of NGOs.

As already indicated, democratisation is important. It is clear that growth is not a sufficient condition for the poor to acquire greater control over their lives and achieve economic and social security. Relying on the market to bring benefits to all devalues those courageous efforts that respect values and ethical principles that are not subordinated to the cold calculus of growth.

In addition to the need for a continuing struggle to democratize and restructure all global and local institutions and to change the root causes of underdevelopment and discrimination, this chapter has tried to argue that the concerns of equity, social justice, gender and ecology, cannot be subordinated to the logic of the market. The Indian case clearly demonstrates that the political goal of self-reliance, political independence, national sovereignty and a marked commitment to the poor needs to be brought back into the center of political concern and action.

6

Children Development Policy and Programming

Several international documents commit governments to meeting the rights and special needs of children. The UN Convention on the Rights of the Child (United Nations, 1989) was the first international agreement to officially recognize the civil, political, economic, social, and cultural rights of children. The Convention, which has now been ratified by 192 countries, legally binds all signatories to uphold children's rights. It contains 54 articles that obligate states to ensure children's rights to survival, protection, development, and participation.

The World Declaration on the Survival, Protection, and Development of Children (United Nations, 1990) and the UN Millennium Development Goals (United Nations, 2000) also focus on the protection of children's rights. More recently, world leaders at a UN General Assembly in 2002 committed themselves to making a "World Fit for Children". In their declaration, they upheld the importance of "Care for Every Child", and agreed that:

Children must get the best possible start in life. Their survival, protection, growth and development in good health and with proper nutrition is the essential foundation of human development. We will make concerted efforts to fight infectious diseases, tackle major causes of malnutrition and nurture children in a safe environment that enables them to be physically healthy, mentally alert, emotionally secure, socially competent and able to learn (UNICEF, 2002).

Against the background of these international commitments, the objective of this chapter is to evaluate the contribution of the Integrated Child Development Services (ICDS) in promoting young children's fundamental rights in India. Specifically, it discusses the role of the ICDS in meeting the rights of children to survival, development, and early education. An overview of the context of early childhood development in India is first provided. Next, the ICDS is evaluated and finally, the chapter considers why meeting children's rights in India are still an unfinished endeavor.

In 2001, there were 157.86 million children in India who ranged in age from birth to 6 years. Of these, an estimated 21 million were infants under 1 year, about 42 million were toddlers between 1 and 2 years, and about 94 million were aged between 3 and 6 years. Services for children below 6 years are provided by the central and state governments, voluntary non-governmental agencies, and profit-making organisations. Early childhood care and education falls under the jurisdiction of the Ministry of Human Resource Development, with the Department of Women and Child Development taking responsibility for overseeing government and governmentaided programmes.

Swaminathan characterizes early childhood services as falling into a "dual track" mode. On one track are government-funded programmes (including those run by voluntary agencies) that are directed at children from economically disadvantaged backgrounds. On the other track are services that are offered by the private sector, which target children from middle- to upper-class backgrounds. The former track aims to promote holistic development, whereas the latter focuses on 3 Rs.

THE INTEGRATED CHILD DEVELOPMENT SERVICES PROGRAMME

The following section outlines the philosophy behind the ICDS, and provides information about its growth and size. Next, the need for such a programme in India is discussed. The support that is given to the programme from the government and international developmental agencies is then described. Finally, the implementation of the programme is discussed. In 1974, the Indian government adopted a National Policy for Children. As a result of this policy, the Integrated Child Development Services (ICDS) programme was launched in 1975.

Under this nationwide programme, children up to the age of 6, and expectant and nursing mothers, benefit from a package of services that includes medical checks, immunisations, referral services, supplementary feeding, pre-school education, and health and nutrition education. The ICDS takes a holistic view of child development, and is an intergenerational programme in that both mothers and children are beneficiaries.

Both the prenatal and postnatal environment are considered, and women between the ages of 15 and 45 years are covered by the programme, as the nutritional status of a woman during her child-bearing years undoubtedly affects the development of her children. The philosophy behind the provision of a package of services is self-evident.

Services are likely to be more effective if they are delivered in an integrated manner and coordinated with related services, such as schemes for ensuring a safe supply of drinking water or for boosting adult literacy. In short, the ICDS is a laudable programme that targets the main components of human resource development: health, nutrition, and education (National Institute of Public Cooperation and Child Development [NIPCCD], 1992).

SIZE OF PROGRAMME

ICDS projects exist in all of India's 28 states and 7 Union territories. States are divided into districts, which cover both urban and rural areas. In rural areas, there is a further division into community development blocks, which comprise 70 to 100 villages. There are 5,652 blocks that are spread out across the country (GOI, 2002b).

The government sanctions ICDS projects, and launched 33 in 1975. There are currently over 5,000 projects. In selecting projects, priority is given to areas with large populations of individuals from scheduled castes or backward communities, drought prone areas, and urban slums. Since the 1980s, the ICDS has been the Indian government's major early childhood intervention strategy, and in 1995 the government made a commitment to universalize the ICDS for all eligible beneficiaries, which led to a marked expansion of the programme.

Since that time, there has been more emphasis on children under 3 years and more focus on integrated early child development. Although 5,614 ICDS projects were sanctioned in 1995, only 4,761 were in operation by September 2002. No other government programme has experienced such a phenomenal expansion, yet there are still many millions of children who do not benefit from early childhood services.

In 1991, the programme covered 12.9 million children and 2.7 million expectant or nursing mothers. The corresponding figures for 2001 were 31.5 and 6 million, which makes the ICDS the world's largest integrated child development programme. This unique community-based programme should cover 54.3 million children and 10.9 million mothers by 2006.

THE NEED FOR AN INTEGRATED CHILD DEVELOPMENT PROGRAMME

"Poverty threatens every right, depriving children of the capacities they require to survive, develop and thrive". The sheer number of children in poverty and other adverse child development indicators have led to the marked expansion of the ICDS. Close to 27 million children (50 every minute) are born in India every year. Only around 34% of these newborns are delivered in an institution, and the majority of the noninstitutional deliveries are attended by untrained midwives.

Due to poor maternal health and nutritional status, about 30% of newborns have low birth weights (below 2.5 kg). The infant mortality rate (IMR), which indicates the number of deaths for every 1,000 live births, has remained at around 70 for several years, although there are wide disparities between regions and between different sections of the population, with lower castes and tribal communities having a higher IMR than the national average. Compared to international reference populations, 47% of Indian children under 3 years are two standard deviations below the international median for weight-for-age.

Approximately 45% of children under 3 years are below the international median height-for-age and 15.5% are below the median weight-for-age. The female to male ratio in India was 933 females per 1,000 males in 2001. More disturbing is the fact that this figure was 927 to 1,000 for the birth to 6 years age group. This may be seen as a testimony to the discrimination against females in Indian society, especially as these low ratios are evident in all age groups, which indicates bias against females.

As a composite indicator, it captures unfavourable practices including female infanticide and feticide and the neglect of girls through inadequate nutrition, inadequate health care, little or no education, early marriage, premature child bearing, and poor maternal nutrition. This anti-female bias is the outcome of cultural, social, and religious beliefs and social norms, and cuts across all strata of society.

Such discriminatory treatment throughout the life cycle of women clearly has several implications for the rights and well-being of Indian children. Millions of children under the age of

6 years live in urban slum areas of India, where civic amenities such as drainage, water, and sanitation are poor. Slums and poor settlements are usually situated on the outskirts of cities beyond the remit of municipal services. These deprived environmental conditions affect the survival, growth, and development of children, and the social indicators for children in urban slums are similar to those for the most backward rural areas.

Despite spectacular progress in some domains, India continues to have high infant and child mortality rates, and about 50% of children below 5 years are moderately or severely malnourished. Promoting the well-being of children from disadvantaged backgrounds has been accorded high priority in the government's Five Year Plans, which are concerned with economic planning. However, the actual implementation of strategies to improve the conditions of underprivileged Indian children has not been optimal and the basic rights of these children have not been met.

GOVERNMENT SUPPORT FOR THE ICDS

Through its policies, which focus on children's rights to survival, development, and education, and its financial assistance, the government has strongly encouraged the development and growth of the ICDS. The Indian Constitution has numerous safeguards to ensure children's rights to survival, protection, and development, and a number of policies are directly concerned with child development. In addition to these policies, there is a wide range of laws that are designed to extensively protect the rights and entitlements that are guaranteed by the constitution. However, despite all of these policy provisions, there is still much to be done to safeguard young children's fundamental rights.

Early childhood policy and programmes in India have tended to respond to context, rather than trying to fit a predetermined model (Evans, 2000). As many children in India are relatively disadvantaged, efforts to operate pre-school programmes that focus on education without acknowledging the primary health and nutrition needs of young children and their families are likely to meet with limited success.

Indeed, a hallmark of the ICDS is its holistic approach to the young child through the promotion of an integrated approach to improvements in health, nutrition, early learning and better parenting; a child-centered curriculum that is structured using a life cycle approach and aims at the development continuum of the child; and emphasis on the developmental needs of children under 3 years. As early childhood services have been indigenously developed, Indian cultural beliefs about child development and childhood have typically been respected, and parental ethnotheories have been taken into account when marketing these services to parents.

It should be noted that 46% of women in India were illiterate in 2001. Convincing these women of the importance of limiting family size, educating their children, and not neglecting female children is comparatively difficult, but very relevant to the success of services that are designed to promote the development and learning of young children.

There is no doubt that contextual factors such as cultural beliefs and practices need to be considered in programme development and implementation. However, there are times when cultural practices are at odds with a children's rights perspective. For example, parents may treat a very sick child with folk remedies of doubtful value rather than taking him/her to a medical practitioner or give preference to a male over a female child. The rationale for funding child development programmes is outlined in various government documents.

Two of the main justifications that are given are similar to those that are given by other governments, but one of them is peculiar to the Indian context. Like others, the Government of India recognizes that early childhood is a critical period in human development, and provides early childhood services for disadvantaged children to enhance their survival and development. It also does so presumably to prevent the development of secondary handicaps and to lower the long-term costs to government that is engendered by the repetition of grades and dropping out of school.

Further, early childhood services are provided to allow mothers, who act primarily as caretakers of young children, to take up industrial employment. However, in the Indian context, early childhood services are provided to encourage female children to attend primary school, thereby ensuring girls has a right to education. In rural areas, girls are typically responsible for looking after their younger siblings, and this deprives them of formal education. In the 1990s, many government-run primary schools were required to establish pre-school classes to enable female children to attend school.

INTERNATIONAL SUPPORT FOR THE ICDS

The ICDS has attracted international support and funding from international development agencies such as UNICEF and the World Bank. UNICEF assists the ICDS by providing weighing scales and vehicles. The World Bank has provided financial support for the ICDS projects in 11 states since 1990, and funds all of the components of the ICDS package. A Child Development Project Office is located in each community development block in which the ICDS programme exists. The office is the basic administrative unit of the ICDS, and each block covers a population of about 100,000 people who live in 100 villages in rural areas and 35,000 in approximately 50 villages in non-tribal areas.

There are typically 100 ICDS centers or Anganwadis (literally courtyard play centers) in each rural and urban project, and 50 Anganwadi Centers (AWCs) in each tribal project. However, the actual number of AWCs differs from block to block because of population density, topography, and communication. The staff for each project includes the Child Development Project Officer, several supervisors who report to the Officer, an Anganwadi Worker (AWW) and an Anganwadi Helper (AWH) for each center.

A medical doctor, a female health visitor, and female health workers from Primary Health Centers in the vicinity work with staff from the Departments of Social Welfare and Women and Child Development to implement the programme. In this section, two national level evaluation studies of the ICDS are discussed. The relationship between Human Development Indicators, such as infant mortality and nutritional status, and the expansion of the ICDS is then considered, because the examination of changes in these Indicators is another way of documenting the impact of the programme.

It is, of course, not possible to retrospectively attribute improvements in human development indicators to one programme when there are a number of government policies and programmes that focus on the improvement of human well-being. However, the ICDS has had a critical role in promoting early development because of its links with other programmes. There have been numerous studies to evaluate the impact of the ICDS on a variety of outcomes. Between 1975 and 1995, 1,029 annual surveys and 720 research studies on the ICDS were conducted.

However, these studies typically focused on small geographical areas, had small sample sizes, and were limited to evaluating a few components of the programme. There have only been two studies with nationally representative, randomly selected samples. These studies, which were conducted by the National Institute of Public Cooperation and Child Development in 1990 and the National Council of Applied Economic Research in 1999, involved the comprehensive evaluation of the ICDS, and will be discussed in the following sections.

This study was undertaken to evaluate the impact of the ICDS on selected outcome indicators; assess variations in the implementation and utilisation of ICDS services in urban, rural, and tribal areas; identify the problems that are associated with the implementation of the ICDS; and assess community perception of and participation in the ICDS. A multi-stage random sampling technique was used in the study, and the sample included 54 rural, 18 tribal, and 18 urban projects that were drawn from 32 states and Union territories.

The total ICDS sample included 700 Anganwadis (378 rural, 196 tribal, and 126 urban) covering 25,864 households, 7,034 children under 3 years, 6,992 children between 3 and 6 years, and 5,124 women. This study was very competently designed and implemented. A multimethod, multi-source data collection strategy was followed. Participants included infants and children, mothers, families, ICDS staff and community members. Children were assessed, adults were interviewed and ICDS records were scrutinised.

A methodological strong point of this study was the inclusion of a control group, as the ICDS was not universalized in 1992. For each ICDS project in the sample, a village near the ICDS block in which the ICDS was not implemented was also selected for study. The non-ICDS areas were similar to the ICDS project areas in terms of level of development and health and education facilities. The non-ICDS group included 54 rural, 28 tribal, and 18 urban units that covered 3,690 households, 994 children below 3 years, 994 children between 3 and 6 years, and 727 women.

The non-ICDS sample did not significantly differ from the ICDS sample in the socio-economic status indicators of income, land ownership, and caste. Over 50 indicators were analyzed, but the discussion here is limited to the findings that are related to pre-natal care and child developmental outcomes. State governments and charitable organisations provide nutritional, health, and education services in both ICDS and non-ICDS blocks.

By comparing the utilisation of heath services in ICDS and non-ICDS blocks, we can deduce the impact of the ICDS. Mothers-to-be in the ICDS areas were more likely to seek ante-natal care (50.2%) and obtain immunisations (46.2%) than in the non-ICDS areas, where only 36.7% of mothers received ante-natal care. Not surprisingly, there were significant differences between the two groups in the utilisation of services that are specific to the ICDS, namely, nutrition and health education and supplementary nutrition.

The evaluation results indicate that the programme had a positive impact on children's health and nutritional status. Compared with the ICDS areas, babies born in the non-ICDS areas had lower birth weights. However, there were no significant differences in the weights of children from the ICDS and non-ICDS areas, although both groups had weights that were under the national norm. The nutritional status of children in the ICDS areas was better than that of children in the non-ICDS areas. In the ICDS areas, 35% of children had normal nutritional status and 10.8% had Grade III or IV malnutrition. The corresponding figures for the non-ICDS areas were 31% and 13.11%, respectively.

About 56% of 3 to 6 years olds who were registered in the Anganwadis received pre-school education there, compared with 8% in the non-ICDS areas. Among the ICDS children of pre-school age, about 50% were able to count up to 50 and count five objects, and about 30% of them were able to recognize and label colors. About half of the children were able to hold a crayon and color a circle. Information about children who ranged in age from 5 to 14 years in ICDS and non-ICDS households was collected.

It is noteworthy that 89% of children who had received pre-school education actually continued their education at the primary level, whereas only 52% to 60% of 5 to 14 year olds who did not receive pre-school education (in either the ICDS or non-ICDS areas) were enrolled in primary schools. In summary, this evaluation study indicates that children in the ICDS programmes had better health, nutrition, and educational outcomes than comparable children who were not enrolled in the programme.

On the basis of these findings, the following recommendations were made: upgrade the physical facilities of the AWCs; improve training and supervision for ICDS staff; enhance the coverage of supplementary nutrition, particularly for children under 3 years; improve the pre-school education component of the programme; provide resources (equipment, food supplements, play materials) to improve the implementation of the programme; increase community participation in the ICDS; and improve the coverage in tribal areas. These recommendations have been largely implemented, but to varying degrees.

THE NCAER STUDY

The NCAER evaluation sought to examine the performance of the ICDS against its stated objectives, and to make recommendations for public policy. This study also used a randomly selected national sample. It was much larger than the NIPCCD study, and included 4,000 ICDS projects, 60,000 AWC, 4,000 Child Development Programme Officers, 4,000 AW supervisors, and 180,000 households. Data were collected through structured interviews of ICDS staff and families who received services and much effort was exerted in training research assistants to ensure that standardized procedures were followed.

However, children were not assessed directly as in the case of the NIPCCD study. Information was collected about the location, physical environment, and resources that were available at the AWCs; the characteristics and training background of the ICDS staff; the functioning of the AWCs; the utilisation of services; and community participation in and perceptions of the ICDS. The data on the AWC and staff are significant, as the effectiveness of the services that are delivered largely depends on the quality of the infrastructure and the resources that are available.

The results indicate that about 65% of eligible children and 62% of eligible women were enrolled in the closest AWC. Food supplements were provided to women and children for more than 21 days in a month in the vast majority of AWCs, and more than 70% of children consumed the cooked meals or ready to eat food in the center. In some states, the majority of women consumed their food supplement at home. When food was taken home, it was either consumed by the beneficiary or shared with other family members.

The problem with the latter is that the food may not reach the intended beneficiary, which sabotages efforts to improve the nutritional status of women and children. In terms of health, the majority of women received ante-natal and post-natal advice from an AWW, and about 80% of children had been immunized against major diseases. In terms of nutritional status, less than 3% of children were severely malnourished, with the exception of the state of Bihar where the figure was 11.3%. It is disturbing to note that despite the emphasis on monitoring children's growth to promote their survival and development, this was only carried out for 30% of the children in the study.

It should be added that weighing scales were available in only 75% of the AWCs in the country. About 60% of eligible children took advantage of the pre-school education component of the ICDS, the effectiveness of which was evaluated by assessing children on their school readiness skills. Only about 30% of children were able to count, read simple words, and distinguish objects. As there was no non-ICDS pre-school group, it was not possible to determine whether or not the pre-school education component of the ICDS was effective compared with a control group.

IMPORTANCE OF NATIONAL LEVEL STUDIES

Taken together, the findings from the two studies indicate that the ICDS has played a significant role in improving the health, nutrition, and education of children. While there have been numerous small-scale studies, it is only the results of these large national level studies that have significantly influenced public policy reinforcing the need for appropriate samples and methodology. However, neither of the studies has actually considered the fiscal efficiency of the programme or looked at the long term impact of the ICDS on children. Indeed, no prospective, longitudinal study of the influence of the ICDS on children has been conducted using a nationally representative sample.

AREAS FOR IMPROVEMENT FOR THE ICDS

The NCAER (2001) made recommendations that were similar to those made by the NIPCCD (1992), which suggests that many of the identified problems have yet to be addressed, despite the enabling policies. Tremendous challenges for the ICDS still exist, with the need to improve training, the content of the programme, and co-ordination between the various programmes that support the development of women and children. It should be pointed out that, through the years, much research has also been critical of the ICDS. Research indicates that in the past the AWCs were perceived as feeding stations, and it is only in the last decade that efforts to strengthen the pre-school education component have been made.

Centers tend to focus on health and nutrition over social and cognitive development, lack curriculum resources, have high adult ratios and large group sizes, and the childcare workers had low levels of professional training. More attention can be directed at providing high quality curriculum materials, enriching the drab curriculum, improving the quality of teaching and learning, and adding school readiness activities.

The pre-school component of the ICDS is considered to be one of the weak points of the programme. Although the ICDS is in the process of being universalized, it has been pointed out that that there is no mechanism to ensure that supplementary nutrition and services actually reach the neediest sector of the population. Furthermore, AWWs are often overworked, and the health, outreach, and education components of the ICDS do not receive adequate attention (World Bank, 1999). Evaluation of the ICDS has focused on its effects on the health and nutrition status of children and not on its pre-school education component.

In the Indian context, the measures that are used to index the success of the programme are extremely important, because evaluation has a very positive backwash effect. For example, when monthly checks on nutritional status are closely monitored by supervisors and Child Development Programme Officers, the AWWs make the assessment of nutritional needs and dealing with malnutrition a priority. As there is no monitoring of other indicators of developmental status, such as cognitive, social, and motor milestones, limited attention is given to the curriculum and the means to facilitate all-round development.

HUMAN DEVELOPMENT INDICATORS

National statistics allow us to examine the relationship between the trajectories of indicators of children's well-being and contemporaneous public policy that is relevant to early child development. Since the 1980s, the ICDS has been the government's primary national strategy for promoting survival, growth, and early childhood development. The ICDS was strengthened and extended in the 1980s, experienced unprecedented growth in the 1990s, and is on track for becoming universalized.

The assessment of the impact of the ICDS on child developmental outcomes based on the results of the national evaluations was presented in the previous section. On the basis of these studies and changes in human development indicators,

I argue that the ICDS has played a critical role in enhancing the survival, growth, and education of children in India. Since independence in 1947, India has made some significant achievements in improving the health of children, but at the same time most of the indicators are very high compared with those in many other developing countries. The IMR decreased from 127 in 1978 to 71 in 1998. There continue to be large variations across states, but the gender differences that existed in 1998 have now almost disappeared.

The child mortality rate (CMR), which is the number of deaths per thousand live births of children under five years, has also declined for both boys and girls. It decreased from 40.4 in 1985 to 24.5 in 1997 for girls and from 36.6 in 1985 to 21.8 in 1997 for boys. Again, there are large inter-state variations, with the CMR ranging from 3 in Kerala to 32.3 in Madhya Pradesh. About 50% of children under 5 years are moderately or severely malnourished. Furthermore, 30% of newborns are significantly underweight and 60% of mothers are anemic.

These figures both reflect and have implications for public policy. Since the period 1975 to 1979, there has been a decrease in the percentage of children with severe and moderate malnutrition, and a corresponding increase in the number of children with mild and normal nutritional status. The widespread prevalence of malnutrition has dire consequences for early child development, and affects children's all-round development and the caretaking capabilities of caregivers. One can compare the national statistics with those obtained from the two ICDS evaluation studies that have been discussed.

It should be noted that the data were not collected in precisely the same time period or in the same location. There are also differences in the source of information in the different studies. Furthermore, ICDS beneficiaries are disadvantaged, and surveys that relate to the general population include people from all social strata. Because of this, it has been argued that when

ICDS studies yield figures that are similar to those in the general population, the ICDS has had a positive impact. The Registrar General and Census Commissioner found that the IMR based on a national sample was 94.5 in 1989, and the NIPCCD study found that it was 71.3 in 1990 for the ICDS sample.

The IMR for a national sample of children was 70 in 1997, and the NCAER (2001) found that it was 41.6 for the ICDS sample in 1999. In terms of health, children who were ICDS beneficiaries showed better nutritional status than those sampled from the general population. This is not surprising, as food supplementation is a cornerstone of the ICDS. In general, the indicators are better for ICDS children than for the general population. Clearly, caution must be exercised in interpreting these findings, because of the aforementioned caveats.

As there are a number of government policies and programmes that focus on the improvement of human well-being, it is not possible to retrospectively attribute improvements to one programme alone, but it is felt that the ICDS has had a critical role in promoting early development in disadvantaged populations. However, mere exposure to early childhood education is not enough to result in positive developmental outcomes, and attention should be directed to the quality of services that are provided.

MEETING CHILDREN'S RIGHTS IN INDIA

Over the last 50 years, India has made tremendous progress in improving the survival and promoting the development of children. In 1949, the IMR was 180 and by 1999 it had been brought down to 70. Although the nutritional status of young children has improved over the years, about half of all children under 5 years of age are still malnourished. This is disturbing given that the country has been self-sufficient in food production since the 1990s, and has considerable food stocks. India's health indicators are very unfavourable by international standards, and given India's remarkable progress in some domains of economic development, these figures reflect the need for continued intervention.

Women's literacy increased from 8.9 in 1951 to 54.2 in 2001, which is important, as maternal literacy is considered to be the best predictor of infant mortality. Why has India been so slow to improve human development indicators, and to what extent is government policy responsible for the current state of Indian children? India has been caught in a vicious cycle of poverty and malnutrition, and breaking this cycle is its most important challenge. The population growth rate, which has now decreased, has also put a strain on resources.

India's population rose from 361 million in 1951 to 1,027 million in 2001. India is now experiencing a demographic transition, but many impoverished families still want to have several children because of cultural beliefs and high IMR. Furthermore, there is an unmet need for contraception. Government policy toward health and child development can be faulted for many reasons. Policies to promote health have not been sufficiently integrated with other policies for economic and social development, including access to school education; the provision of safe drinking water, sanitation, and housing; and the empowerment of women.

There have been low levels of public expenditure on health care, limited access to publie services for impoverished families, and lack of partnership with nongovernmental, charitable organisations. The poor quality of healthcare services in the public sector has led to a growing private sector, and it is estimated that 80% of spending goes on private healthcare, with the poor often seeking private healthcare. Against this backdrop, the ICDS has had more success in states in which the primary health care infrastructure is well developed than it has had in other states, which again highlights the need for inter-sectoral, synergized policies for children.

The philosophy behind the ICDS is indeed consistent with current research on early child development and ways in which to facilitate it. Although the ICDS has attained its goal of improving survival and development, the question of why it has not been more successful must be asked. A discussion of the specifics of past policies and their lack of success is beyond the scope of this chapter. However, a weak link between policy and its implementation is probably the main reason for the slow pace of improvement in the well-being of Indian children.

Not enough support has been given to executing strategy. Some examples that are related to the functioning of the AWCs and the coverage of the ICDS will be used to illustrate this contention. First, although central government funding for the programme has markedly increased over the years, low levels of financial resources have been earmarked for the programme, which affects its quality. For example, the AWC is the focal point of basic health care and thus AWWs are overextended and overworked. The government should fund another AWW for each center. The physical condition of the centers is very poor compared to international standards, and there is a lack of resources.

The government would do well to back up its childfriendly policies with additional resources. When resources are limited, the best way to enhance the quality of education is to improve the quality of training of caregivers. It should be pointed out that attempts are being made to remedy some of the problems that are associated with the poor level of training of AWWs. Another example relates to the coverage of the ICDS. The government planned to universalize the ICDS by 1996 to reach all of the 5,652 blocks in the country.

This has still not happened, and in March 2003 only 4,608 of the 5,652 sanctioned projects had been operationalized. However, by September 2003, this figure had increased to 5,068. Policy goals with regard to expansion of the ICDS have been elusive, and reflect the bureaucratic attitude of devising policies without considering their practical implementation. Policies have not been accompanied by a workable execution strategy, nor have the necessary resources been allocated to achieve universalisation. The coverage of the ICDS has improved, yet only 60% to 70% of eligible beneficiaries are enrolled in their local AWC, and only about 60% of 3 to 6 year olds receive pre-school education.

The poor learning environment in the AWCs, the drab curriculum, and lackluster teaching do not encourage the pre-school child to stay in the center children are often simply taken away after they receive the nutrition supplement. There is a shortage of financial and curricular resources for pre-school education. Efforts to provide high-quality, non-formal early childhood services should be continued. At the same time, attempts to develop alternative, low-cost but effective programmes should be made. Funding from charitable organisations and international agencies can be sought to provide the basic infrastructure to start programmes, which can then be maintained through community support.

Early Childhood Care for Survival Growth and Development (ECC-SGD) is an integrated holistic approach within a rights perspective, to ensure proper childcare leading to the survival, growth, full development and protection of the young child through child centered, family focused and community based interventions /.../ Most of these concepts are incorporated into the ICDS, which have definitely shown its impact especially in the rural scenario. However, the ICDS story is a mixture of successes and embarrassments.

Malnutrition, infant mortality, and birth rates have declined, which has resulted in the enhanced physical well-being of children. With healthier children, more time can be devoted to education, and less time spent feeding children and looking after their health needs. However the pre-school education component of the ICDS is weak and can be much improved.

It appears that an inter sectoral and integrated approach to early childhood services, community participation, and women's empowerment are crucial to the success of child development programmes for children from socially disadvantaged backgrounds, and the ICDS has a significant role in improving children's rights to survival and development, but not their rights to a high-quality early education.

The rapid rate of development in all areas in the early childhood years, research evidence (based on formation of synaptic connections in the brain) regarding occurrence of critical periods related to various domains of development during the early years, and the consequent lasting, and at times irreversible, impact of both favourable and unfavourable experiences have contributed to the understanding that the early childhood years (the first 6-8 years of a person's life) are the most critical for lifelong development.

Four major rights based international declarations/ conventions in the last two decades the LW Convention of Rights of the Child (UNCRC) 1989, the World Conference on Education for All 1990, the World Education Forum 2000, UN Millennium Declaration and Millennium Development Goals - have further contributed to the realisation of the need to invest in Early Childhood Development (ECD), not only for economic reasons but because a stimulating and enriching physical and psychosocial environment is the right of every child. Five of the eight MDGs relate to health, nutrition and education of the young child - thus, ECD is a pre-requisite step towards achieving MDG.

Research around the world has shown that policy planning and programming for ECD has the maximum impact when it is informed by three central tenets of child development. These are: child development is a continuous and cumulative process; the child's health, nutrition and psychosocial development are synergistically interrelated, and; the child's development takes place within a context and is influenced by it.

The implication is that programmes need to address the entire childhood continuum, instead of intervening in any one stage exclusively; all the needs of the child need to be addressed at the same time by adopting a holistic approach to programming; and programmes need to address the child's total context, including poverty reduction and elimination of gender disparity. The rationale for providing early childhood interventions in a developing nation like India stems as much from the fact that poverty, and accompanying deprivation, places a large number of children in the subcontinent 'at risk' as from the changes in the family structure from joint to nuclear, increase in maternal employment outside the home and the demand for quality education from all sectors of the population.

Good quality early childhood interventions enhance preparedness of children, both academically and socially, for formal schooling and result in long term benefits in terms of improving the life chances. Indian children, numbering around 440 million of whom, 158 million are below six years of age, constituting 42 per cent of the country's total population, are not a homogeneous group. Gender, socio-cultural and economic conditions bring diversity in their childhood experiences that impact their development.

More than two-thirds of the country's children are raised in poverty, living in conditions lacking in basic amenities with little or no access to services related to their survival, growth and development. The tenth largest fast-growing global economies, with GDP projected at 9%, India's rank on the Human Development Index, which includes indicators of child mortality, education and child labour, however, has fallen from 124 to 127, which reflects that social development is not an automatic consequence of economic development.

"If all child rights measures were to become a critical measure for HDI, India would fare even worse..." acknowledges The Report of Working Group on Development of Children.

India's progress in the last two decades in promoting child survival, development and education, has been slower as compared to other developing countries, particularly on the Millennium Development Goals. Given the current pace, it is unlikely that the MDG targets - reducing under-5 mortality rate by two-thirds, encouraging universal primary education and eliminating gender disparity in education - would be achieved by 2015.

Various terminologies are used globally to refer to early childhood interventions, and each embodies different perspectives to child development programming depending upon the age group addressed by a particular Programme as well as its thrust. It would be appropriate to deconstruct the scope of each of these perspectives before we proceed further, as each is reflected in child development programming in the Indian context. Early Childhood Care and Education (ECCE) refers to inputs of care and psychosocial stimulation for children between birth to six years of age by providing for their health, nutrition and education needs through a variety of settings such as crèches, home-based parent education programmes and pre-schools.

Early Childhood Education (ECE) programmes focus primarily on one aspect of early childhood interventions - that of providing pre-school education to 3-6 year olds - and operate under various nomenclatures such as preparatory schools, nursery schools and kindergartens. Early Childhood Development and Early Childhood Care and Development adopts a still more holistic and integrated concept to early childhood programmes, as compared to ECCE, by acknowledging the interdependent and synergistic inter-relationship between health, nutrition and psychosocial development and addresses the all round development of the child.

ECCD or ECD programmes take a life cycle approach and reach out to adolescent girls, pregnant and lactating mothers apart from children. In India, child development and education are concurrent subjects which imply shared federal and state responsibility in ECD service delivery. Presently, in India, the government, the private sector and the non-governmental organisations are involved in ECD service delivery, and each sector emphasizes a particular perspective to early childhood interventions.

The public sponsored (government) Integrated Child Development Services (ICDS) and other programmes, largely catering to disadvantaged communities, are the more holistic Programmees of ECD adopting the life cycle approach, and addressing the all round development of the children through meeting their health, nutrition and education needs as well as reaching out to pregnant and lactating mothers and adolescent girls.

The voluntary and non-governmental organisations, largely working in socially and economically backward areas, fulfill a vital need by providing ECCE to communities in difficult circumstances such as tribals, migrant labourers and rural children in specific contexts. The private service providers are fee-charging/profit making initiatives aimed at children of socio-economically better-off families. These, known as nurseries, kindergartens, preparatory schools and pre-primary schools, mosdy provide ECE/pre-school education programmes for 3-5 year olds, to the exclusion of the health and nutrition component.

It is against this backdrop that the present chapter traces the evolution of child development policy and programming in India. Starting with a brief historical perspective, it comments on pertinent constitutional provisions, describes changing perspectives in the five year plans and, after a critical situational analysis of children and programming for children, suggests paradigm changes for future policy planning and programming for effective early childhood interventions. Methodologically, the chapter is based on documentary analysis and literature review.

In ancient India, formal education of the young child began around the age of six or seven years. Until then, multiple caretakers within the extended family provided nurturing care and stimulation that promoted all round development during formative years. Much before the contemporary scientific knowledge of child development was promulgated; the traditional Indian texts chronicled the process of early development, from conception onwards through various stages of the lifecycle.

Embedded in the spiritual context, the scriptures are replete with teachings for parents and family members to guide the process of child rearing, socialisation and learning. The extra-familial institutional history of ECE in India dates back only to the 1890s, when the first kindergarten was started by a Scottish missionary. This was followed by opening of pre-school centers in different parts of the country in the early 1920s and 1930s to cater to children, either of the elite who could pay or of the poor as a philanthropic gesture.

The early pioneers associated with these initiatives were Gijubhai Badhekar, Tarabari Modak and Annie Besant who were inspired and influenced by the work of Montessori. Subsequendy, Indian thinkers such as Mahatma Gandhi, Rabindrarnath Tagore and Zakir Hussain endorsed the importance of formative years and evolved an indigenous philosophy of ECE. By the time of independence, ECE was perceived as a first step in the educational ladder and was primarily imparted in centres owned by private and voluntary organisations. Independence ushered in a new era of child development in the country when the state took up the responsibility for providing for the nation's children.

CONSTITUTIONAL PROVISIONS

The Indian Constitution, framed in 1950, enshrined the vision of the country's leaders for the welfare, protection and development of the nation's children. There are several provisions in the Constitution either as Fundamental Rights or Directive Principles of State Policy that have been used for promoting ECD in the country. The former are justiciable whereas the latter are directives. The Fundamental Right, Article 15(3), empowers the state to practice positive discrimination favouring economically and educationally weaker groups.

Within the Directive Principles of State Policy, there are specific Articles that provide a supportive framework for Early Childhood Development. The relevant Articles are: 24, 39(e) and (f), 42, 45 and 47 which deal with prohibition of deployment of children below 14 years of age in hazardous occupations, protection against exploitation as well as moral and material abandonment; provision of maternity relief; provision of free and compulsory education for children under 14 years; raising the level of nutrition and health, respectively.

It is pertinent here to note as a negative development the Constitution Amendment (Eighty-sixth) Act, 2002 passed by the Parliament which has amended Article 45, splitting the age group 0-14 years into two clear age groups - 0-6 and 614 - covering their educational needs and interests under two separate Articles of the Constitution. Article 21 A, introduced after Article 21, makes the provision of free and compulsory education to children ranging in age from six to fourteen years their Fundamental Right.

Whereas articulating the intent to cater to the needs of children in the age group 0-6 years but leaving it as a directive, the 86th Amendment Act has altered Article 45 (Directive Principle of State Policy) to read: "The state shall endeavour to provide early childhood care and education for all children until they complete the age of six years". ECD professionals, advocates and practitioners have viewed this amendment with distress and concern as it not only de-recognizes the importance of formative years but negates the rights of the young child as well and releases the Government from the obligation to provide ECD services for children below the age of six years.

In order to make the Constitutional provisions obligatory, supportive laws and legislations have been enacted to protect the rights of children. The first set of these laws and legislations pertain to children's right to life and health as well as access to equal opportunities. Some of these provisions, pertinent for children under six, are aimed at prevention of female foeticide, promotion of breast feeding and ensuring growth and development of children with disabilities, respectively.

The second set of laws and legislations relate to providing child care services in specific work situations, where women with infants and young children are employed. Day-care facility in the form of crèches is mandated as a statutory provision under different Labour Acts, subject to fulfillment of certain conditions. Though there are wide gaps in de jure provisions and the defacto realities, yet these laws and legislations have helped to bring forth perceptible change in the status of children.

THE YOUNG CHILD IN THE FIVE YEAR PLANS

Child development and provision for extra-familial care of the young child has been a focus area within the national planning process of independent India, right from the start. However, over the years, the approach towards the planning strategies related to ECD has evolved from welfare to development to rights. The initial four Five Year Plans (1A) focused on multiple, but linear and sectoral, interventions through the sectors of health, education and nutrition to meet the needs of children, especially the deprived and the underprivileged.

The orientation to programming was welfare in nature, wherein children and women were regarded as beneficiaries as the patron state discharged its duty by providing basic minimum services to children. The Fourth Five Year Plan culminated in the adoption of the National Policy for Children in 1974, which defined the role and responsibilities of the State in the nurture and solicitude of the nation's children. The Fifth Plan was a watershed in development programming for children, ushering in the shift in perspective from welfare to development for designing child development interventions, emphasizing integration of and coordination between various services and progammes, which were till now being provided sectorally.

Programming was not seen merely as a welfare activity of the state but a developmental imperative because investment in human capital was seen as a prerequisite for the nation's economic and social development. This approach of the fifth Five Year Plan was translated into a centrally sponsored Integrated Child Development Services (ICDS) Programme launched in 1975 in 33 Blocks in the country.

The Indian government's flagship programme, currendy it is the largest Programme of its kind in the world being implemented through a network of 8.63 lakh 6 village level anganwadi centres set-up across 5,885 development Blocks, covering 60.6 million children from birth to six years of age. Recognizing the synergistic inter-relationship of health, nutrition and education, the Programme incorporates a package of multi-sectoral interventions of health, nutrition and education to ensure the holistic development of the child through a life cycle approach. The Programme also aims to forge linkages with other related services such as safe drinking water, environmental sanitation and schemes/projects for women's empowerment.

The Sixth and Seventh Five Year Plans promoted consolidation and expansion of the programmes started earlier, extending their outreach. A major development towards the end of the sixth plan was the unambiguous articulation, for the first time, of Early Childhood Care and Education (ECCE) as a critical input in the child's development in the National Policy on Education, which devoted an exclusive chapter to it. The Eighth Plan, focusing on human development, not only reiterated its commitment to ensure development of the "every child".

By the Ninth and the Tenth Five Year Plans the development imperative gave way to the rights approach - programming for children was not merely seen as an investment in human resource which would contribute to the country's social and economic fabric but as a means to fulfill the undeniable rights of each child and to enable all to realize their potential. The rights based international declarations/conventions mentioned earlier, ratified and endorsed by India, made policy and programming for ECD an imperative.

During the Ninth and Tenth plan period, some important initiatives which enabled strengthening of policy framework, and led to evolving of innovative interventions, setting up of regulatory mechanisms and monitoring outcomes of interventions included: enactment of the National Health Polity, 2002; adoption of the National Charter for Children, 2003; announcement of the National Common Minimum Programme, 2004; formulation of the National Plan of Action for Children, 2005 and setting up of the Commission for the Protection of Child Rights Act, 2005. Monitorable time-bound targets were set, in the sectors of health, education and nutrition, to assess progress in key indicators of child development, disaggregated by sex, with the aim of bridging gender gaps and improving accountability in service delivery.

MID-TERM REVIEW OF THE TENTH PLAN

The mid-term appraisal of the tenth plan (Planning Commision, 2005) indicated major gaps and inconsistencies in achievement of targets and implementation of activities with respect to survival and development of children - synergy across sectors and services, though articulated in principle and planned for, still remained elusive to achieve. Some landmark decisions which were taken to improve the outcomes in the remaining period of the 10th plan included: universalisation of the ICDS for ensuring coverage of all children by 2012; bringing quality improvements in ICDS services; improving convergence and coordination with allied departments; exponential expansion of day care and crèche facilities in view of inadequate support structures for the care of the youngest children (children under three).

The preceding section highlights the enabling policy framework that India has created for its young children in the last six decades. With ratification of 19 international rights based conventions, efforts are on to integrate their provisions into relevant laws, rules, policies and schemes. There are eight national policies and several acts that aim to safeguard the rights of children. However, while India's policy frameworks have mirrored global paradigm shifts in approaches to planning for children, there are wide gaps in the implementation of the same which is reflected in the poor health, nutrition and education indicators vis-à-vis the young child.

Approximately 2.6 million children under 5 years the in India every year accounting for one in five child deaths in the world, with girls being 50% more likely to die. Around 1.7 million infants the before their first birthday and of these, 1.2 million the before the completion of the first four weeks of life. Neonatal mortality presendy constitutes nearly two-thirds of infant mortality and around half of under-5 child mortality. There has been a significant decline in Infant Mortality Rate (IMR) from 146 per 1000 live births in 1951 to 60 per live births in 2003. However, the decline over the last two decades has been slow - from 79 in 1992-93 to 68 in 1998-99 to 57 in 2005-06.

Gender discrimination is a socio-cultural reality in many parts of India evident in the declining female/male ratio in the age group 0-6 years - from 945/1000 in 1991 to 927/1000 in 2001 and in gender differentials across almost all indicators related to health, nutrition and education. Economically progressive states have recorded the sharpest decline in sex ratio, proving once again that economic development is not always commensurate with progress in social equity.

MORBIDITY INDICATORS

The wide prevalence and resilient persistence of mass under-nutrition in India reflects that oudays for the nutrition sector have not brought about commensurate improvement in quality and coverage of under- trition programmes and nutritional status. One-third of the babies in India are born with low birth weight making India home to nearly 40% of all low birth weight babies in the developing world. Nutritional status of children below three years of age across last two NFHS surveys has shown only marginal improvements.

The reductions were: 'underweight' from 47 to 46 and 'stunted' from 46 to 38, while 'wasted' showed a marginal increase from 16 to 19. Despite India being a traditional society where breast feeding has been the norm, only 46% mothers have been found to practice exclusive breast feeding up to five months. Further, only half the infants in the age 6-9 months receive any complementary foods. The prevalence of malnutrition at 46% co-existing with a rapidly growing economy shows that improvements in survival, development and nutrition indicators of the young child are not a natural fall-out of economic growth.

The high prevalence of micronutrient deficiencies of key vitamins and minerals, such as vitamin A, iron, iodine and zinc in pregnant women and children lead to long term morbidity. It is evident that reductions in mortality and morbidity indicators in India can only be achieved through concerted and inter-linked planning and implementation of nutrition and health programmes.

These programmes need to aim at controlling neonatal mortality by eliminating neonatal tetanus, improving access to obstetric services, providing skilled birth attendants in the community, controlling neonatal and childhood illnesses and above all, preventing malnutrition by promoting appropriate feeding practices such as prompt initiation of breast feeding and timely introduction of appropriate complementary foods.

CHILD PROTECTION

Child protection has not received adequate attention in Indian policy and programming. The changeover to free market economy in India has increased the disparities between the rich and the poor, led to depletion of natural resources, loss of traditional livelihoods, forced migration, consumerism and violence. Changing economic and social structures have led to breakdown of traditional coping mechanisms, community structures and family care systems which provided protection and care to the child.

In the absence of adequate provision of essential child protection services by the state, this has left a large number of children exposed to rights abuse, especially those who are already at risk and disadvantage. In order to redress this long standing gap in policy planning and implementation, the Report of Working Group on Development of Children has explicitly articulated "child protection as an essential component of the country's strategy to place the development of the child at the centre of the eleventh plan."

Consequently, the Integrated Child Protection Scheme (ICPS) has been proposed as a single window government intervention to address issues of child protection and build a secure environment for children through government-civil society partnership. Further, the Juvenile Justice Act, 2000 aims to consolidate the laws relating to juvenile in conflict with law as well as children in need of care and protection, and ensure child friendly approaches in the adjudication and disposition of matters, in the best interest of children and their rehabilitation ultimately.

ACCESS TO ECD PROGRAMMES AND THEIR COVERAGE

In the absence of a comprehensive survey, accurate figures regarding coverage of children below six years of age across the government, NGO and private sector initiatives are lacking.

With respect to ECCE initiatives by the government, the coverage under the various programmes is as follows:

- ICDS: total of about 41 million children - about 18 million below 3 years and about 23 million in the 3-6 age group;
- The Rajiv Gandhi National Crèches Scheme for the Children of Working mothers: .55 million; and
- The pre-primary school. 02 million in the age group 0-5 years. The NGO services for ECCE are estimated to cover anywhere between 3-20 million and the private initiatives for 3-6 year olds cover another 10 million approximately.

Considering only the government sector and the private initiatives (since the variation in the NGO sector figures is too large), we find that of the 60 million children in the 3-6 age group, only 34 million are covered by any kind of pre-school input.

Taking the entire 0-6 years period into account, only 21% are covered by any kind of ECCE service. Not only is this coverage inadequate, the services do not reach small and marginalized groups. The under-threes are neglected in terms of programmes and initiatives in both the public and the private sector, the reason for which in a large part stems from the deeply entrenched patriarchal values and gender bias which fail to recognize the needs of working women that cut across contexts and, in the process, compromises the education of the girl child.

CURRICULUM AND PEDAGOGY OF ECO

In India, various committees have been constituted to outline the methods, pedagogy and curriculum for education, the latest effort being the development of the National Curriculum Framework, 2005 by NCERT (2005). Each of these committees, commissions and documents envisage ECCE to promote all round development of the child through holistic, developmentally appropriate curriculum, based on the active construction of knowledge by the child.

The curriculum is envisaged in three sub-stages - early stimulation for under-threes largely through parental involvement and education in a relatively unstructured mode, the organized centre-based play and development-oriented curriculum for the 3 to 5-year-olds and the school readiness curriculum which overlaps for the 4 to 6-yearolds and includes reading and writing readiness and number readiness, as a preparation for primary schooling.

Additionally, emphasizing continuity of approach and methodology, the pedagogy and curriculum transaction in grades 1 and 2 is expected to be play-way, activity based and experiential. However, this vision regarding the nature of ECD has not translated into reality. Broadly speaking, the services for pre-school children vary immensely in terms of quality in the absence of norms specifying quality indicators, any mechanism of regulation and accreditation of ECCE centres and a nodal body to co-ordinate this.

Generally speaking, the quality of services in the public sector is low. Impact evaluations of the ICDS are inconsistent. On the positive front, the ICDS inputs have resulted in intended child development outcomes such as improved nutritional and health status, reduced mortality and morbidity and enhanced learning capacity, increased enrolment and better performance in the primary school. However, studies have also brought out many weak aspects and mismatches. With respect to the pre-school education component, most studies reveal that the pre-school education component of ICDS does not receive due attention.

Among the six services which are delivered through one functionary for all children up to six years, pre-school education is the one that is most 'time and effort' intensive, if done well. It is, therefore, most often compromised. The private sector is replete with undesirable and damaging educational practices - pre-school education is transacted largely as a downward extension of primary education curriculum with teachers, often with no ECCE training, giving little thought to ECCE as a specific sub-stage of education with its unique pedagogical methods and curriculum. Developmentally inappropriate curriculum is implemented in a rigid, regimented and mechanical manner. While there are excellent models of NGO programmes in ECCE, these have limited geographical coverage with no support/provision for scaling.

CHILD DEVELOPMENT INDEX-WINDOW TO CHILD'S WELLBEING

The Child Development Index computed as a part of a recent study by the World Bank using some important indicators related to survival and development outcomes, helps to assess the situation of the young child in different states of India. The analysis shows that the states fall along a continuum, with those that perform poorly on one indicator performing poorly on most related indicators as well, which highlights the synergistic interrelation between health, nutrition and education in the early years, leading to cumulative disadvantage.

The CDI in states from the north, east and the north-east is lower as compared to others. The implication is for equity by making interventions which are area-specific, groupspecific, culture-specific, setting-specific and age-specific, within the overarching framework of equality.

CHILD BUDGETING - AN INDICATOR OF POLITICAL WILL

The allocation of funds in the country's budget for programmes related to children can be a good indicator of the political will to implement the enabling policy framework. Child Budget analysis has recendy been initiated by the MoWCD and aims to uncover the percentage share of allocation on children in the Union Budget. While there has been an increase in the percentage share of total child budget in the union budget from 2004-05 to 2006-07 (from 2.445% to 4.907 %), yet India, over the years, has not laid adequate emphasis on investments in the social development sector, especially with respect to children.

Within the overall budget of 2006-07, an analysis in terms of sectoral allocation reveals that 'child education' received the maximum funds (3.487%), followed by 'child development' (.830%), then 'child health' (.556%) and then 'child protection' (.034%).

Within the education sector, in most states' and central budgets, the priority was on primary education which consumed more than 50% of the child budget. The actual spending on children below 6 years of age is almost one-eight of that on children in the 6-14 age group, across all states, which shows that the planning process has failed to realize that with 85 % of the brain growth taking place in the early childhood years, investment in ECD is most cost effective than investment at any other stage of life.

TRAINING AND CAPACITY BUILDING

The training and working conditions of the ECD staff are two of the most neglected features of the ECD scenario in the country, which impacts their job performance and motivation. ECD staffs are not recognized as teachers, are poorly paid and have no opportunity for career mobility. In the absence of any regulatory framework governing setting up of ECCE centers, there is no demand for trained staff, unless the leadership of the centre itself is committed to issues of quality.

The existing training programmes in ECD vary widely in terms of their content, methodology, the link between theory and practice, duration and eligibility conditions, corresponding to the range of ECCE programmes in India. Essentially there are two kinds of training provisions - in-service/on-the-job training customized as per the needs of the Programme in the NGO and government sector; and, pre-service training provided by government/private institutions through the face-to-face and the distance mode.

Correspondingly, at one end is the customized 26 day training Programme for the functionaries of the ICDS wherein four days are devoted to training regarding the pre-school education component and qualifications are no bar. This training curriculum does not provide workers with adequate input with ECE, making it difficult for the AWWs to relate theory to practice (i. e., activities to development) or to innovate in the Programme. Many private institutions run their own training courses and while some are good, most of these courses are run for profit making, with no adherence to standard curricula or duration of training.

While the voluntary sector runs qualitatively rich training programmes which are project based, these often do not sustain due to practical considerations. At the other end of the spectrum are the university and government recognized courses. A well established course is the government recognized two year Integrated Pre-primary and Primary Teacher Training Programme offered after completion of class 12, which aims to prepare the teachers for teaching in the pre-school and the first two grades of the primary school.

The open and distance learning mode offers one year training programmes through the national and state level open universities. The curriculum at the senior secondary stage of education (+2) in both the face-to-face and the open and distance learning mode has included early childhood education as an area of vocational education. These are high quality training programmes provided in standard settings, with fixed curricula and duration and standards.

However, the question here is of the limited numbers that can be trained through the face-to-face mode as well as the limited perspective to training programmes in ECE that has been adopted by the National Council of Teacher Education (NCTE), which is a statutory body concerned with maintaining standards in teacher education. NCTE has evolved norms for accreditation of institutions offering Pre primary and Nursery Teacher Training Courses.

Currently, there are 124 NCTE recognized pre-primary and nursery teachers training institutions with an intake capacity of 5938 students in the country, obviously not sufficient to meet the demand for trained teachers. These institutions are functioning in fifteen States leaving twenty States/UTs, which do not have a single recognized Pre School/Nursery Teacher Education Institution. As regards training programmes in ECE, the National Council of Teacher Education has laid down norms for a single teacher education Programme in ECE thus leaving no room to accredit good practices which may function on models other than the singular one laid down by it.

Besides, this single Programme is called 'Certificate in Education', though it has the same training duration, rigour and eligibility criterion as the 'Diploma in Education', defined by the NCTE, which trains teachers for classes 1 to 5. Necessarily, the nomenclature implies an hierarchy which is uncalled for and will perpetuate the problems that the ECCE sector is facing presendy - that of it being the last choice of aspirants who want to join teaching as a profession and reinforcing the low status accorded to ECCE workers in professional hierarchy.

The Certificate in Education also quite clearly curtails the scope of ECD to 6 years of age instead of 8 years which ECD professionals favour. With the grades I and II unambiguously clustered with the higher elementary grades III, IV and V as per NCTE's nomenclature, it is debatable how much of the ECCE philosophy would permeate teaching-learning at the lower primary grades.

PLANNING FOR CHILD DEVELOPMENT

The far from satisfactory status of the Indian child and child development programming shows that a set of policy frameworks and additional resources, by themselves, are not enough. By 2016, about 25 million infants would be in need of immunisation services and their mothers will require maternal health services. Similarly, pre-school education services will need to be provided for 72 million children. What is the way forward in this situation?

The country's planning process needs to incorporate a paradigm shift in child development strategies, involving re-engineering of the whole range of social sector programmes through a review of their concept, approach, content and quality of services. The corner stone of the paradigm shift is the understanding that child survival, development and protection are linked with macro and micro development issues and cannot be conceptualized as a set of activities or measures contained in policy and programmes specifically targeting the child.

These concerns must be addressed within the larger contexts of poverty, deprivation and disparity. Children and their milieu have to be addressed together for programmes to result in tangible outcomes. This involves reexamining the processes of development planning and implementation at many levels, involving paradigm shifts, as discussed further. First, the country's planning processes and systems need to be re-oriented to focus on 'Children' as a category such that while policies and plans are being formulated, the impact of these on children's development, and their context, is kept in mind.

Therefore, ministries and departments across the board need to review their own policies, programmes, services, laws, budget and procedures to examine how they can incorporate and integrate better development, participation and protection of the child. There needs to be a shift from focus on inputs designed to meet the needs of children as per sub-stages in a fragmented and discrete manner to focus on outcomes by planning interventions comprehensively keeping the whole child, hisor her context and the life cycle in perspective.

Second, ECCE needs to be valued unequivocally and, along with its recognition as a vital developmental need of the child and it needs to be recognized as part of mainstream education in India. Many of the problems which beset the sector today originate from its ambivalent status in nation's plans - while various national documents recognize ECD as the foundation for all other initiatives, political actions do not match the stated intent. The third paradigm shift has to be in terms of providing and assuring quality education for all.

The few good quality ECD programmes are high in cost and the deeply entrenched social divides prevent a large segment of the population from accessing these. While we need diverse models to cater to different contextual realities and multiple needs, each of these models must conform to a common quality framework. Fourth, ensuring quality ECCE for all requires norms and standards at a national level to be created with respect to five major quality dimensions of ECCE - curriculum, staff/teachers, teacher-child ratio, infrastructure and supervisory mechanism.

Along with this, regulatory framework and mechanisms need to be put into place and adherence to them ensured through various strategies. Fifth, given the wide inter-state variations in priorities and outcomes for children's development, the planning, implementation and monitoring processes need to be de-centralized to allow for local specificity and prioritisation.

The shift needs to be from supply driven approach to demand driven need assessment and bottom-up approach, from normative service delivery mechanisms with rigid financial provisions to flexible need based management procedures of governance and performance-based accounting system. This calls for organisational reforms in service delivery leading to involvement of Panchayati Raj Institutions, along with building their capacities for taking on these responsibilities effectively by vesting them with adequate powers and resources.

Sixth, multiple models of training need to be created and recognized in order to train personnel working in various programmes under diverse contexts, including mobile training, formal university degree courses and Programme specific training courses. Seventh, intentional, strategic, flexible and organized advocacy at all levels using different approaches is an essential step to creating a value for ECCE, understanding its nature and purpose as well as generating demand for quality. So far, advocacy has largely been carried out as isolated attempts by the NGO sector and has had a limited impact.

The government needs to take a lead preparing requisite materials and leading campaigns, and, if need be, create a dedicated advocacy unit at the central level. Eighth, research on early childhood education takes place in the country but it does not feed into policies and programmes. The link between research and action needs to be made more vibrant.

Lastly, and most importantly, there has to be commensurate enhancement in allocation of resources by the government. Along with this, there needs to be a shift from federal financing as the sole source of child interventions to public-private partnership leading to sharing of responsibility in providing services for children.

Just prior to the initiation of the Eleventh plan period, the Department of Women and Child Development was elevated to the status of the Ministry of Women and Child Development in February, 2006. The Ministry now has the enhanced mandate of dealing not only with policy relating to children but also a comprehensive range of programmes relating to child survival, development, protection, education and participation. The vertical and lateral links among these have to be recognized to ensure holistic approach to child's rights. The Ministry would also need to play the coordinating role with all other sectors.

The Working Group on Development on Children for the Eleventh Five Year Plan has recommended that the guiding principles of National Plan of Action for Children, 2005, which has adopted the child rights perspective to address children's issues and emphasize holistic programming, should form the guiding principles for the Eleventh plan. The Eleventh Plan states clearly that 'children and their development are central to the Eleventh Plan' and enjoins the Planning Commission to lay the foundation for adequate resource allocation to ensure children's wellbeing.

It identifies the Constitution of India and the UNCRC as the guiding framework for realizing all rights of all and approaching and addressing the child as a whole person. To conclude, over the years there has been a growing recognition in India about the need for providing interventions for the young child. Granting children the right to live with dignity and having access to opportunities for their holistic development may seem a dream today, but appropriate actions backed up by supportive political will can make this achievable in the foreseeable future.

7

The Globalisation of Poverty

The late 20th century will go down in world history as a period of global impoverishment marked by the collapse of productive systems in the developing world, the demise of national institutions and the disintegration of health and education programmes. This "globalisation of poverty"- which has largely reversed the achievements of post-war decolonisation-was initiated in the Third World coinciding with the onslaught of the debt crisis. Since the 1990s, it has extended its grip to all major regions of the world including North America, Western Europe, the countries of the former Soviet block and the Newly Industrialized Countries (NICs) of South East Asia and the Far East.

In the 1990s, famines at the local level have erupted in sub-Saharan Africa, South Asia and parts of Latin America; health clinics and schools have been closed down; hundreds of millions of children have been denied the right to primary education. In the Third World, Eastern Europe and the Balkans, there has been a resurgence of infectious diseases including tuberculosis, malaria and cholera.

FAMINE FORMATION IN THE THIRD WORLD

From the dry savannah of the Sahelian belt, famine has extended its grip into the wet tropical heartland. A large part of the population of the African continent has been affected: 18 million people in Southern Africa (including 2 million refugees) are in "famine zones" and another 130 million in 10 countries are seriously at risk. In the Horn of Africa, 23 million people (many of whom have already died) are "in danger of famine" according to a United Nations estimate. In the post-independence period extending through the 1980s, starvation deaths in South Asia had largely been limited to peripheral tribal areas.

But in India today, there are indications of widespread impoverishment among both the rural and urban populations following the adoption of the 1991 New Economic Policy under the stewardship of the Bretton Woods institutions. More than 70 per cent of rural households in India are small marginal farmers or landless farm workers, representing a population of over 400 million people. In irrigated areas, agricultural workers are employed for 200 days a year and in rain-fed farming for approximately 100 days. The phasing out of fertilizer subsidies-an explicit condition of the International Monetary Fund (IMF) agreement-and the increase in the prices of farm inputs and fuel is pushing a large number of small- and medium-sized farmers into bankruptcy.

A micro-level study conducted in 1991 on starvation deaths among handloom weavers in a relatively prosperous rural community in Andhra Pradesh sheds light on how local communities have been impoverished as a result of macroeconomic reform. The starvation deaths occurred in the months following the implementation of the New Economic Policy: with the devaluation and the lifting of controls on cotton yarn exports, the jump in the domestic price of cotton yarn led to a collapse in the pacham (24 meters) rate paid to the weaver by the middleman (through the putting-out system).

"Radhakrishnamurthy and his wife were able to weave between three and four pachams a month, bringing home the meagre income of 300 to 400 rupees (US$12 to 16) for a family of six; then came the Union Budget of 24 July 1991, the price of cotton yarn jumped and the burden was passed on to the weaver. Radhakrishnamurthy's family income declined to Rs. 240-320 a month (US$9.60 to 13.00)." Radhakrishnamurthy of Gollapalli village in Guntur district died of starvation on 4 September 1991. Between 30 August and 10 November 1991, at least 73 starvation deaths were reported in only two districts of Andhra Pradesh. There are 3.5 million handlooms throughout India supporting a population of some 17 million people.

ECONOMIC "SHOCK THERAPY" IN THE FORMER SOVIET UNION

When assessing the impact on earnings, employment and social services, the post-Cold War economic collapse in parts of Eastern Europe appears to be far deeper and more destructive than that of the Great Depression. In the former Soviet Union (starting in early 1992), hyperinflation triggered by the downfall of the ruble contributed to rapidly eroding real earnings. Economic "shock therapy" combined with the privatisation programme precipitated entire industries into immediate liquidation, leading to lay-offs of millions of workers.

In the Russian Federation, prices increased one hundred times following the initial round of macroeconomic reforms adopted by the Yeltsin government in January 1992. Wages, on the other hand, increased tenfold. The evidence suggests that real purchasing power plummeted by more than 80 per cent in the course of 1992. The reforms have dismantled both the military-industrial complex and the civilian economy. Economic decline has surpassed the plunge in production experienced in the Soviet Union at the height of the Second World War, following the German occupation of Byelorussia and parts of the Ukraine in 1941 and the extensive bombing of Soviet industrial infrastructure.

The Soviet gross domestic product (GDP) had by 1942 declined by 22 per cent in relation to pre-war levels. In contrast, industrial output in the former Soviet Union plummeted by 48.8 per cent and GDP by 44.0 per cent between 1989 and 1995, according to official data, and output continues to fall. Independent estimates, however, indicate a substantially greater drop and there is firm evidence that official figures have been manipulated.

While the cost of living in Eastern Europe and the Balkans was shooting up to western levels as a result of the deregulation of commodity markets, monthly minimum earnings were as low as ten dollars a month. "In Bulgaria, the World Bank and the Ministry of Labour and Social Assistance separately estimated that 90 per cent of Bulgarians are living below the poverty threshold of U.S. $4 a day." Old age pensions in 1997 were worth two dollars a month, Unable to pay for electricity, water and transportation, population groups throughout the region have been brutally marginalized from the modern era.

POVERTY AND UNEMPLOYMENT IN THE WEST

Already during the Reagan-Thatcher era, but more significantly since the beginning of the 1990s, harsh austerity measures are gradually contributing to the disintegration of the welfare state. The achievements of the early post-war period are being reversed through the derogation of unemployment insurance schemes, the privatisation of pension funds and social services and the decline of social security. With the breakdown of the welfare state, high levels of youth unemployment are increasingly the source of social strife and civil dissent.

In the United States, political figures decry the rise of youth violence, promising tougher sanctions without addressing the roots of the problem. Economic restructuring has transformed urban life, contributing to the "thirdworldisation" of western cities. The environment of major metropolitan areas is marked by social apartheid: urban landscapes have become increasingly compartmentalized along social and ethnic lines. Poverty indicators such as infant mortality, unemployment and homelessness in the ghettos of American (and increasingly European) cities are in many respects comparable to those prevailing in the Third World.

DEMISE OF THE "ASIAN TIGERS"

More recently, speculative movements against national currencies have contributed to the destabilisation of some of the world's more successful "newly industrialized" economies (Indonesia, Thailand, and Korea), leading virtually overnight to abrupt declines in the standard of living. In China, successful poverty alleviation efforts are threatened by the impending privatisation or forced bankruptcy of thousands of state enterprises and the resulting lay-offs of millions of workers. The number of workers to be laid off in state industrial enterprises is estimated to be on the order of 35 million.

In rural areas, there are approximately 130 million surplus workers. This process has occurred alongside massive budget cuts in social programmes, even as unemployment and inequality increase. In the 1997 Asian currency crisis, billions of dollars of official central bank reserves were appropriated by institutional speculators. In other words, these countries are no longer able to "finance economic development" through the use of monetary policy. This depletion of official reserves is part and parcel of the process of economic restructuring leading to bankruptcy and mass unemployment. In other words, privately held capital in the hands of "institutional speculators" far exceeds the limited reserves of Asian central banks. The latter acting individually or collectively is no longer able to fight the tide of speculative activity.

GLOBAL FALSEHOODS

DISTORTING SOCIAL REALITIES

The increasing levels of global poverty resulting from economic restructuring are casually denied by G7 governments and international institutions (including the World Bank and the IMF); social realities are concealed, official statistics are manipulated, economic concepts are turned upside down. In turn, public opinion is bombarded in the media with glowing images of global growth and prosperity. As expressed in one *Financial Times* article, "Happy days are here again ... a wonderful opportunity for sustained and increasingly global economic growth is waiting to be seized."

The world economy is said to be booming under the impetus of "free market" reforms. Without debate or discussion, so-called "sound macroeconomic policies" (meaning the gamut of budgetary austerity, deregulation, downsizing and privatisation) are heralded as the key to economic success. In turn, both the World Bank and the United Nations Development Programme (UNDP) assert that economic growth in the late 20th century has contributed to a remarkable reduction in the levels of world poverty.

DEFINING POVERTY AT "A, DOLLAR A DAY"

The World Bank framework departs sharply from established concepts and procedures for measuring poverty. It arbitrarily sets a "poverty threshold" at one dollar a day, labeling population groups with a per capita income above one dollar a day as "nonpoor." This subjective and biased assessment is carried out irrespective of actual conditions at the country level.

With the liberalisation of commodity markets, the domestic prices of basic food staples in developing countries have risen to world market levels. The one dollar a day standard has no rational basis: population groups in developing countries with per capita incomes of two, three or even five dollars remain poverty stricken (i.e. unable to meet basic expenditures on food, clothing, shelter, health and education).

ARITHMETIC MANIPULATION

Once the one dollar a day poverty threshold has been set, the estimation of national and global poverty levels becomes an arithmetic exercise. Poverty indicators are computed in a mechanical fashion from the initial one dollar a day assumption. The data is then tabulated in glossy tables with forecasts of declining levels of global poverty into the 21st century. These forecasts of poverty are based on an assumed rate of growth of per capita income; growth of the latter implies pari passu a corresponding lowering of the levels of poverty.

For instance, according to the World Bank's calculations, the incidence of poverty in China should decline from 20 per cent in 1985 to 2.9 per cent by the year 2000. Similarly, in the case of India (where according to official data more than 80 per cent of the population (1996) have per capita incomes below one dollar a day), a World Bank "simulation" (which contradicts its own "one dollar a day" methodology) indicates a lowering of poverty levels from 55 per cent in 1985 to 25 per cent in the year 2000.

The entire framework built on the one dollar a day assumption is tautological; it is totally removed from an examination of real life situations. No need to analyze household expenditures on food, shelter and social services; no need to observe concrete conditions in impoverished villages or urban slums. In the World Bank framework, the "estimation" of poverty indicators has become a numerical exercise.

THE UNDP FRAMEWORK

While the UNDP Human Development Group has in previous years provided the international community with a critical assessment of key issues of global development, the 1997 Human Development Report devoted to the eradication of poverty conveys a viewpoint similar to that advanced by the Bretton Woods institutions. According to the UNDP, "the progress in reducing poverty over the 20th century is remarkable and unprecedented.... The key indicators of human development have advanced strongly." The UNDP's "human poverty index" (HPI) is based on "the most basic dimensions of deprivation: a short life span, lack of basic education and lack of access to public and private resources."

Based on the above criteria, the UNDP Human Development Group comes up with estimates of human poverty which are totally inconsistent with country-level realities. The HPI for Colombia, Mexico and Thailand, for instance, is around 10 to 11 per cent. The UNDP measurements point to achievements in poverty reduction in sub-Saharan Africa, the Middle East and India which are totally at odds with national estimates of poverty. The human poverty estimates put forth by the UNDP portray an even more distorted and misleading pattern than those of the World Bank. For instance, only 10.9 per cent of Mexico's population is categorized by the UNDP as "poor."

Yet this estimate contradicts the situation observed in Mexico since the early 1980s: a collapse in social services, the impoverishment of small farmers and a massive decline in real earnings triggered by successive currency devaluations. According to one report:

[R]eal income [in Mexico] fell between 1982 and 1992 [following the adoption of IMF prescriptions]. Infant deaths due to malnutrition tripled. The real minimum wage lost over half its value; and the percentage of the population living in poverty increased from just under one-half to about two-thirds of Mexico's 87 million people. A recent OECD study confirms unequivocally the mounting tide of poverty in Mexico since the signing of the North American Free Trade Agreement (NAFTA).

DOUBLE STANDARDS IN THE "SCIENTIFIC" MEASUREMENT OF POVERTY

Double standards prevail in the measurement of poverty The World Bank's one dollar a day criterion applies only to "developing countries." Both the Bank and the UNDP fail to acknowledge the existence of poverty in Western Europe and

North America. Moreover, the one dollar a day standard contradicts established methodologies used by western governments and intergovernmental organisations to define and measure poverty in "developed countries."

In the West, methods for measuring poverty have been based on minimum levels of household spending required to meet essential expenditures on food, clothing, shelter, health and education. In the United States, for instance, the Social Security Administration (SSA) in the 1960s set a "poverty threshold" which consisted of "the cost of a minimum adequate diet multiplied by three to allow for other expenses." This measurement was based on a broad consensus within the U.S. Government.

The U.S. "poverty threshold" for a family of four (two adults and two children) in 1996 was U.S. $16,036. This figure translates into a per capita income of U.S. $11 a day (compared to the one dollar a day criterion of the World Bank used for developing countries). In 1996, 13.1 per cent of the U.S. population and 19.6 per cent of the population in central cities of metropolitan areas were below the poverty threshold. Neither the UNDP nor the World Bank undertakes comparisons in poverty levels between "developed" and "developing" countries.

Comparisons of this nature would no doubt be the source of "scientific embarrassment," as the poverty indicators presented by both organisations for Third World countries are in some cases of the same order of magnitude as (or even below) the official poverty levels in the United States, Canada and the European Union. In Canada, which occupies the first rank among all nations according to the same 1997 Human Development Report published by the UN, 17.4 per cent of the population is below the national poverty threshold, compared to 10.9 per cent for Mexico and 4.1 per cent for Trinidad and Tobago, according to UNDP's HPI.

Conversely, if the U.S. Bureau of Census methodology (based on the cost of meeting a minimum diet) were applied to the developing countries, the overwhelming majority of the population would be categorized as "poor." While this exercise of using "Western standards" and definitions has not been applied in a systematic fashion, it should be noted that with the deregulation of commodity markets, retail prices of essential consumer goods are not appreciably lower than in the United States or Western Europe. The cost of living in many Third World cities is higher than in the United States.

Moreover, household budget surveys for several Latin American countries suggest that at least 60 per cent of the population in the region does not meet minimum calorie and protein requirements. In Peru, for instance, according to household census data, 83 per cent of the Peruvian population was unable to meet minimum daily calorie and protein requirements following the 1990 IMF sponsored "Fujishock." The prevailing situation in Sub-Saharan Africa and South Asia is more serious, where a majority of the population suffers from chronic undernourishment. Poverty assessments by both organisations take official statistics at face value.

They are largely office-based exercises conducted in Washington and New York with insufficient awareness of local realities. For example, the 1997 UNDP Report points to a decline of one third to one half in child mortality in selected countries of sub-Saharan Africa, despite declines in state expenditures and income levels. What it fails to mention, however, is that the closing down of health clinics and massive lay-offs of health professionals (often replaced by semi-illiterate health volunteers) responsible for compiling mortality data has resulted in a de facto decline in recorded mortality.

VINDICATING THE "FREE" MARKET SYSTEM

These are the realities which are concealed by the World Bank and UNDP poverty studies. The poverty indicators blatantly misrepresent country-level situations as well as the seriousness of global poverty. They serve the purpose of portraying the poor as a minority group representing some 20 per cent of world population (1.3 billion people). Declining levels of poverty including forecasts of future trends are derived with a view to vindicating free market policies and upholding the "Washington Consensus" on macroeconomic reform.

The "free market" system is presented as the most effective means of achieving poverty alleviation, while the negative impact of macroeconomic reform is denied. Both institutions point to the benefits of the technological revolution and the contributions of foreign investment and trade liberalisation, without identifying how these global trends might exacerbate rather than abate poverty.

THE CAUSES OF GLOBAL POVERTY

The global decline in living standards is not the result of a scarcity of productive resources as in preceding historical periods. The globalisation of poverty has indeed occurred during a period of rapid technological and scientific advance. While the latter has contributed to a vast increase in the potential capacity of the economic system to produce necessary goods and services, expanded levels of productivity have not translated into a corresponding reduction in levels of global poverty.

On the contrary, downsizing, corporate restructuring and relocation of production to cheap labour havens in the Third World have been conducive to increased levels of unemployment and significantly lower earnings to urban workers and farmers. This new international economic order feeds on human poverty and cheap labour: high levels of national unemployment in both developed and developing countries have contributed to depressing real wages. Unemployment has been internationalized, with capital migrating from one country to another in a perpetual search for cheaper supplies of labour.

According to the International Labour Organization (ILO), worldwide unemployment affects one billion people, or nearly one third of the global workforce. National labour markets are no longer segregated: workers in different countries are brought into overt competition with one another. Workers' rights are derogated as labour markets are deregulated.

World unemployment operates as a lever which "regulates" labour costs at a world level. Abundant supplies of cheap labour in the Third World (e.g. China with an estimated 200 million surplus workers) and the former Eastern block contribute to depressing wages in developed countries. Virtually all categories of the labour force (including the highly qualified, professional and scientific workers) are affected, even as competition for jobs encourages social divisions based on class, ethnicity, gender and age.

PARADOXES OF GLOBALISATION

Micro-Efficiency, Macro-Insufficiency

The global corporation minimizes labour costs on a world level. Real wages in the Third World and Eastern Europe are as much as seventy times lower than in the United States, Western Europe or Japan: the possibilities of production are immense given the mass of cheap impoverished workers throughout the world. While mainstream economics stresses efficient allocation of society's scarce resources, harsh social realities call into question the consequences of this means of allocation.

Industrial plants are closed down, small and medium-sized enterprises are driven into bankruptcy, professional workers and civil servants are laid off and human and physical capital stand idle in the name of "efficiency." The drive toward an "efficient" use of society's resources at the microeconomic level leads to exactly the opposite situation at the macroeconomic level. Resources are not used "efficiently" when there remain large amounts of unused industrial capacity and millions of unemployed workers. Modern capitalism appears totally incapable of mobilizing these untapped human and material resources.

Accumulation of Wealth, Distortion of Production

This global economic restructuring promotes stagnation in the supply of necessary goods and services while redirecting resources toward lucrative investments in the luxury goods economy. Moreover, with the drying up of capital formation in productive activities, profit is sought in increasingly speculative and fraudulent transactions, which in turn tend to promote disruptions on the world's major financial markets.

In the South, the East and the North, a privileged social minority has accumulated vast amounts of wealth at the expense of the large majority of the population. The number of billionaires in the United States alone increased from 13 in 1982 to 149 in 1996. The "Global Billionaires Club" (with some 450 members) has a total worldwide wealth well in excess of the combined GDP of the group of low income countries with 56 per cent of the world's population. Moreover, the process of wealth accumulation is increasingly taking place outside the real economy; divorced from bona fide productive and commercial activities.

As noted in Forbes Magazine, "Successes on the Wall Street stock market [meaning speculative trade] produced most of last year's [1996] surge in billionaires." In turn, billions of dollars accumulated from speculative transactions are funneled toward confidential numbered accounts in the more than 50 offshore banking havens around the world.

The U.S. investment bank Merrill Lynch conservatively estimates the wealth of private individuals managed through private banking accounts in offshore tax havens at U.S. $3.3 trillion. The IMF puts the offshore assets of corporations and individuals at U.S. $5.5 trillion, a sum equivalent to 25 per cent of total world income. The largely ill-gotten loot of Third World elites in numbered accounts is placed at U.S. $600 billion, with one-third of that held in Switzerland.

Increased Supply, Reduced Demand

The expansion of output in this system takes place by "minimizing employment" and compressing workers' wages. This process in turn backlashes on the levels of consumer demand for necessary goods and services: unlimited capacity to produce, limited capacity to consume. In a global cheap labour economy, the very process of expanding output (through downsizing, layoffs and low wages) contributes to compressing society's capacity to consume.

The tendency is therefore toward overproduction on an unprecedented scale. In other words, expansion in this system can only take place through the concurrent disengagement of idle productive capacity, namely through the bankruptcy and liquidation of "surplus enterprises." The latter are closed down in favour of the most advanced mechanized production. Entire branches of industry stand idle, the economy of entire regions is affected and only a part of the world's agricultural potential is utilized.

This global oversupply of commodities is a direct consequence of the decline in purchasing power and rising levels of poverty Oversupply contributes in turn to the further depression of the earnings of the direct producers through the closure of excess productive capacity. Contrary to Say's Law of Markets, heralded by mainstream economics, supply does not create its own demand. Since the early 1980s, overproduction of commodities leading to plummeting (real) commodity prices has wreaked havoc, particularly among Third World primary producers, but also (more recently) in the area of manufacturing.

Global Integration, Local Disintegration

In developing countries, entire branches of industry producing for the internal market are eliminated while the informal urban sector-which historically has played an important role as a source of employment creation-has been undermined as a result of currency devaluations and the liberalisation of imports. In sub-Saharan Africa, the informal sector garment industry has been wiped out and replaced by the market for used garments, imported from the West at U.S. $80 dollars a ton.

Against a background of economic stagnation (including negative growth rates recorded in Eastern Europe, the former Soviet Union and sub-Saharan Africa), the world's largest corporations have experienced unprecedented growth and expansion of their share of the global market. This process, however, has largely taken place through the displacement of preexisting productive systems, i.e. at the expense of local-level, regional and national producers.

Expansion and profitability for the world's largest corporations is predicated on a global contraction of purchasing power and the impoverishment of large sectors of the world population. Survival of the fittest: the enterprises with the most advanced technologies or those with command over the lowest wages survive in a world economy marked by overproduction. While the spirit of Anglo-Saxon liberalism is committed to "fostering competition," G-7 macroeconomic policy (through tight fiscal and monetary controls) has in practice supported a wave of corporate mergers and acquisitions as well as the bankruptcy of small- and medium-sized enterprises.

In turn, large multinational companies (particularly in the US and Canada) have taken control of local-level markets (particularly in the service economy) through the system of corporate franchising. This process enables large corporate capital ("the franchiser") to gain control over human capital, cheap labour and entrepreneurship. A large share of the earnings of small firms and/or retailers is thereby appropriated, while the bulk of investment outlays is assumed by the independent producer (the "franchisee"). A parallel process can be observed in Western Europe.

With the Maastricht Treaty, the process of political restructuring in the European Union increasingly heeds to dominant financial interests at the expense of the unity of European societies. In this system, state power has deliberately sanctioned the progress of private monopolies: large capital destroys small capital in all its forms. With the drive toward the formation of economic blocks both in Europe and North America, the regional- and local-level entrepreneur is uprooted, city life is transformed, individual small scale ownership is wiped out.

"Free trade" and economic integration provide greater mobility to the global enterprise while at the same time suppressing (through non-tariff and institutional barriers) the movement of small local-level capital. "Economic integration" (under the dominion of the global enterprise), while displaying a semblance of political unity, often promotes factionalism and social strife between and within national societies.

THE ONGOING INTERNATIONALISATION

THE DEBT CRISIS

The restructuring of the global economic system has evolved through several distinct periods since the collapse of the Bretton Woods system of fixed exchange rates in 1971. Patterns of oversupply started to unfold in primary commodity markets in the second part of the 1970s, following the end of the Vietnam War. The debt crisis of the early 1980s was marked by the simultaneous collapse of commodity prices and the rise of real interest rates. The balance of payments of developing countries was in crisis, and the accumulation of large external debts provided international creditors and "donors" with "political leverage" to influence the direction of country-level macroeconomic policy.

THE STRUCTURAL ADJUSTMENT PROGRAMME

Contrary to the spirit of the Bretton Woods agreement of 1944, which was predicated on "economic reconstruction" and stability of major exchange rates, the structural adjustment programme (SAP) has, since the early 1980s, largely contributed to destabilizing national currencies and ruining the economies of developing countries. The restructuring of the world economy under the guidance of the Washington-based international financial institutions and the World Trade Organization (WTO) increasingly denies individual developing countries the possibility of building a national economy.

The internationalisation of macroeconomic policy transforms countries into open economic territories and national economies into "reserves" of cheap labour and natural resources. The state apparatus is undermined, industry for the internal market is destroyed, national enterprises are pushed into bankruptcy These reforms have also been conducive to the elimination of minimum wage legislation, the repeal of social programmes and a general diminution of the state's role in fighting poverty.

"GLOBAL SURVEILLANCE"

The inauguration of the WTO in 1995 marks a new phase in the evolution of the post war economic system. A new "triangular division of authority" among the IMF, the World Bank and the WTO has unfolded. The IMF has called for more effective "surveillance" of developing countries' economic policies and increased coordination among the three international bodies, signifying a further infringement on the sovereignty of national governments.

Under the new trade order (which emerged from the completion of the Uruguay Round at Marrakesh in 1994), the relationship of the Washington-based institutions to national governments is to be redefined. Enforcement of IMF-World Bank policy prescriptions will no longer hinge upon ad hoc country-level loan agreements (which are not "legally binding" documents).

Henceforth, many of the mainstays of the structural adjustment programme (e.g. trade liberalisation and the foreign investment regime) have been permanently entrenched in the articles of agreement of the WTO. These articles set the foundations for "policing" countries (and enforcing "conditionalities") according to international law. The deregulation of trade under WTO rules combined with new clauses pertaining to intellectual property rights will enable multinational corporations to penetrate local markets and extend their control over virtually all areas of national manufacturing, agriculture and the service economy.

ENTRENCHED RIGHTS FOR BANKS AND MNCS

In this new economic environment, international agreements negotiated by bureaucrats under intergovernmental auspices have come to play a crucial role in the remolding of national economies. Both the 1997 Financial Services Agreement under the stewardship of the WTO and the proposed Multilateral Agreement on Investment under the auspices of the OECD provides what some observers have entitled a "charter of rights for multinational corporations."

These agreements derogate the ability of national societies to regulate their national economies. The Multilateral Agreement on Investment also threatens national-level social programmes, job creation policies, affirmative action and community-based initiatives. In other words, it threatens to lead to the disempowerment of national societies as it hands over extensive powers to global corporations.

Ironically, the ideology of the "free" market upholds a new form of state interventionism predicated on the deliberate manipulation of market forces. Moreover, the development of global institutions has led to the development of "entrenched rights" for global corporations and financial institutions. The process of enforcing these international agreements at national and international levels invariably bypasses the democratic process. Beneath the rhetoric of so-called "governance" and the "free market," neoliberalism provides a shaky legitimacy to those in the seat of political power.

The manipulation of the figures on global poverty prevents national societies from understanding the consequences of a historical process initiated in the early 1980s with the onslaught of the debt crisis. This false consciousness has invaded all spheres of critical debate and discussion on the "free" market reforms.

In turn, the intellectual myopia of mainstream economics prevents an understanding of the actual workings of global capitalism and its destructive impact on the livelihood of millions of people. International institutions including the United Nations follow suit upholding the dominant economic discourse with little assessment of how economic restructuring backlashes on national societies leading to the collapse of institutions and the escalation of social conflict.

THE EMERGENCY

Prime Minister Indira Gandhi did not go to Mexico City for the United Nations International Women's Year Conference as she had planned. She had some troubles at home. The Gujarat elections, considered by many to be a forecast of forthcoming nationwide elections, had gone against her, with the opposition "Peoples Front" winning a narrow victory.

The Allahabad High Court had declared her guilty of election malpractices, a decision that nullified her victory in 1972 and thus her position as the Prime Minister, though the court had granted a 'Stay' until her appeal was heard by the Supreme Court. And the opposition right wing parties plus the Socialists under the leadership of Jayaprakash Narayan had announced a national agitational campaign to demand her resignation. But the most powerful woman in the world was able to manage her own affairs.

On June 27, a State of Emergency was declared which gave the President full power to handle what was said to be a "right wing conspiracy" that included calls to the military to revolt and which aimed at preventing the democratically elected government from functioning. Arrests of all top opposition leaders, including Jayaprakash Narayan himself and a number of his supporters within the Congress Party were made.

Public meetings and demonstrations were banned in most places throughout the country; those attempting to organize such meetings in protest against the Emergency were arrested and total press censorship was instituted. On June 28, the Prime Minister declared that a new economic programme would be announced, but assured industrialists that there would be no further nationalisations. At the same time Agriculture Minister Jagjivan Ram announced that the Emergency would make it possible to procure grain levies from rich peasant and merchant hoarders.

Arrests of smugglers and hoarders were announced and merchants were forced to display their prices. On July 1, a government ordinance amended the Maintenance of Internal Security Act (MISA) to make it possible to detain anyone arrested under it up to one year with no accounting, and it was ordered that no one could move the court for any hearings under the constitutional provisions guaranteeing fundamental rights. Then on July 2 the new 21 point Economic Programme was proclaimed.

In contrast to earlier programmes emphasizing rhetoric of socialism and promising both to curb monopolies and rely on the public sector, this one consisted of a number of very concrete and unexceptionable measures designed to give something to practically every sector of the population without any attack on basic bourgeois interests.

It included price reduction measures; implementation of land-ceiling laws; measures to halt bonded labour in agriculture; measures to liquidate rural indebtedness; review of laws of minimum agricultural wages; measures to increase irrigation and power supply; measures to improve the supply of cheap cloth; measures against tax evasion and smuggling; schemes for workers' association in industry; liberalisation of investment procedures; income-tax relief to the middle classes; and provisions of cheap hostel food, books and stationery for students.

A pervasive theme of all these measures was an increase in industrial and agricultural productivity. The measures and the Emergency were welcomed by representatives of big business. On July 5, the Government announced the banning of 26 organisations including the Rashtriya Swayamsevak Sangh (a Hindu communal organisation, one of whose members had earlier assassinated Gandhi), the Jamaat-i-Islami (a Muslim communal organisation), the Anand Marg (a political-religious sect with probable CIA connections), and ten factions of the Communist Party of India (Marxist-Leninist).

This was followed by arrests of members of these organisations. On July 6, the Prime Minister told union leaders and workers not to engage in strikes or agitations during the Emergency. Strikes have not been directly banned and some have gone on since the Emergency. But gate meetings and public meetings have all been banned, no agitational material can be published and the arrests of local militants for carrying on strike activities have made them almost impossible.

In addition the Emergency has been used to enforce further anti-labour measures, for instance the Unfair Labour Practices Law in Maharashtra which makes lightning strikes, gheraos, sit-down strikes and other forms of militant action impossible to carry on without losing union recognition and incurring the risk of arrest. At the same time at an all India level the Congress-sponsored Indian National Trade Union Congress (INTUC), the CPI-sponsored All India Trade Union Congress (AITUC), and the right socialist Hind Mazdoor Sabha (HMS) were quick to assure Mrs. Gandhi of their full support and to promise no strikes.

These unions have since actively worked together at state and local levels as coopting agents within the unions. In terms of the working class the emphasis of the Emergency was thus on ending "turmoil" and increasing production; the productivity emphasis was linked with checks on bureaucratic corruption and inefficiency; and white collar employees, especially those in government service, were put under speed-up pressure and forced to meet time clocks in a way they had not for some time.

The pro- MoscowCommunist Party of India (CPI) not only announced its full support of the Emergency and widely publicized it as an attack on a "right reactionary conspiracy," but it also began to emerge as an increasing partner of the Congress Government. Congress President D. K. Borooab, in a statement on July 2, said that various sections of the people should be organized for implementing the measures of the new economic programme.

The ideological theme of the Emergency was to be both self-discipline (the Prime Minister said that she would prefer that newspapers should censor themselves rather than having the government do it, and she has made much of Vinoba Bhave's statement that the Emergency was 'anushasanam parva', a Sanskritic phrase drawn from the ancient epics meaning an "era of self-discipline") and mobilisation reaching down to the lowest levels of the population.

And the CPI proposed both to help enforce discipline and to provide the cadres for mobilisation. The first issue of *New Age* after the declaration of Emergency declared that there should be vast changes in the orientation of their cadres; that instead of nationwide campaigns, strikes, bandhs and agitations there should be renewed "constructive work" moving to every group in the masses for implementation of the government's programme.

In the months after the Emergency they have sponsored with the Congress a series of "anti-fascist conferences" throughout the country designed to provide ideological support to the programmes and they have attempted to form "vigilance committees" together with Congress cadres in the factories to promote discipline and production. There was little immediate public reaction against the Emergency.

By and large the workers, peasants and middle class masses saw it as an attack on rightists, not on them; they showed almost no inclination to go to the defense of the arrested leaders; and they seemed inclined to wait to see whether the slight initial downturn in prices and the promised new measures would really indicate a fundamental change. And the actual events of the Emergency make this "wait and see" attitude quite understandable. First, it is a fact that the majority of arrests have been of "rightists."

The government very early stopped publishing the total numbers of arrests, but the figure of 60,000 that is being published in some external and underground newspapers is probably correct. However, this figure does not consist simply of "political prisoners." First, a very large percentage does consist of smugglers, hoarders and black marketeers. Second, another large proportion is members of right wing parties and direct supporters of the J. P. movement, and while these have had some base among the petty bourgeoisie and rural elite they have had almost none among the workers and rural poor; indeed the arrests of members of right wing parties has been a bonus factor for the Emergency as far as the masses have been concerned.

Finally, a large percentage of the actual left activists arrested were arrested for planning agitations against the Emergency or for direct association with the J. P. movement, and again a large percentage of these have been subsequently released. Within the left, the CPI (M) claims to have the largest number of arrested members of any political party, about 2-3000 mostly in the states of West Bengal and Kerala. (More were probably initially arrested but since released.)

The Socialists have close to this amount, though the attack on them has been more widespread and more directly connected with the J. P. movement. "Naxalite" or CPI (ML) arrests have been much smaller, largely because they have not had as large a base and because much of the leadership was underground anyway. Finally, the impact of the Emergency has varied widely between states: "left" arrests concentrated in Bengal and Kerala, arrests of intellectuals occurring in Delhi (some 300 college teachers, mostly right wing, were arrested, and a number of Marxist students) but not so much elsewhere, and very little enforcement of the Emergency in opposition governed Tamil Nadu and Gujarat.

The pattern of arrest, then, was not such as to convince the workers and rural poor that the Emergency was against them. Further, while the attack on the democratic rights of the masses was there from the beginning, it was not clear that this meant an attack on their living standards. Some wage raises were granted immediately after the Emergency, and it was not really until the government announced in September that the traditional bonus of the workers would be lowered from 8 per cent to 4 per cent that an anti-working class thrust became clear.

In the meantime there has been significant effort to isolate the organized workers by hammering on the theme that national development means productivity and discipline and by making large-scale promises to the rural poor (land ceiling promises, agricultural wages, debt relief, construction of house-sites for landless labourers) and to the urban masses at the level of consumption (debt relief again, and promises of lower prices). Thus, illusions about the Emergency and its promises of development and reform have been rapidly vanishing among the organized workers in spite of extensive collabourationist efforts of the right communists, but they still remain at quite a high level in the rural areas and among unorganized and middle class sections in the cities. It is a fact that Indira Gandhi's popularity, which was declining, increased immediately after the declaration of Emergency and that it remains high.

8

Poverty and Sustainable Development

The ability of mountain ecosystems to provide for the growing number of people, elsewhere on Earth, is fast approaching many of its limits. It is quite disturbing to note that, under intense anthropogenic pressure, a minimum of 140 plants and animal species are condemned to extinction each day; forests are vanishing at a rate of some 17 million hectares per year - an area about the size of Finland. The optimal management of resources, particularly bioresources, which is fundamental to long term survival and well-being of societies in the mountains, is governed by the mountain specificities, viz. inaccessibility, fragility, marginality, diversity, niche and adaptability.

Further, enhancement of production through the application of modern technologies in mountain ecosystems is restricted by these mountain specificities. Slope, altitude, terrain conditions, seasonal hazards (landslide, slips, snow, etc.) make mountain areas inaccessible, manifesting in isolation, distance, poor communication and limited mobility with serious socio-cultural and economic dimensions. High vulnerability of natural resources, mainly because of slope and altitude, in association with geologic, edaphic and biotic factors make mountain areas highly fragile.

Inaccessibility and fragility result in limited external linkages and replication of external experiences, slow pace of transformation/development, intra-regional imbalances and under-utilisation of regional potential, low-regenerative capacity of nature, low productivity, limited production options, high overhead costs of resource use, labour intensive and limited physical and economic inputs. These conditions make the area, people and production systems in mountains marginal with marginal options.

These specificities, therefore, have a definite role on the use of natural resources and mode and pace of development. In addition, non-focused development interventions in the mountain regions, based on uncritical evaluation of economic growth models with gross disregard to ecology and its specificities and socio-cultural matrices of mountain people, have aggravated this situation; the development interventions largely involved conflict between man and nature. The Indian Himalayan region (IHR), 250-300 km across, stretches over 2500 km from Jammu and Kashmir in the west to Arunachal Pradesh in the east.

It covers partially/fully 12 states of India, viz., Jammu and Kashmir, Himachal Pradesh, Uttaranchal, Sikkim, Arunachal Pradesh, Nagaland, Manipur, Mizoram, Tripura, Meghalaya, Assam and West Bengal. The region has a total geographical area of about 591 000 km^sup 2^, inhabited by 51 million people representing 18% area and 6% of total population of India. The region supports about 8000 species of flowering plants (47.06% of the total flowering plants of India), of which 80% are endemic to the region.

However, despite the policy stipulations, e.g. Forest (Conservation) Act of 1988, that a minimum of 60% of its total geographical area should be under forests, only 21.78% area is under forests and, already 17 medicinal plants are listed in the Red Book of Indian Plants. The people of the IHR, like elsewhere in other mountain ecosystems, arc heavily dependent for their living on their immediate natural resources and production from primary sectors such as agriculture, forestry, livestock, etc. This dependency of the continually growing population on these finite resources, and lack of viable technologies to mitigate the mountain specificities and enhance the production to meet the demand, are depleting and marginalising the scarce resources effecting poverty.

ECOLOGICAL POVERTY

In mountain regions like the Indian Himalayan Region (IHR), for a number of reasons, poverty can not be understood and measured independent of ecological wealth. Poverty itself, despite decades of research, lacks a universally agreed-upon definition. It is defined as inability to attain a minimum standard of living and people are considered poor when they cannot secure a minimum standard of well-being and when they have limited or restricted choices and opportunity for a tolerable life.

Further, the poverty line based on purchasing power parity (PPP) differs from country to country and even between states within a country, i.e. in India during the IX Plan, the poverty line varied in different states and ranged from Rs. 13 000 to Rs. 19 650 per annum. The World Development Report (1992) defined the poverty line as annual per capita income less than US$ 420. The other definition of poverty, based on consumption, comprises two elements: (1) the expenditure necessary to buy a minimum standard of nutrition and other basic necessities, and (2) a further amount reflecting the cost of participating in the everyday life of society.

The development process in IHR has not been able to introduce suitable interventions and technologies to mitigate mountain specificities enhancing the production system, and to combat poverty of the growing population. Despite voluminous development interventions, poverty is rampant and increasing in all the states of the IHR with the exception of West Bengal, where it is decreasing in the country. It should be mentioned that only one district of West Bengal, Darjeeling, falls in IHR.

Apart from technologies, there are many other aspects to consider while determining poverty in IHR; the major one being that, in this mountain ecosystem, like elsewhere in other mountains, poverty cannot be understood and measured independent of ecological wealth. The reasons to call poverty in IHR ecological poverty are that, in this subsistence-oriented mountain economy, barter/exchange dominates market transactions, and households perform a variety of subsistence activities that often are not reflected in income accounting.

The popular indicators of poverty, whether they are based on income or consumption, are not all-inclusive because of a variety of factors, such as the non-monetised nature of economy of this mountain region, cultural values, and rich natural resource and other niche-based opportunities available to the people. Therefore, comprehensive measures such as the Quality of Life Indicators or Human Development Index are better approximations, although not without their own problems, in determining poverty in this mountain region.

The appropriateness of monetised or quantifiable indicators, e.g. per capita income or gross domestic product (GDP), may not be exactly the most suitable indicators for measuring the quality of life for mountain people like IHR, and the substantive implications of ecology on poverty necessitate labelling it as ecological poverty. The development interventions aiming to combat poverty also, consciously or unconsciously, ignored the adaptive measures that include ecological and cultural values, indigenous and traditional knowledge, and socio-economic practices.

This prevailing situation of IHR demands a closer look at the various factors, such as mountain specificities, in the functioning of the ecosystem in order to reach some conclusion about the dynamics of poverty. Keeping this in view and taking the central Himalayan region of IHR as a case study, an effort has been made here to understand how various factors influence poverty (ecological poverty) and determine sustainable development in mountain ecosystems.

CASE STUDY: THE CENTRAL HIMALAYAN REGION OF INDIA

The Central Himalayan region of India, with a geographical area of 53 485 km^sup 2^, forms a part of Western Himalaya which is recognised as a sub-centre of diversity of plant genetic resources. Further, there are 26 'hot-spots' identified in India where there are high rates of deforestation and endemicity. One of these is the Himalayan belt as a whole constituting one mega hot-spot; eight areas in the Himalaya are especially critical and the Central Himalayan region is one of these eight critical areas. Despite being ecologically rich and unique, the region is highly fragile geologically and vulnerable seismologically.

Within an altitudinal variation ranging from 200 m to more than 8000 m asl, the region comprises five lithotectonically and physiographically distinct subdivisions, namely, the Outer Himalaya comprising the Tarai and Bhabhar, Sub-Himalayan belt of the Siwalik, the Lesser Himalaya, the Great Himalaya and the Trans-Himalaya or Tethys. Human habitation in the region is found up to an altitude of 3500 m asl. The region supports 8 479 562 persons who constitute about 0.8% and 21.4% of the total population of Indian Republic and Indian Himalayan Region (IHR), respectively.

The decennial growth rate of the population of the region for the decade 1991-2001 was 19.2%. The sex ratio of the population has substantially changed from 936 in 1991 to 964 in 2001, which is higher than that of India. The literacy rate was 72.3% in 2001; the rate for males is 84% against 60.3%

for females. The people of the Central Himalayan region of India are largely dependent for their living on their immediate bioresources.

The region is experiencing major difficulties in sustaining its growing population on its overall environmental resources - land availability, forests and grasslands, water resources. Much of the environmental resource degradation is governed by mountain specificities, viz. inaccessibility, fragility, marginality, diversity (heterogeneity), niche (natural suitability) and adaptability (human adaptation) and growing population. The human population of the region is increasing at an exponential rate of 1.8% per cent per annum and is doubling in 27-30 years. The climate of the region is quite harsh, particularly in winter when temperature goes occasionally below freezing point.

Forest is the basis of life for the people and the prime store house of bioresource of the region. Classification of land under forests by ownership in the region shows that about 69.2% of the forests belong to forest department; 23.3% are civil soyam while 6.9% and 0.6% are Panchayat forests and private forests. Though, it is claimed that the area under forests in the region is above 60% of the total area, many studies report the area under forests to be much less.

The forest cover, from 1972-75 to 1980-82, reduced by 10.15% in Indian Himalaya region (IHR), and 18.8% in Indian Central Himalaya. Distribution of forests, as interpreted by Landsat imagery for the years 1980-82, showed that only 28.6% of the total area of region was under forests; out of this good tree cover (crown cover > 60%) existed only on 15.45% of forest land, medium (30-60% crown cover) and poor tree cover (10-30% crown cover) existed on 52.3% and 32.2% of forest lands, respectively.

The State of Forests Reports, 1991, of the Ministry of Environment and Forests, estimated the forest area of Central Himalayan region of India as only 44.08% of the total area. Irrespective of the area under forests, the commonly agreed fact is that the health of forests is deteriorating under growing anthropogenic and other pressures. Though, there is substantial growth in human population in the region, the area available for cultivation is not increasing proportionately, rather it shows a decreasing trend. The per capita land holding from 1980-81 to 1990-91 decreased from 0.15 ha to 0.11 ha.

The net area sown is only 12.6% of the total land and nearly 70% of the operational holdings are owned by marginal farmers. Though all the major rivers originate from this region, hardly 20% of its cultivated area is irrigated because of geomorphological factors rendering more than 80% of the rest of the cultivated area to be rainfed. The per capita cultivated land in Central Himalaya is lesser than that of Himalaya (0.16 ha) and India (0.2 ha).

Agriculture in the region is strongly related to ecological specificities and socio-economic and cultural conditionings. The agro-ecosystem is holistic in composition including agriculture, forests and livestock. A topo-sequence is maintained with forests or uncultivated land or support area at the top, the village in the middle and the agricultural lands below the village on terraced spurs in slopes ranging from 8-45[degrees].

The region supports about four million livestock according to the Livestock Census of 1993. Mainly cows, followed by oxen and she buffalo, obviously indicate the need-based composition and the availability of fodder to maintain such livestock. Local breeds constitute about 94% of the total animal population.

The per family and per capita availability of animals were 3.52 and 0.68, respectively in 1993. The livestock population in Central Himalaya has increased frum 3 774 000 in 1961 to 3 897 000 in 1993 in absolute numbers, the increase is about 123 000. However, after converting the animal type to a standard animal unit, the absolute increase of units is 242 000, which is almost double the livestock population. This is due to an increase in buffalo population. Buffalo are stall-fed and the green fodder is usually obtained from forests and grasslands.

SITUATION OF ECOLOGICAL POVERTY IN THE REGION

In the Central Himalayan region there is a continued increase in population from year to year, whereas there is minimal or no technological intervention to enhance production and sustain the population. Extensive and rapid technological intervention is restricted by mountain specificities. While the population during the decade 1981-1991 grew at the rate of 22.5%, the production during this period grew at 12.1%.

Further, while the population is increasing, food production is gradually decreasing from 1 320 482 tons in 1980-81 to 1 506 897 tons in 1989-90, hut in 1990-91 it decreased to 1 486 943 tons. Under the prevailing ecological situation, it is difficult to reverse the deficit in food, as it is not possible to bring more land under cultivation since it docs not exist. Additional land for agriculture could only be brought into cultivation by encroaching forest land which is not advisable. Agriculture is also influenced by altitude, size of farm, and availability of uncultivated land, particularly forests. Forests surrounding a village support cultivation by supplying organic matter and plant nutrients to cultivated land and, therefore, has been defined as support land.

Agriculture is sustained by a flow of organic matter and plant nutrients from support land to cultivated land and by the recycling of organic matter and plant nutrients in crop residues. Livestock are dependent on green leaves obtained from forests as fodder, and the cultivated land is dependent on animal dung used as compost, apart from animals (bullock) used for ploughing.

The dry leaves, also obtained from forests, are used as bedding for animals and as compost in cultivated land. Indirectly, by supplying firewood, the forests also support cultivation; in the absence of which livestock dung would be used as fuel, seriously interrupting the flow of organic matter and plant nutrients to cultivated lands.

It has been established that each unit of agronomic production in the region is obtained at the expense of about seven units of energy from the adjacent forests in terms of fodder, firewood and leaves for compost. Against the requirement of 18 ha of forest land, including 5-12 ha of well-stocked forests, per hectare of cultivated land, the ratio of forests to agricultural land is only 1.33: 1 and the ratio of well-stocked forests to agricultural land is only 0.84: 1.

Because of their location on terraced spurs in slopes ranging from 8-45[degrees], cultivated lands are small and highly fragmented; most plots being smaller than 0.02 ha and distributed at different locations. This small size and rainfed nature are inappropriate for introduction and replication of modern inputs and technological interventions. Many studies report that high-yield crops produce more than traditional varieties in irrigated cropfields, but in the rainfed fields there was no difference and crop residue yield was almost the same.

The traditional varieties yield about 1.8 times more crop residue in rainfed fields when grown using the farmers' manuring practices. In this ecosystem, straw yield is as important as grain yield to local people and can ease the pressure on forest and grasslands. The women in the region are the life blood and labour source of the economic structure of the agricultural system. The women generally work more than 15-18 h a day, attending cattle, collecting fuel, fodder and water, in addition to the normal duties at home.

As production from primary sources in the region cannot sustain the food requirement of its populace for more than 4 to 6 months, men migrate to the lower plains for seasonal earning, entrusting further responsibilities on women. About 30-40% of men migrates to the plains; in some villages one-third of a family migrate. Grazing intensity is high, but each ha can only support 2 units of livestock, while cattle/ha in Central Himalaya are 7.99.

The green fodder requirement has been estimated as 259 lakh mt per annum, but present production is only 52 lakh mt, both from forests and agriculture. At present a substantial portion of the gap is met from extensive lopping of trees. Further, in view of poor availability of alternative sources of energy, such as LPG or solar energy, biomass serves as the major source of energy and is obtained from fuelwood. Rough estimates of fuel wood requirement reveals that about 25.04 lakh mt is required annually, against the present availability of 13.20 lakh mt.

The rest is obtained from forests by the women carried on their heads. Decrease in protective vegetation below 60%, has increased the rate of erosion in the catchment of Central Himalayan rivers. Erosion has increased five-fold to 1 mm per year. The rivers carry large amounts of sediment at the rate of 16.5 ha-metre per 100 km^sup 2^ of the catchment area per year.

Further, the loss of forests has reduced the capacity of mountain slopes to absorb and filter rain water leading to drying up of springs and consequent dwindling of water resources. A survey in the Gaula river catchment in Nainital district of the Central Himalaya revealed that about 45% of springs have gone dry or become seasonal. The drying up of streams has resulted in more work for women as they have to walk longer distances to collect water for domestic use. In some villages, in order to collect water, fodder and fuel, women travel 10 km every day.

DEVELOPMENT OPTIONS TO ALLEVIATE ECOLOGICAL POVERTY

Solutions to ecological poverty in Central Himalaya are to be sought within the mountain specificities and adaptability of people which is governed by sociocultural principles. Attributes for sustainable development here should include use of natural regeneration processes, use of niche, multiple use, local availability, flexibility, accessibility, use of indigenous knowledge, low input, realisation of local milieu and people's participation.

People and population dynamics such as growth, distribution, density, in-and-out migration, have vital effects on mountain specificities. Socio-economic factors such as ethnicity, type of economic activity and resource management practices play a major role in determining the pace of development. Some of the dynamics affect the specificities and thus the productivity of the area and the biodiversity in the short or long term, while others mitigate the specificities through adaptability and niche.

Moreover, since demographic behaviour is related to productivity, understanding of specific demographic issues like migration and population pressure and incorporation of these into productivity programmes will result in multiple benefits. Understanding how local and indigenous people are associated with resource use and management, their needs and uses, their economic relations with the resources, etc., will help in the productivity of the resources.

Identification of social, cultural, economic and political issues such as gender, poverty, education, land tenure, legal rights, trade, debt, will help in understanding how they affect productivity. There is a necessity to know how gender is related to the population-resource relationship, and to identify women's role in development and planning. The development process will include options which have larger human dimensions such as socio-economic conditioning and cultural principles, simple technologies, indigenous knowledge, innovation and practices.

SIMPLE TECHNOLOGIES

In the Central Himalayan region as much as 70% of the populations are engaged in the primary sector, i.e. agriculture, livestock, forestry, plantations, for their livelihood. For enhancement of production in this sector, advanced technological inputs are either not available or, if available, are not ecologically appropriate. Technological inputs, so far, are marginal and remained confined to agriculture, in the form of high-yield varieties, pesticides, insecticides and chemical fertiliser.

Simple and cheaper technologies already in use in the region have potential to promote socio-economic development of the people and ensure regeneration of degraded mountain lands, blending development with conservation. These include medicinal plants, tea, apiculture, mushrooms, floriculture, and cash crops like cardamom, seasonal and off-season vegetables and integrated fish farming.

Simple technologies that would promote the economy and help conserve resources are biocomposting, vermicompost, biofertilizer, polypit, polytrench and polyhouse. Improving underutilized lands/wastelands through silvi-pastoral practices and multipurpose tree planting, hedgerows, agroforestry and bio-fencing will help conserve soil, and promote yield income. Value-addition using traditional practises such as water harvesting, fermentation, and products of bamboo will also promote the economy. These simple technologies are cheap, flexible, accessible, acceptable and appropriate to promote natural regeneration processes and the economy.

POPULATION CONTROL

The primary task in mitigating ecological poverty is to control population growth, a well-recognised national as well as international problem. The population of the region is almost doubling in 27-30 years, posing a serious threat to its natural resources and biodiversity. Studies carried out in the region have established that literate women have lower fertility, and use methods of contraception. It is therefore, important to accord priority to female education so that changes in nuptiality behaviour can be brought about consequently reducing birth rates.

Studies in the region have also revealed that scheduled castes and tribes have more surviving children that other group. The region is largely inhabited by caste Hindus (91.8%)

including scheduled tribes, a small population of Muslims (4.85%) and Sikhs (2.68%). Since, the scheduled caste and scheduled tribe population in the region constitute only 13.0% and 3.54%, respectively, in comparison to 16.73% and 8.08% in India; the region is advantaged in that these minority groups will not aggravate the growth rate.

INDIGENOUS KNOWLEDGE, INNOVATIONS AND PRACTICES

In their efforts to survive in remote places having inadequate or no infrastructural facilities, the people of the Central Himalaya have evolved unique indigenous knowledge, innovation and practices (KIP). These are based on locally available bioresources, and play a pivotal role in promoting the economy and in conserving resources. Understanding them is of paramount importance in sustainable development, as they provide a historical continuity of 'living in harmony with nature'.

For example, the traditional practice of multiple cropping, best suited for rainfed agriculture and prevalent in this region, is based on indigenous knowledge. Further, different land races and crop varieties, have probably evolved according to native micro-climate, soil conditions and tolerance to various biotic and abiotic stresses; thus minimizing the risk of crop failure due to pathogens or climate. Cross-breeding of animals by high altitude communities and selective killing of male buffalo calves to reduce pressure on fodder are indigenous strategies adopted to use and conserve scarce natural resource.

The male buffalo consumes twice the amount of fodder and has no value except for breeding. Socio-cultural practices like polyandry, used to control population by the Jaunsari tribal community of the region, division of community forest into compartments and compartment rotation to allow natural regeneration, ethnomedicine, ethnoveterinary practices, development of sacred groves that admix religion and science, are other indigenous practices for conservation of bioresources.

Considering the role of indigenous systems in resource management and sustainable development of local people, the Convention on Biological Diversity (1992) has recognized it as a tool for resource conservation through Article 8(J): '. . . respect, preserve and maintain knowledge, innovations and practices of indigenous and local communities embodying traditional life styles relevant for the conservation and sustainable use of biological diversity . . .', and Article 10(C): 'protect and encourage customary use of biological resources in accordance with traditional cultural practices that are compatible with conservation or sustainable use requirements'.

Undisputedly, the role of indigenous knowledge is pivotal in the region in sustainable use and conservation of resources; however, they are fast disappearing resulting in habitat loss leading to loss of resources. The indigenous knowledge, innovation and practices arc being threatened and eroded by growing tide of technification. Indigenous knowledge is scattered and associated with low-prestige rural life and even those who are its bearers may believe it to be inferior.

There is also a need to explore possibilities for their value addition and validation through appropriate science and technology inputs which would rejuvenate and enhance the efficiency of the products and improve their economic potential. So far, the people of the region have failed to obtain meaningful economic importance from their indigenous knowledge. Value addition could ensure conservation through enhanced income generating potential of bioresources. The value addition of indigenous knowledge and practices has remained unattended mainly due to lack of exposure and entrepreneurship of the local communities.

DEVELOPMENT APPROACH

Development, to be successful, should embrace participatory and bottom-up approaches in which the locals should be recognized as actors, analysts and partners. In this approach, the relationship of planners with the people needs to embrace tenets like enabling, supporting and empowering, instead of controlling, inducing and motivating.

The traditional economy of people of the region is primarily built around the forests, since they extract a major portion of their food, fodder, fuel, fruits, edible roots, and medicines, from the forests, apart from forests acting as support land to agriculture. Conservative estimates indicate that the Central Himalayan region harbours more than 700 species of medicinal plants out of the 1748 species of medicinal plants reported in Indian Himalayan Region.

There are in-built safeguards which are socially sanctioned and culturally patterned in the use of medicinal plants. These regulatory practices are being ignored by unscientific and non-regulated collection of medicinal plants and ineffective organized management control over the sale of medicinal plants. Seventeen Himalayan medicinal plants, more than half of them from this region, are listed in the Red Data Book of Indian Plants.

Since as much as 65% of the region is under forest, and out of it 65% is already conserved as reserved forests, either to bring more area under forests for conservation or more forests under reserved category would be inappropriate. Rather, proper use and conservation of forests based on a community participatory approach is fundamental for its economic development. Forest management programmes that anticipate peoples' participation need to have potential to increase production and productivity. Good forest cover would result in (1) affording long-range ecological security for the conservation of water, soil and biodiversity, (2) meeting the needs of goods and services of the people, and (3) amelioration of degraded areas and wastelands so as to enhance the productive capacity of such derelict lands and many others.

A successful Programme with conservation in focus must incorporate scientific input compatible with social needs and aspirations. People's participation, being a social phenomenon, takes a long time to evolve. Participation involves decision-making, implementation, sharing the benefits, monitoring and evaluation. A number of factors - physical, biological, economic, political, social, cultural, and historical are generally encountered in the process.

Further, lack of commitment of development agents to adopt a participatory approach, unwillingness of project officials to give up control over project activities and decisions, lack of incentives and skills among project staff to encourage them to adopt a participatory approach, limited capacity of local level organisations, mistrust between shareholders, vested interests, lack of committed leadership to motivate the villagers, intra-village conflicts, competition between various government departments with variant approaches to a single Programme, a subsistence economy that enforces food insecurity, people's aspiration, lack of awareness, are other critical factors that affect participation.

However, creation of a common platform, identification of most pressing common problems, socialisation of costs and surpluses, a democratic decision-making process, social reform with strict discipline, cooperative management systems, a special focus on women, facilitating village organisations and need-based planned socio-economic development, not only mitigate impacts of above inhibitors but also invigorate participation.

Development, and hence poverty reduction, as argued by Amartya Sen in his Development as Freedom, essentially depends on expanding the freedom of choice. In mountain regions like Central Himalaya, considering that the people are disadvantaged in resource use by mountain specificities, they necessarily opt for development(s) that suits their eco-cultural conditioning. Imposed conventional development paradigms will only restrict their freedom of choice.

For their survival in this ecosystem, based on generations of practical experience, requires indigenous and simple technologies and practices that have minimal dependence on external input. Inaccessibility as a limiting factor could be mitigated, with minimal dependence on external inputs, especially transport cost. Fragility as a limitation could be mitigated by blending conservation with high productivity through adoption of traditional strategies, institutional measures and socio-economic matrices of the local communities.

Marginality needs to be tackled by traditional strategics to upgrade marginal resources. Location technologies and institutional management based on folk knowledge and local concerns can well accommodate diversity and niche. The loss of forests cover in the region is resulting in loss of habitat, biotic extinctions and deteriorating quality of life for the locals. Restoration of forest health based on a community participatory approach would help control poverty.

There is a need to understand, respect, strengthen and encourage community-oriented development endeavours based on ecological, social and cultural principles. This advocates value-added growth with a holistic approach including ecology, resources, culture and population dynamics. In brief, ecological poverty can be fought by focusing on activities with minimal dependence on external input resources, blending of technological and institutional measures with conservation, location-specific simple and useful technologies and institutional management, and use of folk knowledge and local concerns.

Of the 63.72 million ha of forest cover in India (almost all is state owned and controlled) over 40% is degraded, with a crown density of less than 0.4. This degradation of forests is mainly ascribed to rigid state control and the resulting disempowerment and displacement of indigenous tribal and hill communities, accompanied by the disintegration of community-based resource management. Consequently, the government of

India made a major policy shift in 1988 and switched to Joint Forest Management (JFM).

JFM is an evolving community forestry Programme, which sets out to establish management 'partnerships' between local forest-dependent communities and the state forest department for the sustainable management and joint benefit sharing of public forest land. To accomplish this, JFM seeks to shift the existing inequitable distribution of management control by directly involving local people and institutions in forest management. JFM does not involve the transfer of ownership of forests, but attempts instead to restructure the formal system of access, decision-making, and sharing of benefits to account for the needs of local communities.

So far, 22 state governments have issued orders for implementation of JFM and the states have evolved their own mechanisms of involving local communities in conformity with the proclaimed policy. About 36130 Village Forest Councils are managing a total of 10.25 million ha of forest area in the country. Tamil Nadu, the southern state of India, has a geographic area of 13 million ha, which constitutes 3.96% of the land area of the country.

The total population of the state is 55.86 million (1991 census) accounting for 6.60% of the country's population. The recorded forest area is 2.26 million ha, which is 17.40% of the land area of the state. But the actual forest cover, as assessed through remote sensing, is only 1.71 million ha-a mere 13.13% of the land area. Not only that, but half of this actual forest cover has a crown density of less than 0.40. There are 15 822 villages in the state, of which 1405 abut forests.

The total population of these forest villages is estimated to be 3.11 million, a large percentage of whom constitute the most disadvantaged section of society (based on per capita income, literacy rate, nutritional and health status, and lack of access to social and technical services). Because of their remoteness, thin and scattered population, modern development and amenities have not reached them. Nor do they have political clout, as most of these people are tribals and scheduled castes. Rigid state control and indiscriminate removal of bamboo and other trees by industries in the past have degraded the forests, aggravated poverty of forest communities and jeopardized the ecological and hydrological balance of the area.

THE TAMIL NADU FORESTRY PROJECT

Tamil Nadu Forestry Project (called the Project hereafter) is a Japan Bank for International Cooperation (JBIC) funded US$100 million Joint Forest Management (community forestry) project being implemented in Tamil Nadu state since 1997-1998. In the project, degraded forest microwatersheds, together with abutting hamlets, or habitation or revenue villages are selected.

The forest area is divided into three zones - Lower or Utility zone, Middle or Asset creation zone and Upper or Eco-restoration zone. Normally, the area for all three zones is 250 ha, in which the zone-wise gap planting is taken up. The uniqueness of the project is that it has a provision of US$12000 for village development alone, under buffer zone activities over a period of 3 years. The aim is to reduce the dependence of villagers on forests by providing alternate income generation activities.

In each of the identified management units, a people's representative body, the Village Forest Council (CFC), is formed, and is fully involved in the planning and execution of works, protection, harvesting and benefit sharing in the management unit with a focus on degraded forests. One male member and one female member from each household, provided that they are willing, are enrolled as its members. Any person who opts out from membership of the Council is not entitled for any benefit. The VFC meets as and when called for but, in any case, at least once in 3 months.

Each Village Forest Council elects an executive committee in such a manner that one hamlet elects at least two members; each Council elects a minimum of 5 and maximum of 15 members to the Executive Committee. The Panchayat (lower tier of local self-government in India) members of the management unit are co-opted as ex-officio members of the Executive Committee (EC). The members of the EC elect its president from themselves who is also President of the Council.

The forest ranger concerned is the member secretary of the EC who facilitates the election of members and the president of the EC. The EC is responsible for day-to-day activities of the Council and meets at least once a month. A memorandum of understanding is signed at the start between the District Forest Officer (on behalf of Forest Department) and the Council president. This details the roles and responsibilities of the Forest Department and Council - the partners in JFM. All the councils are being registered under the Societies Registration Act 1975.

The Government order sanctioning the funds from the JBIC soft loan had the Programme objective of increasing the tree cover through involvement of the people. But once the Programme was launched, it was continuously reviewed, modified, and broadened in consonance with feedback from the people and field officers. It was found that unless those dependent on the forest (wood cutters and grazers) are weaned away by providing alternate livelihoods for themselves, the social fencing would not be established.

The money for the buffer zone residents (for development of forest dependents) was increased to US$12 000 from US$6000. The individual grants were converted into interest-free loans so that the VFC can build up its corpus fund and extend loans to the remaining forest dependents for acquiring productive assets. The VFC president was made joint signatory for withdraw of funds and submission of accounts.

One landmark order came from the state government, for the involvement of all other departments, such as the public works, electricity, health, agriculture, animal husbandry and tribal development departments, to give priority for holistic development of these micro-watersheds. Not only that, the involvement of other departments is monitored and guided by a state committee headed by the Chief Secretary and at the district level by the Collector. All department heads at state and district level are members of these committees. Spurred by its success, the JBIC has extended the project until 2004-2005, and has also consented to fund a second phase to cover the remaining forest villages.

FORESTRY PROJECT AND POVERTY ALLEVIATION

The accepted view in the world is that poverty is about more than inadequate income or human development - it is also about vulnerability and lack of voice, power and representation. With this multi-dimensional view of poverty comes greater complexity in poverty reduction strategies because more factors - such as social and cultural forces -need to be taken into account.

Based on the study of earlier programmes and interviews with poor people in different countries, the World Development Report aptly proposed a three-pronged strategy for attacking poverty: promoting opportunity, facilitating empowerment, and enhancing security. In this strategy, none of the elements can be said to be more important than the others as they are all deeply complementary.

Progress in reducing the scourge of poverty is possible by tackling one element and leaving the other two untouched. For instance, wage work will improve the income of the poor and may also improve their well being if is given for a long period but, once this is withdrawn, the people may relapse into the same poverty vortex. Hence, for sustainable alleviation of poverty, actions will be necessary on all three fronts - opportunity, empowerment and security - because of their complementarity and mutual reinforcement.

Though it was never explicitly intended, even at later stages, broadening of the Project in response to field needs has caused it to evolve into a sustainable poverty alleviation Programme from a mere greening project. As elucidated below, at the local level it abundantly provides all three elements of the comprehensive poverty alleviation strategy advocated by World Development Report.

OPPORTUNITY

Tree assets

In the forest area of around 250 ha of each micro-watershed, 77 000 saplings are planted, with deliberate emphasis on non-timber forest products (NTFPs). The species used include Azadirachta indica, Phyllanthus emblica, Syzizium cumini, Tamarindus indica, Bassia latifolia, Terminalia bellerica. In addition, 25 000 saplings are distributed to the villages for growing on their own lands.

The WC members are given the right to collect NTFPs and a share in the final harvest. Assuming a realistic survival of 50% of saplings to become trees, there will be 38 500 trees in the forest area, which will yield various NTFPs. This produce can be sold directly or after processing and value addition. Already, many of the older VFCs having semi-evergreen forests are getting more than US$4000 annually from sale of NTFP.

Water harvesting structures

In the forest area, water harvesting structures such as percolation ponds and check dams are made to help in raising the water table and recharging bore wells in adjoining agriculture lands.

In a state like Tamil Nadu, where annual rainfall is not more than 700 mm and mostly in the monsoon season, these water harvesting structures have caused complete transformation of the village economy by raising the water table. In most places, the cropping intensity has increased and people have shifted to the cultivation of high water use crops such as sugarcane and rice.

Improvement in basic infrastructure

There are instructions from the government to all other line departments to dovetail their development and infrastructure activities in Project villages as a priority. There is a committee at the state level headed by the Chief Secretary and at the district level headed by the District Collector to guide, steer and oversee coordination by all other departments.

There is a substantial improvement in basic infrastructure such as roads, electricity, drinking water and schools, in most of the watersheds. From the project funds, 30% of the buffer zone funds is spent on creation of community assets like community halls, threshing floors, etc.

Promotion of alternate livelihoods

From buffer zone funds, village youths are given free training to enable them to become drivers, electricians, television mechanics, etc., Apart from that, the women and elders are trained in various village level activities such as rope making, pickle making, tailoring, embroidering or soap making, so that they obtain a steady income from alternate sources and need not cutwood for their livelihoods.

Literacy

The forest villages have a high incidence of illiteracy. After adoption of the watersheds, the people have been motivated to admit their children to the schools. Wherever schools were not available, they have been opened through the education department or charitable organisations. Adult education classes were taken in some villages. In one tribal village, namely Chellapanthoddi, the WC itself started a school, which was later taken over by a charitable organisation.

Provision of milch cattle and other productive assets

The forest dependents are given interest-free loans from the buffer zone fund to buy high quality milch cattle. Similarly, skilled women and other persons are given loans to buy tailoring machines, tools, etc.

Wage work

Out of US$60 000 spent in each programme micro-watershed, around US$36 000 pays for the wage work of local people in planting or civil structures (mainly for materials). In the first 3 years, this substantial wage employment on their doorstep has provided a big boost and enabled the people to make full use of the infrastructure and productive assets. Another hallmark of the programme is transparency, as all the expenditure is done through the WC.

Empowerment

A Panchayat comprises a group of villages having a population of 6-10 000 whereas a forest village has a population of not more than 600. Thus, forest villages generally constitute only a hamlet of the Panchayat and do not have any control or say in Panchayat affairs, leaving the forest people absolutely powerless. But the formation of WCs has provided a real chance for their empowerment.

The entire planning, execution and monitoring of the programme is done by the VFCs, whose day-to-day affairs are looked after by its executive committee headed by an elected President. The annual NTFPs revenue of some of the VFCs has already exceeded US$4000 and, from the initial money of US$12 000 for buffer zone, some VFCs have developed a corpus fund of US$24 000, as they charge interest of 1% per month from the beneficiaries.

The Council president and the concerned range officer jointly sign all the accounts and fund applications. Council presidents are ex officio members of the district JFMC, which is headed by a District Collector. This imparts more prestige and glamour to the post of president. Consequently, this post has become so much coveted.

Women's empowerment is given due emphasis and one third of the Executive Committee posts are necessarily held by women. In each village, one or two women's self-help groups are formed and are encouraged to undertake economic activities individually or jointly using credit from the buffer zone fund.

Security

Restocked forests provide households with a means for diversifying their subsistence and income-generating activities, optimising their labour resources during different seasons, and insuring against the risks of agricultural failures. Improvements in village infrastructure and diversification of income generation activities have enhanced security. The rebuilding of the forests and water harvesting structures has reduced vulnerability to drought, which is the most common risk.

The drought-proofing of these areas has gone a long way towards improving agriculture income on a sustainable basis. The training in alternate livelihoods has also made a significant contribution in reducing vulnerability to natural vagaries. The forest trees are perennial assets available for generations and, by their nature, each successive year their yield increases and susceptibility to natural vagaries decreases.

Even last year, when the rainfall in the state was the lowest in a century, Neem tree seed collection proved to be a good source of income for the poorest of the poor. Not only that, in most of the villages, group insurance has been provided to all the council members from public sector insurance companies for three years. Thus, the Project amply provides the three elements - opportunity, empowerment and security at the local level for effective poverty alleviation.

The latest satellite data show substantial improvement in forest cover and density in the state, the increase is one of the highest in the country. A visit to the forest villages is enough to gauge the palpable improvement in dwellings and living standards of the majority of families. With these three pillars of poverty alleviation properly placed, we do not see any reason for a relapse into the vortex of poverty.

The remaining households will also be able to cross the poverty line with the support of VFCs. No other government programme in India has had such a comprehensive approach to poverty alleviation. Integrated watershed development programmes incorporate multisectoral integration for promotion of economic opportunities but they are unable to empower the poorest of the poor. Most of other states in India are also implementing community forestry projects but they lack integration of other departments and the amount spent for alternate income generation is very low. Hence, these latter projects are not able to make a lasting and real impact on forest conservation, apart from poverty reduction.

CONSTRAINTS

The Tamil Nadu Forestry Project is a massive Programme which has acquired a poverty alleviation approach in the course of its implementation, as the feedback from people and field officers was continuously used for broadening the project. Depending on the dedication of field officers, cooperation by the district administration and interest of the villagers, some of the 1118 villages covered so far have not been provided with all the components described above. In spite of the emphasis on micro-planning through people involvement, the top-down approach is not completely eliminated in the project.

The extent of the forest area to be treated in each micro-watershed is fixed, irrespective of the size of adjoining reserved forests. The number of seedlings to be planted per hectare is also constant as per the project document, irrespective of the actual needs. Similarly, the buffer zone amount for each watershed is US$12 000 whereas the number of households varies. Planting of the full 250 ha is done in the first year and the buffer zone and maintenance are completed in 3 years. Consequently, there is no provision for the creation of alternate employment and assets after 3 years.

Also, the attention of field officers shifts to new villages and the task remains half done in the earlier villages. It would be much better if tree planting was staggered over 5 years and the buffer zone and asset creation was continued for at least 10 years in each village. The cooperation of departments needs to be further enhanced and strengthened. The Tamil Nadu Forestry Project was conceived, sanctioned and launched as a mere community forestry-based greening project.

However, the flexibility, participatory approach, continuous monitoring, review and readjustment have transformed it into a sustainable poverty alleviation project for the forest communities. It very vividly demonstrates that the ultimate solution for forest conservation in India and other developing countries lies not merely in community forestry but in keeping a broad approach to alleviate poverty in the most comprehensive and sustainable way through promotion of opportunity, facilitating empowerment and enhancing security.

No biodiversity conservation Programme can succeed unless it adequately caters to the development needs of the people. The project also underscores the need for present-day foresters to comprehend social and economic issues in addition to the technical issues for the successful take up of forestry projects. However, restocking of forests and poverty alleviation are long processes so that the duration of forest development projects should be not less than 10 years. Supporters of minimum wage laws argue that the setting of a minimum wage improves the economic conditions of low-wage workers.

However, if increasing the minimum wage reduces the employment of this group of workers, the overall effect on income distribution is ambiguous. It is all the more important, therefore, to assess the relevance of the minimum wage as a wage policy tool after the labour market liberalisation that occurred in the 1980s and 1990s. On the one hand, minimum wages seem to be received by a greater share of the working population, partly because the low level of the minimum wage in some countries provided more incentive to comply with the law.

On the other hand, a high proportion of the new jobs created in the developing world are in the informal sector where the minimum wage is weakly, if at all, enforced. In Latin America, for example, 85 per cent of newly created jobs are in the informal sector. In Africa, the percentage of the labour force working in the formal sector declined between 1990 and 1999. What are the consequences of this trend? Other questions this chapter attempts to answer centre on the effect of the minimum wage on the level of employment.

What is the sign of the relationship, if any? What are the competing theories that explain the link between the minimum wage and employment? Have they received any empirical support in developing countries? Finally, there remains the most ambitious question of all: ultimately, what is the effect of a change in the minimum wage on poverty? In other words, does a higher minimum wage push workers into or out of poverty? Who are the workers most at risk? Is it possible to test the minimum wage effect in a dual sector economy with a sizeable informal sector?

The lack of data makes such an analysis difficult. One of the most severe limitations in studying minimum wages is the unavailability of time series data for many developing countries, especially in Africa. Moreover, many countries also lack information on basic variables like the share of workers receiving minimum wages, the degree of compliance with minimum wage laws, the distribution of minimum wage earners by sex or by population group (e.g. youth, urban, etc.).

However, a recently released database does provide information on the minimum wage at several points in time (from the 1970s to the late 1990s) for approximately 30 developing countries, mainly in Latin America and Africa. Thailand and the

Philippines are also represented in the sample. This data set has made it possible to test simple equations that relate changes in minimum wages to variations in employment and poverty.

The discussion opens with a review of recent developments in the literature on the minimum wage and a summary of the main results of the studies. This section is followed by an overview of low-wage labour market conditions, including trends in minimum wage levels, country evidence on compliance and the characteristics of minimum wage earners. A third section investigates the response of employment and poverty levels to changes in minimum wages using the above-mentioned data set. A concluding section summarizes the main findings and presents some policy recommendations.

THE EFFECT OF MINIMUM WAGE ON EMPLOYMENT AND POVERTY

Minimum wage and employment: Predictions

The standard model predicts that employment will fall if the wage is exogenously raised. The higher the minimum wage, the more unemployment there will be. In developing countries, minimum wage law generally applies to a small formal sector.2 Often, though, the minimum wage law does not cover all workers of the formal sector-excluding, say, part-time workers or workers in some industries- while in a few cases, there is also a lower limit imposed on wages paid to informal-sector workers.

The terms "informal" and "uncovered" are therefore not exactly equivalent. The following discussion, however, is concerned with substitution effects and with changes in relative wages in two parts of the economy: one with and another without a minimum wage. In the long run, substitution of capital for labour and changes in relative wages can be expected to occur in both the uncovered and the informal sectors as a result of changes in the minimum wage, though probably more immediately in the informal sector. Informal and uncovered are thus used interchangeably.

In the presence of an extended informal sector, the effect of the minimum wage is twofold. Firstly, the introduction of a minimum wage results in a decrease of employment in the covered sector since labour demand in the neoclassical model is a decreasing function of wage. Secondly, workers who lose their jobs in the covered sector will work in the uncovered sector, thereby depressing wages in this part of the economy.

As some of these workers have reservation wages above the wage equilibrium that prevails in the uncovered sector, total employment is less than employment in the absence of a minimum wage. The ultimate effect on employment is therefore highly dependent on the size of the minimum wage increase and also on substitution effects between formal and informal employment.

Formalizing the effects of the minimum wage when there is an uncovered sector, Fields (1994) showed that the effect of the minimum wage on unemployment effectively depends on three factors: the elasticity of demand for labour in the covered sector, the elasticity of wage in the non-covered sector and the size of the minimum wage rise. These factors ensure that the overall effect is ambiguous: Other things being equal, "a higher minimum wage can result either in more unemployment in equilibrium or in less unemployment in equilibrium, depending on parameter values".

INTRODUCING EFFICIENCY WAGE THEORY

The model developed by Agenor and Aizenman departs from neoclassical theory in assuming that skilled workers are paid an efficiency wage. These authors argue that a reduction in the minimum wage increases the demand for unskilled workers in the formal sector and contributes to a decrease in labour supply in the informal sector, thus leading to an increase in the informal sector wage. Thus, as the wage paid to unskilled workers in the informal sector rises, the wage paid to skilled workers is rated up. In turn, the wage increase for skilled workers reduces their employment.

Efficiency wage theory is also able to account for the spike in wage distribution - i.e. concentration of wages at the minimum

- that occurs even in firms exempted from the wage floor, as in the United States for example. A similar phenomenon was observed in Papua New Guinea after the 1992 drop in the minimum wage: new entrants in large firms were paid wages higher than the minimum wage that was supposed to apply to them. One explanation is that workers perceive the old minimum wage as the fair wage.

INTRODUCING FIRMS' REACTION TO THE MINIMUM WAGE

De Fraja builds on the idea that firms respond to an increase in the real minimum wage by making working conditions harder. In this model, jobs with harder working conditions are better paid and workers have different preferences as regards working conditions. In the absence of minimum wage regulations, the firm would not require a worker who prefers lighter working conditions to work harder, because it would have to compensate her for that. With the introduction of a minimum wage, the firm requires more effort from that worker.

This model is able to account for the evidence that, for a moderate increase in the minimum wage, the overall effect on employment seems negligible. It is also possible that firms offset the effect of the minimum wage by reducing non-wage compensation. For instance, employers may react to a rise in the minimum wage by increasing investment in fixed and human capital, with the effect of increasing aggregate employment.

The very fact that firms may respond to an increase in the minimum wage otherwise than by dismissing employees is important. It means that the participation of workers' and employers' organisations in the determination of the minimum wage may greatly contribute to the success of any minimum wage policy. According to Islam and Nazara (2000), consultations with unions and business organisations in Indonesia contributed to making minimum wage increases harmless to employment over 1990 and 1998.

Controlling for the level of GDP and location, these authors found no evidence of a negative relationship between the ratio of minimum to average wages and wage employment in that country. Lastly, it has also been argued that a rise in the minimum wage may not lead to a decrease in employment because an increase in aggregate demand may offset the "disemployment effect" of the minimum wage.

REMOVING THE HYPOTHESIS OF FREE COMPETITION

In the monopsony theory, firms are price-takers in the product market, but have some degree of market power in the labour market. This hypothesis corresponds to the situation of agriculture in Morocco, for example: the low mobility of labour ensures that, in a given area, a few large farmers deal with a given number of employees. In Morocco, there is a minimum wage specific to agriculture, which is substantially below the minimum wage payable in other sectors and seems more or less enforced.

When firms are confronted with an increase in the minimum wage above the going wage (which is less than the worker's marginal productivity in the case of a monopsony), monopsony theory predicts that the best strategy is to increase the level of employment. Indeed, Azam found a positive relationship between the minimum wage and employment in wheat farming in Morocco over the period 1971-89. Controlling for the market price of wheat and other cereals, an increase in the real minimum wage in agriculture is found to increase wheat production and therefore the demand for labour. The minimum wage thus increases employment and, as the agricultural labourers are amongst the poorest workers, contributes to alleviating poverty.

INTRODUCING EFFICIENCY WAGE IN THE MONOPSONY CASE

Further research suggested an alternative explanation for Azam's findings on Morocco. His explanation assumes that the setting of a minimum wage relieves the employer from the burden of finding out the appropriate wage which, for each employee, would minimize labour costs while ensuring that the employee's household can survive.

In this model, the minimum wage works in the common interest of the employers, by preventing some kind of opportunistic behaviour. Hence, each of them has an incentive to monitor compliance by the others. In turn, this incentive explains why the agricultural wage is enforced in Morocco. In this country, there seems to be a collective interest in enforcing the minimum wage.

Introducing household labour supply

A rise in the minimum wage may also reduce the labour supply of other members of households affected by the rise and thereby contribute to the reduction of unemployment.

Including job search friction/reservation wage

In a model where workers and jobs are heterogeneous, time is needed to ensure that each worker's profile matches her/his own job type. The effect of setting a minimum wage in this context is to increase the reservation wage and therefore the quality of the match between jobs and workers' profiles.

Minimum wage and employment

The ambivalence of the theoretical predictions has prompted a large number of studies using empirical data. There are two main procedures for estimating the effect of the minimum wage on employment. The first and most simple is to regress employment changes on the minimum wage, controlling for other factors.

Estimations typically relate changes in employment over time to variation in the level of the minimum wage (often relative to the average wage), output growth, controls for changes in labour supply (e.g. the ratio of economically active to total population), educational attainment and a time trend. To account for the effect of the minimum wage in the uncovered sector, the coverage-weighted sum of the ratio of the minimum wage to average wage is often used as an independent variable in place of the minimum wage.

Bell estimated the impact on employment of the erosion of the minimum wage in Mexico and of its increase in Colombia in the 1980s. She found significant minimum wage effects in Colombia but not in Mexico. In Colombia, an increase of 15 per cent in the real minimum wage is found to have reduced employment by 5 per cent over the period 1977-87. In Mexico, the very low value of the minimum wage may well explain the finding that no disemployment is observed for this country.

The real minimum wage lost 45 per cent of its value in Mexico in the 1980s, whereas it increased by roughly the same proportion in Colombia by 1988. While Bell's analysis is restricted to the manufacturing sector, another study on Mexico focuses on the impact of the minimum wage on overall employment. This study identified strongly differentiated impacts by sex: reductions in the Mexican minimum wage between 1970 and 1990 were found to have increased the employment of women aged 15-64 and to have reduced the employment of older male workers.

As in industrialized countries, the minimum wage is suspected of having a negative effect on youth employment in developing countries, though there is little evidence on this question for lack of disaggregated data. In France, a cross-section study investigated the responsibility of the minimum wage for keeping the youth unemployment rate as high as 20 per cent since 1983.

Empirically, the study regressed the yearly youth unemployment rate over the log of minimum wages - using the unemployment rate of prime-age adults (25-49) to control for business cycle variation - and the log of the number of subsidized jobs for youth over the number of youth unemployed and the schooling rate during the period 1970-1994. No impact of minimum wage on youth unemployment could be identified.

The method of regressing the minimum wage at time t (or t-1) raises two caveats. First, it requires changes in demand and supply factors to be controlled. Most notably, controls for final product demand in low-wage industries are also lacking. Secondly, the minimum wage is possibly endogenous, as minimum wage and output may well be determined by the same factors. The second procedure for estimating the minimum wage effect on employment is the so-called "natural experiment approach" introduced by Card and Krueger.

These authors analysed the increase in the minimum wage in New Jersey in 1994, using as a control group the neighbouring state of Pennsylvania where the minimum wage was left unchanged. Basically, they compared employment growth between the two states following the rise in New Jersey's minimum wage. No disemployment effect was evidenced. This conclusion, though challenged by several researchers, was confirmed again by Card and Krueger, using another set of employment data provided by the Bureau of Labour Statistics. In another study, the authors analysed the effect of the 1991 increase in the federal minimum wage in Texas.

Looking at differences in employment growth between restaurants that had to adjust their wages to the new minimum and restaurants that were paying wages above the new minimum, they found weak evidence of a positive employment effect of the increase in the minimum wage. The "natural experiment" method has been heavily criticized because it is difficult, in practice, to define a proper control group. There is always concern that the change in employment observed for the control group may not reflect what would have happened to firms subject to the minimum wage regulations in the absence of those regulations.

EMPLOYMENT DISTRIBUTION EFFECTS

Another possible effect of a minimum wage increase is to alter the distribution of employment as between demographic groups. For example, a decrease in the minimum wage may cause a shift away from older workers towards younger workers, as appears to have happened in Mexico in the 1990s. The skill profile of minimum wage workers may also shift - away from those with more formal education towards those with little education.

As already mentioned, Feliciano also reported large swings in the estimated effects of minimum wages by sex for Mexico, with a decline in the minimum wage having a positive effect on the employment of women. Similarly, a differential impact of the minimum wage by sex and age was also found for the United States. By affecting the distribution of employment across population groups, changes in real minimum wages might have an impact on household poverty, an issue that is examined in the next section.

MINIMUM WAGE AND POVERTY

Much of the justification for minimum wage regulation centres on the objective of providing income support to the poor. It seems, however, that while some low-wage workers may gain from a minimum wage increase, others lose, depending on its employment effects and its impact on average earnings.

Raising the minimum wage level in developing countries may contribute to widening the gap between workers in the covered sectors and the others. It would thus generate further poverty in relative terms. For example, this argument has been developed in work on Malawi. Malawi has a small urban sector and a large and impoverished, mainly informal, rural sector.

Different minimum wage rates apply in towns and rural areas, and rates have been periodically increased but not sufficiently to compensate for the rise in consumer prices. According to Livingstone, increasing the minimum wage within such a context would only result in driving workers from the rural areas to towns, where they would look for a job but not necessarily find one. Therefore, the most efficient way of lifting workers out of poverty is to raise the price of labour through rural development, not to increase the minimum wage in urban areas.

There is at least one counter argument. In some developing countries, unskilled wages account for a higher proportion of the income of poor urban people than in developed countries where the poor are more likely to benefit from social income. Thus a minimum wage increase may lift relatively more low-paid workers out of poverty in developing countries. Furthermore, changes in the minimum wage may alter the labour supply behaviour of other members of the households of minimum wage earners, with an effect on well-being.

To summarize, the effects on poverty are fourfold. Firstly, some workers lose their job in the covered sector and, in the absence of unemployment benefits, receive zero income. Secondly, some workers previously employed in the covered sector find a job in the uncovered sector and, depending on the inter-sectoral wage differential, may fall into poverty. Thirdly, some workers who keep their jobs in the covered sector earn more due to the introduction or increase of the minimum wage.

A proportion of them might escape poverty depending on the level at which the minimum wage is set. Fourthly, a family may react to a decrease in the minimum wage earned by one family member by increasing labour participation in the informal sector. Theory thus offers no clear predictions as to the effect of the minimum wage on poverty, as the overall effect depends on the value of several elasticities that are, themselves, difficult to predict. As the effect on uncovered workers remains unclear, it makes sense to test the data by regressing change in poverty rates on changes in the minimum wage. Theory, however, suggests that increases in the minimum wage might reduce poverty if the employment effect of minimum wage is small.

MINIMUM WAGE AND WAGE INEQUALITY

At least two studies have shown that the minimum wage may have a strong effect on observed wage inequality. The United States, for instance, experienced a dramatic increase in wage inequality during the 1980s, primarily between more and less educated workers and between more and less experienced workers. A recent study concluded that most of the growth in inequality in the bottom categories of wage distribution is attributable to erosion of the real value of the minimum wage during the 1980s. The impact of the minimum wage on the lower wage categories was also confirmed by data on the Netherlands.

POVERTY AND LOW-PAID EMPLOYMENT

Low-paid employment is usually defined in terms of earnings below 66 per cent of the median. The poverty rate among the working age population has been shown to be systematically higher in OECD countries where lowwage employment is more developed. More specifically, poverty is quite considerable among households with dependent children when the head of household is in low-paid employment. However, the vast majority of two-adult households with at least two wage earners are out of poverty.

Conversely, and somewhat obviously, the highest poverty rates are found in households with no adults at work. A similar relationship between the number of employed individuals per household and poverty has been observed in Chile. In 1994, poor Chilean households were about the same size as the national average; only the proportion of those at work differed, with 0.8 persons employed in poor households as against 1.2 for those not living in poverty. A poverty-reduction alternative to an increase in the minimum wage may thus be to have individuals in the lowest decile working.

Financing minimum wage: Wage subsidies for unskilled workers? It is often argued that minimum wages should be subsidized to promote social integration through employment of the least skilled workers in the context of declining demand for unskilled labour. Subsidizing enterprises that employ workers whose wages are below a certain level has indeed been suggested as a mechanism to protect income for the poor in Latin America. Yet, as the Bank has rightly pointed out, there are problems with subsidizing firms in order to increase employment or support the income of the poorest workers.

Besides being difficult to monitor, subsidies may also generate poverty traps because they reduce the incentive for firms and workers to raise productivity and wages above the threshold level. While wage subsidies may be provided on a temporary basis with the above effect, it seems that social welfare measures aimed at encouraging labour force participation may turn out to be detrimental to minimum wage earners in the long run. The very idea of subsidizing work may easily be taken to imply that the work performed is not valuable. This, in turn, will put downward pressure on the non-subsidized minimum wage with the result that the minimum wage may again become the maximum wage.

EVIDENCE

Empirical evidence suggests a negative correlation between minimum wages and poverty. Using a sample of developing countries, Lustig and McLeod regressed change in poverty on a number of explanatory variables of poverty, including real wages (either minimum wage or average wage) and the growth in per capita income. The level of human capital of the population and the share of agricultural employment are also among the independent variables they consider, together with real public spending, terms of trade, unemployment rate divided by the number of years in the interval, inflation (if minimum wage is increased infrequently), and education expenditure as a percentage of GDP. Their sample contains 22 countries and more than 40 time periods. The results suggest that higher minimum wages have a stronger impact in diminishing poverty than do higher average wages. Lustig and McLeod also found that the effect of the minimum wage on poverty is slightly higher in recovery periods. The analysis is replicated for several measures of poverty, including the poverty gap, the income gap and the per capita calorie intake.

Another study compares the situation of Costa Rica and Colombia both of which adopted a policy of increasing the minimum wage relative to the average wage during the adjustment process of the 1980s - with that of Chile and Guatemala, which experienced a relative decline in their minimum wages.

This study concludes that minimum wage adjustments - together with lower unemployment and inflation - contribute to explaining why poverty did not rise in Colombia between 1984 and 1988, despite tough fiscal and exchange-rate policies. It also argues that the rise in the minimum wage relative to the average wage in Costa Rica protected the position of the lowest-paid workers. In sharp contrast, a poor macroeconomic policy and a decline in the minimum wage relative to the average wage lead to increased poverty and reduced GDP growth in Guatemala.

On the one hand, the foregoing literature review invites the conclusion that for low levels of minimum wage, theoretical effects on the level of employment are fairly small, except where all the hypotheses of perfect competition are met. On the other hand, empirical studies lead to different conclusions. However, there does seem to be a correlation between the minimum wage and the reduction of poverty.

Recent developments in minimum wages

How does the behaviour of minimum wages in developing countries relate to the theoretical predictions and empirical findings of the studies reviewed above?

Instability of minimum wage

In real terms, minimum wages are widely believed to have declined worldwide during the adjustment crisis of the 1980s before recovering modestly in the 1990s. While this picture holds in the case of many Latin American countries, the evidence is more mixed in the cases of Asia and Africa.

STRUCTURAL ISSUES

Calculated on the basis of the IMF Consumer Price Index (CPI), the value of real minimum wages and that of average wages appear to have fluctuated widely in the developing countries over the period 1980-1998. Increases of 30-40 per cent and decreases in the order of 15 to 20 per cent are common for both variables. Such extreme changes illustrate the difficulty of measuring real wage behaviour in countries with huge inflation rates. However, much less variation has occurred in the variable of primary interest here, namely, the ratio of minimum to average wage.

In some countries, the minimum wage appears to have been relatively stable over time in relation to average wage. Internal stability, however, does not imply lack of variation across countries. For example, minimum wage levels in Malawi and Bolivia represented less than 20 per cent of those countries' average manufacturing wages, whereas the ratio was around 40 per cent in Botswana and increased modestly from 48 to 54 per cent in Thailand during 1986-1994.

In other countries, by contrast, the ratio of minimum to average wages fluctuated over time. A deterioration of the ratio indicates that the wage gap widens between unskilled workers paid the minimum wage and skilled workers. The Philippines, for instance, experienced a continuous decline in the ratio, from more than 60 per cent in 1981 to around 35 per cent in 1992. Similarly, in Ecuador the minimum wage represented a much larger proportion of the average wage in 1980 - at 65 per cent - than in 1989, when it reached 45 per cent.

In El Salvador, by contrast, the ratio almost doubled, from 21 per cent in 1984 to 42 per cent in 1991. A comparison of the ratio between OECD and Latin American countries in the 1990s undertaken by the Inter-American Development Bank (1998) showed that the minimum wage represented more than 70 per cent of the average wage in Venezuela, Italy and El Salvador. At the opposite end of the distribution, the ratio was less than 35 per cent in a group of countries that included Bolivia, Brazil, Chile and Spain.

Finally, the minimum wage was close to half the average wage in Switzerland, Colombia and Sweden. Within the sample selected for this chapter, some of the countries have a national minimum wage (e.g. Algeria, Colombia, and Togo), while others set minimum wages by sector (e.g. Burkina Faso, the Philippines). Furthermore, countries may have adopted regional minimum wages (Mexico, Thailand, etc.).

In Peru and Turkey, only the capital city is covered. The approach followed in defining the value of the minimum wage was to select the lowest minimum wage series with the most comprehensive coverage within an economy. In cases where such series were very short or where there was not enough information on the data, the next best series were selected, i.e. the next lowest wage series with the most comprehensive coverage.

COUNTRY EVIDENCE

In Latin America, minimum wages tended to decline during the 1980s and have since become largely non-binding. Overall, minimum wages in Latin America lost more than 30 per cent of their value in real terms between 1980 and 1990. With the period of modest recovery that followed (+ 1 per cent a year), the minimum wage was still below its 1980 value in most countries by the end of the 1990s. In Bolivia, El Salvadör, Mexico and Peru, its 1997 level was equivalent to one-third of its 1980 level. The minimum wage dropped relatively more and then recovered less than average industrial wages during 1980-1990.

As a result, low-paid workers were disproportionately affected by the recession. In Chile, the minimum wage lost two-thirds of its value between 1980 and 1987, but has since been increasing again. Studies on Ghana show that the minimum wage applying to publicsector workers was halved in real terms during the period from the 1970s to the early 1990s. The same sharp drop is observed for starting wages in the manufacturing sector.

Since GDP per capita increased steadily over the same period, these findings mean that workers in the manufacturing sector failed to benefit from the rise in aggregate income that followed the introduction of the country's structural adjustment Programme in 1983. The Government of Zimbabwe adopted an interventionist wage policy in the 1980s. As a result, the minimum wage increased in real terms until 1990-91. However, some studies argued that this policy failed to ensure growth of income and wage employment in the formal sector, so that the minimum wage policy was progressively abandoned.

Foroma argues that job losses due to the setting of minimum wages were particularly severe during the mid-1980s, but provides no evidence to back up this claim. As the author himself notes, "it is difficult to quantify the impact that job security legislation and the minimum wage had on investment because other strong factors (such as foreign exchange shortages and price and exchange controls) were also at play".

In India, the minimum wage applies to a small formal sector and varies across occupations, industries and states. Minimum wages are not regularly adjusted to price increases so that most states have been paying workers a cost-of-living allowance to compensate for inflation. As a result, minimum wages decreased in real terms between 1983 and 1988 in half of the major Indian states, while they increased between 1988 and 1994 in most states.

In Papua New Guinea, minimum wage regulation was introduced in 1972 and then dropped in 1992. By 1995, it seemed that real wage decreases had been substantial for both skilled and unskilled labour. In the case of unskilled workers, however, the wage decrease was inferior to that allowed by the reduction in the minimum wage: wages received by unskilled workers in 1995, while below the pre-1992 official minimum wage, were well above the new minimum. One reason is that, although the new minimum wage applied only to newly hired workers, large regulated firms was reluctant to discriminate between new workers and existing employees performing the same job.

The minimum wage in Puerto Rico, which is imposed by the Federal Government of the United States, was increased gradually between 1974 and 1983. By 1983, Puerto Rico had the same minimum wage as the United States. But many studies have concluded that Puerto Rico's minimum wage increase resulted in a decline in employment, though Card and Krueger cast some doubt over this interpretation of their findings. The above evidence shows that the stated goal of providing low-paid workers with a decent livelihood is not systematically reflected in the process of adjusting minimum wages, which differs by country.

In Indonesia, the minimum wage is adjusted according to changes in labour productivity, employment growth and per capita GDP. In Thailand, minimum wage adjustments used to be based on changes in the CPI, but since 1990, they also depend on GDP growth. As a result, the minimum wage has been growing faster than the average wage. In the Philippines, the CPI seems to be the main criterion for updating minimum wages, though 11 criteria should in theory enter into the determination of the minimum wage. In Mexico, the objective of maintaining or increasing the purchasing power of the minimum wage came into conflict with other objectives of structural adjustment policy.

After the debt crisis of 1982, the reduction of inflation became the main consideration in fixing the minimum wage as adjustments were indexed to expect future inflation. Such conflicts between the objectives of economic policy also occur in industrialized countries. In the United States, for example, changes in the level of the minimum wage can mostly be traced to political pressures during the adoption of the Minimum Wage Bill, rather than to the aim of lifting low-income households out of poverty.

In conclusion, the minimum wage is a very unstable variable in some cases, both in real and in relative terms. In some cases, workers seem better protected against increases in consumer prices than they are in others, and the minimum wage follows variations in the average wage more closely.

Compliance

In principle, the setting of the minimum wage provides a floor to workers' earnings. However,. the legislation of most countries excludes certain groups of workers from the scheme, who thus legally earn sub-minimum wages (e.g. part-time workers, the self-employed). In addition to those workers who are excluded by law, some workers earn wages below the minimum because the employer fails to comply with the legislation. Gindling and Terrell, for example, estimate the number of workers earning wages below the statutory minimum in Costa Rica. Their study concluded that onethird of the workers in the covered sector (full-time employees) were paid less than the minimum wage, with the same proportion in the uncovered sector (part-time workers and the self-employed).

In Guatemala, the National SocioDemographic Survey estimated that persons working 40 hours a week or more and whose income was less than the minimum wage of the branch of activity concerned accounted for 49.4 per cent of urban employment in 1987 and 53.5 per cent in 1989. As documented by several studies, most governments appear not to enforce strict compliance with minimum wage legislation. In Ecuador, for example, the fine for non-compliance with labour legislation cannot exceed five times the national minimum wage regardless of the severity of the violation and the number of workers involved.

In the Philippines, the ILO (1997) reports a low level of compliance due to the absence of real penalties for underpayment of the minimum wage. In Chile, 9.4 per cent of wage earners were paid less than the minimum wage in 1994. In Indonesia, about 15 per cent of workers in manufacturing are paid less than the minimum wage, and the proportion rises to 26.9 per cent for women and 20.6 per cent for workers under 25. In India, a statutory minimum wage applies to the informal or unorganized sector, which represents more than 90 per cent of the labour force.

In general, however, minimum wage levels are not enforced: for agricultural labour, actual earnings were on average below the minimum wage in almost all states. Non-compliance is widespread, and not only among small-scale enterprises. A study conducted by the ILO (1997) revealed that 63 per cent of the workers in micro-enterprises in Costa Rica received sub-minimum wages, the proportion being 46 per cent in Panama, 38 per cent in Venezuela, 28 per cent in Chile, 19 per cent in Mexico and 16 per cent in Colombia and Brazil.

But the same study also found that 8 per cent of the workers in Mexico's large enterprises (those employing more than 300 workers) earned wages at or below the minimum wage. An OECD study, however, found contrasting results as to the extent of non-compliance by microenterprises in seven developing countries. According to its authors, most micro-enterprises in these countries respected minimum wage laws with the exception of those in the two poorest countries of their sample, namely, Niger and Swaziland.

All else being equal, non-compliance is expected to be more widespread the higher the ratio of minimum to average wages. This positive relationship was found for 12 Latin American countries. Non-compliance levels were estimated to be below 10 per cent in countries where the minimum wage is below 30 per cent of the average wage (Argentina, Chile, and Bolivia) and more than 35 per cent in those where the minimum wage is at least 60 per cent of the average wage, as in Paraguay, El Salvador and Venezuela. Sub-minimum wages are also rather common in developed countries. In 1990, 7 per cent of wage earners in France -mostly young people employed in publicly funded programmes - had wages below the statutory minimum, while 6.6 per cent were paid the minimum wage. In the United States, 4.5 per cent of all employees had wages below the minimum wage and 13.2 per cent at the minimum in 1981.

SECTORAL AND INDIVIDUAL CHARACTERISTICS

The proportion of the labour force receiving the minimum wage differs by sector. In some countries, many minimum wage workers are found in export-oriented activities. In Chile, for example, a quarter of the workers in agriculture were paid at, or below, the minimum wage in 1994. In such cases, it is often suspected that a higher minimum wage - when compensated by an increase in product prices - may have an adverse effect on the volume of exports.

However, if the minimum wage applies mainly to the service (and/or public) sector, its impact on the price of goods produced for export may be quite small. Again in the service sector, workers may be less likely to lose their job because of technology or mechanisation so that a higher minimum wage may only marginally affect employment. When civil servants and state-firm workers are covered by minimum wage regulations, the state must collect the resources to finance the additional costs resulting from higher minimum wages.

Similarly, a high minimum wage may induce teenagers to leave secondary school early and start working instead. The incentive to leave school may be higher in industrialized countries where minimum wage laws mainly benefit teenagers, young workers and workers with low levels of education (like secondary school dropouts), although there are some exceptions. In other countries, minimum wages have little impact on exports. For example, Standing, Sender and Weeks argue that the minimum wage would not affect South African export since the main export industries tend to have relatively high wages.

The situation looks different in Mexico where there exists a massive, low-paid export processing industry called "maquiladoras". Maquiladoras are factories located in low-wage regions, in which workers assemble imported materials for export. The maquiladoras of Tijuana, for example, mainly employ women - married women, women with children, and women with low levels of education - who earn less than women in the service and trade sectors whatever their educational levels, and less than self-employed women, except those at the lowest educational level.

In Chile, more men are paid the minimum wage, especially in rural areas, where the labour force participation of women is low. One study on Costa Rica showed that workers earning below the minimum wage are disproportionately women, non-heads of household, under 19 years of age or older than 60, have low education and live in rural areas outside the Central Valley. In cases where women make up the majority of the lowest paid workers, a decrease in the minimum wage can contribute to widening the wage gap between women and men.

According to the study by Fortin and Lemieux, something along those lines happened in the United States between 1979 and 1991, when the decline in the minimum wage contributed to setting back the wage gap by 7.5 percentage points at the 10th decile. In another study, Fortin and Lemieux show that about one-third of women's wage inequality in the United States is attributable to the decrease in the minimum wage over the period 1979-1988.

POVERTY OF MINIMUM WAGE WORKERS

The position of minimum wage earners and their families in relation to overall income distribution depends not only on their level of earnings but also on household structure and labour supply, and non-wage income. There is some scattered evidence on the poverty of minimum wage earners in developing countries. In Chile, less than 50 per cent of minimum wage earners are considered to be poor.

There is more evidence in industrialized countries. In France, households with the highest proportion of individuals paid the minimum wage are in the third lowest income decile, while one-third of minimum wage earners in Spain are in the bottom decile of household income. What emerge first from the overview in this section are the wide variations in the minimum wage in real terms, which are much less pronounced in its relation to the average wage.

Second, the ratio of minimum to average wages varies across countries and, in some countries, over time. Furthermore, there are legal sub-minimum wages and little enforcement of minimum wage regulations in several countries. And finally, minimum wage earners do not seem to belong systematically to the poorest segments of the population.

EMPIRICAL ANALYSIS

Most of the minimum wage data used in this section is drawn from a database created in early 2000, while a few other data were provided by ILO field offices and national labour ministries.

The data on other variables like GDP growth, GDP per capita, share of GDP spent on education and working-age population - are taken from the World Development Indicators. The ILO provided the figures on employment, informal employment and unemployment. The CPI data come from the IMF.

EFFECT ON EMPLOYMENT

Minimum wage and the informal economy

The relationship between the growth of the informal economy and changes in the minimum wage in Latin America is analysed on the basis of time series data provided by the ILO Regional Office in Lima. Informal-sector employment is understood to include all ownaccount workers - except professionals - and all workers in establishments with fewer than six or 11 workers, depending on survey methodology. A very minimalist equation is tested: on the labour-supply side, change in GDP per capita should measure the income incentive associated with the supply of labour in the informal economy, while on the labourdemand side, log changes in the ratio of minimum to average wages represent changes in the flexibility of the labour market for unskilled labour relative to more skilled labour.

The independent variable is the annual change in the log of the share of the informal economy. In other words, the exercise is really a regression of cross-section of panel data. The results of this regression suggest that increases in per capita GDP tend to reduce urban informal employment significantly. In contrast, changes in the ratio of minimum to average wage seem to have no significant impact on the relative size of the informal economy.

Using changes in real minimum wages instead of changes in that ratio does not improve the significance of the coefficient. This result tends to support the view that labour market rigidity and, more specifically, wage rigidity introduced by minimum wage regulation is not the main cause of informal sector growth in Latin American economies.

MINIMUM WAGE AND OVERALL EMPLOYMENT

The results show that GDP growth is positively correlated with employment growth whatever the other factors controlled. The effect of other variables is much more unstable, e.g. that of an increase in the real wage rate. From the second regression, increases in the real average manufacturing wage appear to have a significant negative impact on the level of employment, though the t is rather low at 1.5. In none of the cases is there any significant effect of changes in the ratio of minimum to average wages that would explain variations in employment. Restricting the analysis to manufacturing employment or excluding specific geographic areas like Africa leads to the same conclusion. These results may partly be explained by the extent of non-compliance in developing countries, which can be expected to reduce the employment effects of minimum wages.

Another simple explanation for the generally small disemployment effect caused by minimum wages may be the decrease in the real minimum wage experienced by many countries during most of the 1980s. Indeed, a low value of the minimum wage is unlikely to cause much unemployment. There is a simple way of checking for such an effect: if the minimum wage has a negative impact on employment, the negative impact can be expected to be stronger in countries with a relatively high minimum wage. Yet such cross-section analysis leads to no significant result on the data set used here.

EFFECT ON POVERTY

Poverty line

The data are presented by region. North African countries have a relatively high minimum wage, with more than US$100 a month, while the minimum wage is under US$50 a month in all sub-Saharan African countries except Senegal. The figure for most Latin American countries is between US$40 and US$70, with a few countries enjoying a much higher minimum wage (Chile, Paraguay and Costa Rica). Three of the five Asian countries have minimum wages above US$ 100 a month.

The minimum wage is above the poverty line at US$1 per day in most, though not all, countries. But it is below the poverty line at US$2 a day in all sub-Saharan African countries except Senegal and in a few countries of Latin America. Obviously, when comparing the minimum wage level and the poverty line, it should also be borne in mind that a minimum wage earner may provide the main income of a household.

Several measures of poverty are used: the share of the population living below the national poverty line and the share of the population living with less than US$1 and US$2 a day. What is more striking is the finding that this relationship persists after controlling for the average wage. The relationship between the minimum wage and poverty remains negative when the level of development, as approximated by per capita GDP and location, are introduced as explanatory variables. The effect of the regional dummies is estimated with respect to the effect of poverty in Thailand and the Philippines. The regression shows that for a constant level of GDP per capita and average wage and controlling for location, a higher national minimum wage is associated with a lower rate of poverty.

Using the estimated coefficients, it is possible to calculate the elasticity of poverty with respect to changes in the minimum wage. This value is often estimated by computing it at sample mean, where the minimum wage is - in this case - US$214 a month and the poverty rate, 31.6 per cent. The elasticity at sample mean is 0.459, i.e. a 1 per cent increase in the minimum wage produces a 0.46 per cent reduction in the level of poverty. Finally, the fit of the regression is rather good.

The above analysis is based on the national poverty line. But the regression can also be run on a smaller group of countries using the US$1- or US$2a-day poverty line. The shares of population below these poverty lines are taken from the World Bank. The level of the minimum wage in dollars is not significantly associated with the share of population living on less than US$1 a day. In fact, none of the independent variables can explain the level of poverty using the US$ 1a-day threshold.

This result confirms intuitive assumption that minimum wages in developing countries do not apply to the poorest share of the population, but rather to the relatively less poor among the low-income population. Indeed, the minimum wage in dollars is a significant determinant of the larger share of the population living on less than US$2 a day. However, the coefficient of the minimum wage becomes insignificant when adding controls for GDP per capita, average wage and location.

As this study focuses on poverty, wages in dollars are expressed using the purchasing power parity conversion factor developed by the World Bank. Estimating the equations with wages expressed in dollars using the official exchange rate leads to the same conclusion as to the impact of average and minimum wages on poverty. In conclusion, there are indications that a higher minimum wage is associated with a lower level of poverty.

This result per se does not imply that setting a higher minimum wage would reduce poverty; it is merely the sign of a correlation between the two variables. For instance, the correlation could indicate that countries with a high minimum wage are also more committed to the reduction of poverty and have developed social policies targeting the poor. Furthermore, there seems to be little relation, if any, between the minimum wage and extreme poverty as measured against the international poverty line of US$1 per day. However, the results are an indication that minimum wages may be an efficient channel of poverty reduction.

UNEMPLOYMENT

Indicators of poverty other than poverty lines have been suggested to measure the minimum wage effect, such as the level of unemployment. Lustig and Mcleod, for example, evaluate the effect of changes in real minimum wages on changes in unemployment rates controlling for real public spending, human capital and terms of trade. Their study concludes that the real minimum wage increases unemployment, a result that is often quoted in the literature.

The way the independent variable "unemployment" is defined is not clear from this analysis as "the unemployment variable is the change in the unemployment rate divided by the number of years in the interval"; it is therefore difficult to reproduce these results. However, based on a larger sample of 40 observations, the result turns out to be the opposite: an increase in the minimum wage relative to the average wage reduces the unemployment rate. This result remains remarkably stable across specifications and when various definitions of the variables are used. Therefore, no conclusion will be inferred as to the link between the unemployment rate and the minimum wage. After years under attack for its negative effect on low-paid employment, the minimum wage seems to be back in favour as a means of providing unskilled workers with a decent living. Several factors are responsible for the renewed interest in the minimum wage as a tool of market policy.

First, several studies from the 1990s showed that the minimum wage had little, if any, disemployment effect. Second, there is currently a shift towards a new human rights approach that focuses on the right to decent employment. Within this context, this chapter has been concerned with the impact of the minimum wage not only on employment, but also on the level of poverty. From the theoretical literature review on the minimum wage, it was concluded that the static model of pure and perfect competition - i.e. homogeneity of goods and workers, perfect information, many small suppliers and buyers - is a unique case where the minimum wage has a definite negative effect on employment.

If one of the hypotheses of perfect competition is removed (e.g. workers are heterogeneous or paid the efficiency wage, or if there are a few employers) or dynamics are introduced (minimum wage affects household labour supply or aggregate demand), the impact of the minimum wage on employment cannot be predicted. This seems also to apply in an economy with a sizeable informal sector. It is therefore not surprising that many empirical studies failed to find evidence of a negative effect on employment for moderate increases in the minimum wage.

As regards the impact of the minimum wage on the level of poverty in developing countries, one empirical cross-country study showed that increases in the minimum wage are associated with a lower level of poverty when other factors are held constant. The present chapter shows evidence of high instability of the minimum wage in real terms in many developing countries. The ratio of minimum to average manufacturing wages is shown to vary considerably both between countries and within countries over time.

In some countries, the minimum wage appears to be relatively stable over time in relation to the average wage, though such internal stability does not imply lack of variation across countries. For example, minimum wage levels represented less than 20 per cent of the average manufacturing wage in Malawi and Bolivia, as against 40 per cent in Botswana; and in Thailand the ratio increased modestly from 48 to 54 per cent over the period 1986-1994. In other countries, however, the ratio of minimum to average wages has fluctuated widely over time. This variety of minimum wage data was used in this chapter to assess the impact of the minimum wage on employment and poverty. The relationship between the growth of the informal economy and changes in the minimum wage was analysed using time series data on the informal economy in Latin America. To that end, a simple reduced form was tested.

On the labour supply side, change in GDP per capita should measure the income incentive associated with the supply of labour in the informal economy, while on the labour demand side; change in the ratio of minimum to average wages represents changes in the flexibility of the labour market for unskilled labour relative to more skilled labour. The dependent variable is annual change in the share of the informal economy.

The results of this regression suggest that increases in per capita GDP tend to reduce urban informal employment significantly. In contrast, changes in the ratio of minimum to average wages seem to have no significant impact on the share of the informal economy. This result tends to support the view that labour market rigidity and, more specifically, low-wage rigidity is not the main explanation for the size of the informal sector in the Latin American countries.

One of the main objectives of this study was to determine the relationship between changes in employment and changes in the ratio of minimum to average wages (which measures the relative price of unskilled labour and, thereby, the bite of the minimum wage in the wage structure). A regression was thus estimated that relates changes in the ratio of employment to population to the following variables: changes in the ratio of minimum to average wages, growth of the real average wage, changes in the terms of trade, GDP growth and changes in educational levels.

The results suggest that, other things being equal, the minimum wage level has an insignificant effect on the level of employment. The number of countries in the sample made it possible to estimate the effect of the minimum wage on the level of poverty, using cross-section data. As expected, the level of the minimum wage (in United States dollars) is a negative and significant determinant of the level of poverty.

What is more striking is that this relationship persists after controlling the level of development, as approximated by GDP per capita, average wage in manufacturing and location. The regression shows that for constant levels of GDP per capita and average manufacturing wage, and after controlling for location, a higher minimum wage is associated with a lower national level of poverty. This analysis was based on national poverty lines. But with a smaller group of countries, the regression could also be run using the US$1- or US$2-a-day international poverty line.

The result shows that the level of the minimum wage in dollars is not significantly associated with the share of the population earning less than US$1 a day. This result confirms the intuitive assumption that minimum wages in developing countries do not affect the poorest population groups, but rather the upper levels of the low-income population. In contrast, the minimum wage in dollars does correlate with the share of the population earning less than US$2 a day. Yet the minimum wage is still not significantly associated with a lower level of poverty at US$2 a day when other factors are held constant.

In conclusion, an analysis of the data gives strong support to the idea that the minimum wage may bring positive results in poverty alleviation by improving the living conditions of workers and their families, while having no negative effects in terms of employment. There is no evidence either of any effect of the ratio of minimum to average wages on the size of the informal economy in Latin America. Yet the consequences of setting a minimum wage are manifold and go beyond the impact this may have on levels of employment and poverty.

Raising the minimum wage may have an effect on incentives to provide training and enhance productivity, as well as on working conditions and prices. These and other such effects, however, have received little attention even within the context of the more industrialized developing countries. The idea that a decent minimum wage may induce firms in these countries to use their labour force more efficiently has been little explored so far.

Bibliography

Amarendra, 1998. Poverty, Rural Development and Public Policy. Deep & Deep Publication Pvt. Ltd., New Delhi.

Chakravarty Sukhamoy, 1989. Development Planning the Indian Experience. Oxford University Press, Delhi.

Deaton, Angus, and Alessandro Tarozzi. 2000. Prices and Poverty in India. Mimeo. *Research Program in Development Studies*, Princeton University.

Drθze, Jan and Amartya Sen. 1995 *India: Economic Development and Social Opportunity.* New Delhi: Oxford University Press.

Drθze, Jan, and P.V. Srinivasan. 2000. Poverty and Inequality in India: Evidence from Regional Data. *Journal of Quantitative Economics*, 16:1: 33-50.

Economic Survey, 1998-99. Ministry of Finance, Economic Division.

Government of India 2000. Economic Survey, 1999-2000. Ministry of Finance, New Delhi.

Haq Mahbub Ul, 2000. Reflections on Human Development. Oxford University Press, New Delhi.

Jha, Raghbendra. 2000. Reducing Poverty in India: Has Liberalization Helped? UNU/WIDER Working Paper No. 204.

Kotwal, Ashok and Mukesh Eswaran. 1994. *Why Poverty Persists in India: A Framework for Understanding the Indian Economy.* Oxford University Press.

Lal, Deepak, Rakesh Mohan, and I. Natarajan. 2001. Economic Reforms and Poverty Alleviation: A Tale of Two Surveys. *Economic and Political Weekly (*March 24): 1017-28.

Murthy Ranjani K.; Rao Nitya, 1997. addressing poverty. Friedrich Ebert Stiftung (India office) New Delhi.

Parikh Kirit S. 1999. India Development Report 1999-2000. Oxford University Press, New Delhi.

Planning Commission, 1981. A Technical Note on the Sixth Plan of India 1980-85. Government of India, New Delhi.

Planning Commission, 1986. A Technical Note on the Seventh Plan of India, 1985-90, New Delhi.

Ravallion, Martin, and Gaurav Datt. 1996. How Important to India's Poor is the Sectoral Composition of Economic Growth? *World Bank Economic Review*, Vol.10 : 1-26.

Reserve Bank of India. 2001. *Handbook of Statistics on Indian Economy.*

Ravallion, Martin, and Gaurav Datt. 1999. When is Growth Pro-Poor? Evidence from the Diverse Experiences of Indian States. World Bank Policy Research Working Paper No. 2263, Washington, D.C.

Sachs, Jeffrey, Nirupam Bajpai, and Ananthi Ramiah. 2002. Understanding Regional Economic Growth in India. Harvard Center for International Development Working Paper No. 88.

Sen, Abhijit, 2000. Estimates of Consumer Expenditures and Its Distribution: Statistical Priorities after NSS 55th Round. *Economic and Political Weekly* (December 16): 4499-4518.

World Bank, 2002. The India Poverty Project: Poverty and Growth in India, 1951-94. At

World Bank. 2000. *India: Reducing Poverty, Accelerating Development*. Oxford University Press for the World Bank, Washington, D.C.

INDEX